THIS REMARK

THIS REMARKABLE GIFT

Being gay and Catholic

Maurice Shinnick

ALLEN & UNWIN

First published in 1997 by

Allen & Unwin
9 Atchison Street
St Leonards NSW 2065
Australia
Phone: (61 2) 9901 4088
Fax: (61 2) 9906 2218
E-mail: frontdesk@allen-unwin.com.au
URL: http://www.allen-unwin.com.au

National Library of Australia
Cataloguing-in-Publication:

Shinnick, Maurice.
This remarkable gift: being gay and Catholic.

Bibliography.
Includes index.
ISBN 186448 462 4.

1. Catholic gays. 2. Homosexuality—Religious aspects—Catholic Church. 3. Gays—Religious life. 4. Church work with gays. I. Title.

282.08664

Set in 10.5/12 pt Goudy Old Style by DOCUPRO, Sydney
Printed by KHL Printing Co Pte Limited, Singapore

10 9 8 7 6 5 4 3 2 1

For Frank
a brother of generosity, courage and integrity
1931–1996

Let there be unity in what is necessary,
freedom in what is doubtful,
and charity in everything.

The Second Vatican Council

The Bible contains six admonitions to homosexuals
and three hundred and sixty-two admonitions to heterosexuals.
That doesn't mean that God doesn't love heterosexuals.
It's just that they need more supervision.

Lynne Lavner

Contents

Conventions and Abbreviations

CONVENTIONS

The term *Magisterium*, which refers to the teaching role of the pope, the Catholic bishops and the various Congregations that make up the Roman Curia, can be used individually or collectively to describe their teaching. The context will make clear what aspect of the *Magisterium* I am referring to in the book.

The Holy See is often called simply *The Vatican* after the city-state where the pope and various Congregations work. I frequently use the term *Vatican* when referring to the Roman Curia, or more particularly the Sacred Congregation for the Doctrine of the Faith.

Most documents by the pope or the Vatican Congregations are divided into numbered paragraphs or articles. Throughout the book I have used the article number rather than the page number of the document in the references. It needs to be noted that the English translation of papal and Vatican documents rarely uses inclusive language. I regret this convention. But I have quoted precisely from the documents, including italics where found in the original English translations. Likewise, most papal and Vatican documents are known by their Latin title (usually taken from the first words of the document). I use the Latin titles in the notes for these and for other publications frequently referred to in the text. Full publication details are given in the bibliography.

I use the word *church* in the following ways: *Church* when referring to a particular church when I need to be specific: for example, [Catholic] Church, [Anglican] Church. I use *church* when referring to the Christian church or churches in general.

The designation of gay men and lesbian women takes various forms in the book. This is partly to give variety. It is also an attempt to respect the diversity of choice made by gay and lesbian people themselves. All Vatican documents use the term *homosexual persons*, and only the *1975 Declaration* uses the term *lesbian*.

Scripture quotations are from the Jerusalem Bible translation unless otherwise stated.

ABBREVIATIONS

1975 Declaration	*Declaration on Certain Questions Concerning Sexual Ethics*. Congregation for the Doctrine of the Faith.
1986 Letter	*Letter to the Bishops of the Catholic Church on the Pastoral Care of Homosexual Persons*. Congregation for the Doctrine of the Faith.
1992 Considerations	*Some Considerations Concerning the Response to Legislative Proposals on the Non-discrimination of Homosexual Persons*. Congregation for the Doctrine of the Faith.
The AIDS Crisis	*The AIDS Crisis: A message to the Australian people*. Australian Catholic Bishops Conference.
Apostolicam actuositatem	*Apostolicam actuositatem: Decree on the Apostolate of Lay People*. Second Vatican Council.
Called to Compassion	*Called to Compassion and Responsibility: A Response to the HIV/AIDS Crisis*. National Conference of Catholic Bishops (USA).
Catechism	*Catechism of the Catholic Church*. The Holy See.
Code Canon Law	*The Code of Canon Law*. The Holy See.
Dei verbum	*Dei verbum: Dogmatic Constitution on Divine Revelation*. Second Vatican Council.

Dignitatis humanae	*Dignitatis humanae: Declaration on Religious Liberty*. Second Vatican Council.
Ecclesial Vocation Theologian	*Instruction on the Ecclesial Vocation of the Theologian*. Congregation for the Doctrine of the Faith.
Evangelium Vitae	*Evangelium Vitae: The Gospel of Life*. Encyclical letter of Pope John Paul II.
Familiaris Consortio	*Familiaris Consortio: The Role of the Christian Family in the Modern World*. Apostolic Exhortation of Pope John Paul II.
Gaudium et spes	*Gaudium et spes: Pastoral Constitution on the Church in the Modern World*. Second Vatican Council.
Homosexual People in Society	*Homosexual People in Society: A contribution to the dialogue within the faith community*. Catholic Council For Church And Society (The Netherlands).
Human Sexuality	*Human Sexuality: A Catholic Perspective For Education And Lifelong Learning*. National Conference of Catholic Bishops (USA).
Humanae Vitae	*Humanae Vitae: Of Human Life*. Encyclical letter of Pope Paul VI.
The Interpretation of the Bible	*The Interpretation of the Bible in the Church*. The Pontifical Biblical Commission.
Life in Christ	*Life in Christ: Morals, Communion and the Church*. Second Anglican–Roman Catholic International Commission.
Lumen Gentium	*Lumen Gentium: Dogmatic Constitution on the Church*. Second Vatican Council.
Many Faces	*The Many Faces of AIDS: A Gospel Response*. National Conference of Catholic Bishops Administrative Board (USA).
Nostra aetate	*Nostra aetate: Declaration on the Relationship of the Church to Non-Christian Religions*. Second Vatican Council.
A Note	*A Note on the Teaching of the Catholic Church Concerning Homosexual People*. Cardinal Basil Hume.
NRSV	*New Revised Standard Version*. The Holy Bible.

Observations	*Observations on the Catholic Church's Teaching Concerning Homosexual People*. Cardinal Basil Hume.
Pastoral Care	*An Introduction to the Pastoral Care of Homosexual People*. Catholic Social Welfare Commission: Catholic Bishops of England and Wales.
Pastores Dabo Vobis	*Pastores Dabo Vobis: I Will Give You Shepherds*. Post-synodal Apostolic Exhortation of Pope John Paul II.
Principles to Guide	*Principles to Guide Confessors in Questions of Homosexuality*. National Conference of Catholic Bishops (USA).
Quaker View	*Towards A Quaker View of Sex*. A Group of Friends.
Redemptor Hominis	*Redemptor Hominis: The Redeemer of Man*. Encyclical letter of Pope John Paul II.
Tolerance	*Tolerance: A Christian Perspective on the International Year for Tolerance*. Australian Catholic Social Justice Council.
Unitatis redintegratio	*Unitatis redintegratio: Decree on Ecumenism*. Second Vatican Council.
Ut Unum Sint	*Ut Unum Sint: That They May All Be One*. Encyclical letter of Pope John Paul II.
Veritatis Splendor	*Veritatis Splendor: On Certain Fundamental Questions of the Church's Moral Teaching*. Encyclical letter of Pope John Paul II.

Acknowledgments

This book emerged from the thesis *This Remarkable Gift: A Dialogue on Homosexuality for the Catholic Community* prepared for a Master of Theology degree through the Melbourne College of Divinity. I am grateful to my supervisor, Bishop Andrew St John, Assistant Bishop to the Anglican Archbishop of Melbourne. Bishop Andrew's knowledge and pastoral sensitivities gave guidance throughout the research.

Allan Patience, Professor of Asian Studies and Political Science at the Victoria University of Technology, has given me constant encouragement. He has kindly given me access to his library, and helped me enormously to understand more clearly modern social theory as it relates to gay and lesbian issues. I thank him for being an invaluable critic of my thinking, research and writing. Fr Laurence McNamara CM, lecturer in moral theology at St Francis Xavier Seminary, Rostrevor, South Australia, has been supportive of this research, has shared his insights, and has provided theological resources. I thank him. Fr Augustine Fitzsimons CP of Adelaide has been a source of constant encouragement and wisdom. He has always kept before me the importance of the ecumenical dimension to each and every endeavour. Thank you.

I thank all who have provided me with valued resources for this research: Martin Pendergast of Catholic AIDS Link, London; Leonard Schmidt, former National Co-ordinator of Acceptance-Australia; Roger Swanson, Co-ordinator of Assent, Wellington,

New Zealand; Stephen Getman, Operations Director, Dignity/USA, Washington; Dr Simon Rosser of Minneapolis, USA; Fr Robert Carey of Catholic News Service, Adelaide; and Ms Mary Newport, Director of the Australian Catholic Bishops' National Media Office in Canberra; and Warren Featherstone. The staffs of Imprints Bookshop, Adelaide, and Hares and Hyenas, South Yarra, have been invaluable in assisting me to access the most recent writings.

My thanks go to Sr Enid Wood OP, and Sr Joan Gillen RSM, both of Adelaide, and Philip Cain of Melbourne, for reading the text and making valuable suggestions. Ms Helen Fox and Wun Tudo have patiently rescued me from several computer-induced traumas, and for that I am very grateful. The staff of Imprints Bookshop, Adelaide, and Hares and Hyenas, South Yarrra, have been imvaluable in assisting me to access the most recent writings.

Over the years members of Acceptance-Adelaide and many associated with the Adelaide Diocesan AIDS Council and its Centre have shared their stories with me. I thank my gay brothers and lesbian sisters for that trust. I am particularly grateful to those men and women who have allowed their story to be told in this book. May their words give heart to others. Dr Bob Lyons, former Chairperson of the Adelaide Diocesan AIDS Council, and Mrs Geraldine Rice, Director of the Family Life Programme within the Catholic education system in Adelaide, have given me much appreciated insights into the needs of gay and lesbian teenagers.

While working on the research I was very much encouraged by Robbie Guevara, Mark Hennessy, Maxine and Geoff Coffey, Jeff Hood, Marie London, Kevin Rybak, Arthur Williams, Eric Clarke, Lonia Catalano, Gordon Carter, Fr Senan Ward OSA of AIDS Pastoral Ministry (Melbourne), Rev. Dr Ken Sinclair SSS, as well as Fr John Barry OSA, Miss June Cochrane and parishioners of St Joseph's at South Yarra. I appreciated the support of Bruce Abaloz, Jeannette McGregor, Anne-Maree Neill, Lindsay Worthington, Carey Parsons and Andrea Gladwell, volunteers with the Victorian AIDS Council. Cafe 151 at South Yarra was an oasis of hospitality and friendship. I thank Gordon Hood and John Harber.

This work would not have been possible without the permission of Archbishop Leonard Faulkner to undertake study leave. He has always been an example of how to develop an inclusive Church where all can feel respected. The Jordan-Kennedy Committee and the Board of the Diocesan Presbytery Fund made available the finances necessary for the study leave. I record my thanks to them, and my particular appreciation to John Mahoney of the Catholic Finance and Property Office for his constant practical advice and help. The people of St Brigid's Parish, Kilburn, have shown unfailing support and interest. I thank them along with Rev. Dr James McEvoy and Sr Josephine Weatherald RSM who continued pastoral ministry among the people at Kilburn. I thank my family for their support, and especially my sister, Sr Veronica Shinnick DC, whose example of respect for those experiencing alienation is always inspirational. Monsignor Ian Dempsey AO, VG has been unfailing in his support. Dr Robert Gillen of Adelaide encouraged me to pursue my dream of further study, and affirmed the important relevance of this research. I will always be grateful to him for his guidance.

Ms Elizabeth Weiss of Allen & Unwin has been a gracious adviser and publisher. She has gently eased me into the publishing world. My thanks also to Rowena Lennox and Emma Cotter for their support.

Lastly, my deepest gratitude is for my brother Frank, whose goodness, wisdom, courage, faith and kindness have nourished me in countless ways throughout this research. He has been the best of teachers.

While so many people have been involved in this project in one way or another, I take full responsibility for the finished product. Their conclusions might well be different from mine, but in that difference lies the seed for dialogue.

Introduction

This is a dangerous book. Homosexuality is one of the most volatile issues in contemporary ethics. It arouses the passions of people. But this is not a book meant to cause anger. It is meant to encourage, indeed plead for, dialogue. Some will be upset by an appeal to re-examine Christian and Catholic teaching on the subject. Others will regret that the book does not go far enough. Whatever our present position on the matter, we have to deal with homosexuality as communities, as church members, as families and as individuals. The present climate is putting people's lives at risk, their freedoms at stake, and their reputations under threat. For gayness is a shocking 30 per cent factor in teenage suicides. There *is* discrimination in the workplace and in neighbourhoods. And some live in fear of being 'outed' to their families and significant others.

In 1984 I was appointed by my archbishop as chaplain to a new group in the Catholic Church in Adelaide: *Acceptance*. Established in Sydney some ten years earlier, this small national organisation tries to provide pastoral, emotional and spiritual support to gay and lesbian Catholics, their families and friends. When this appointment received widespread media coverage in 1986 I was amazed at the ferocity of opposition that came from some sections of the Church.

What was heartening was the sensitive support that came from brother priests. The Church in Adelaide has had a long tradition of reaching out to those who feel alienated from the community. Its many welfare services have always worked within a policy of non-discrimination.

Those people who opposed both my appointment and the very existence of the group, acted on the assumption that members of Acceptance were what they termed 'practising homosexuals'. What homosexual people, and gay men in particular, *did* was far more important to them than *who they were*. When pushed to explain what they meant by 'practising homosexuals' they could rarely articulate an answer. Those who did, reluctantly named 'sodomy' or 'anal intercourse' as the reason for their objection. They may be surprised to know that many gay men have no attraction to such activity. Furthermore, they may be even more surprised to know that some heterosexual married couples include anal sex in their sexual repertoire. Even so, what is noteworthy is the obsessive preoccupation with the alleged sexual practices of gay people. In my twenty-six years of being a priest I have never heard it asked if members of Church youth organisations, singles groups, or associations for the separated, widowed or divorced were 'practising heterosexuals' (whatever this may entail).

The literature, propaganda and speeches that emerge from fundamentalist Christians, the politics of the Right, and sections of the Catholic Church leave me bewildered. Why are they so angry and obsessively bitter and violent in their words directed towards homosexual people and concerning homosexuality itself? Why are they so frightened about two men loving each other or two women loving each other? Especially when they seem to take for granted, or are indifferent to larger and frighteningly violent issues in society. Gay men and lesbian women are portrayed as enemies of the family, but no one actually explains how this is so. This is despite the fact that there are many gay and lesbian relationships today that would match those of many married heterosexual couples for trust, honesty, fidelity, commitment and love.

This book emerges out of many years of working pastorally with gay men and lesbian women, both from within and beyond the Church. It comes out of the experiences of a broad range of friends who have shared their stories with me. It is shaped by a passion for justice which has been formed in me by my parents, brothers and sisters. It is an expression of concern for my Church which too quickly is becoming fragmented—by intolerance and self-righteousness; by *factions unable or unwilling to participate in dialogue*. It is informed by my ministry among people living with HIV and AIDS, and by the sadness of having to officiate at the funerals of friends. It is above all an attempt to stand with my gay brothers and lesbian sisters, who for all the advances of the last thirty years, rarely feel at home within the Church.

This is a frustrating book. It is like a buffet meal. The many and varied dishes are placed on the table and one is invited to taste a little of everything. As interesting as such a meal can be, it often does not satisfy hunger in the same way as a home-cooked three-course meal does. So here many voices on the topic of homosexuality are gathered together, so that we get a taste of the breadth, if not the depth, of recent intellectual developments. A glance through the bibliography will reveal how fertile the literature is, coming increasingly—and probably surprisingly so—from the churches. The book offers an overview of what is being said on the topic by gay and lesbian people themselves, by the Protestant, Anglican and Catholic communities, at the official level and among theologians—as well as an overview of developments within the social sciences. Each chapter could well be developed into a book of its own. But in *This Remarkable Gift* there is an attempt to give the reader a general overview of the situation. What is alluded to here is that there is no one homogeneous form of homosexuality; rather, there is a growing awareness of *homosexualities* which in different cultural settings are lived and expressed in a variety of ways—all reflecting the complexity of human nature and the diverse complexity of God.

It is particularly the gathering together of material produced by the various churches that may contain heartening news for gay and lesbian Christians, because theology is not a museum of ancient teachings, but a vibrant science engaged in the search for truth and values. It affirms human dignity, respects conscience, promotes justice and works for love in all things.

Many gay and lesbian Christians have been deeply hurt by their churches. They have sought understanding and guidance, especially in their adolescent years, and received too often only pious platitudes or terrifying condemnation. Such experiences lead to alienation, bitterness and resentment towards the church. It helps then to explain why some sections of the gay community taunt the Christian church, trying to provoke a defensive response (and usually succeeding). Others leave the church community sad that they have been forced into a choice. A person cannot run away from his or her sexuality. It is part of who each person is, each and every day. It is often in order to survive in a complicated and divisive world that many feel that they have to distance themselves from the church of their upbringing. But there are those who stay within their church, determined to live life with as much harmony as possible between their sexuality and their spirituality. Theirs is a maturing faith because they have had to make a commitment to church without compromising their own identity. They invariably have a deep faith in God, and the following of Christ in love is what gives shape to their church affiliation and daily living. For all their efforts they are nonetheless criticised for staying in the church both by fellow Christians and by sections of the gay community. Such people are the real pioneers of an emerging *gay and lesbian theology*, developing a Christian ethic appropriate to their situation in life. No dialogue on homosexuality can take place unless gay men and lesbian women are part of it. Those in the church, and those estranged from it, all have something valuable and essential to contribute. And no experience should be lost to the cause of searching for a fuller truth. The Scriptures intimate over and over again how those judged as outcasts, or as being 'on the edge', have actually been the ones through whom God has worked most powerfully.

The discussion within the churches about homosexuality has been robust over the past thirty years. This has led to shifts in pastoral responses to gay and lesbian members—sometimes with the appallingly patronising 'love the sinner, hate the sin' approach, but at other times demonstrating a respect for the individual and his/her conscience. What is happening at the local parish level can be in sharp contrast to the dogmatic attitudes expressed in church statements.

Parents with a church affiliation often agonise over their gay sons and lesbian daughters. 'Will they be saved?' is asked with great concern. They fear that their children's 'life-style' will put their immortal souls in danger. Yet they know so little about this so-called 'life-style'. Their imagination is fed by a media that seeks to sensationalise, a gay flamboyance that sets out to shock, and by the teaching of some churches that portrays their children as perverted deviants who are an abomination to God, instead of reflecting aspects of Him. All of this challenges the love they have for their son or daughter, and they feel lost in a sea of confusion. Hopefully the work of Scripture scholars and theologians in wrestling with this issue will bring to parents a sense of hope and comfort. In the midst of the ambiguities of life, and there are many of them, God certainly does not abandon His people. Some of His official (largely self-appointed) spokespersons may. God doesn't.

Until quite recently the theological training of the clergy was quite inadequate regarding the whole realm of human sexuality, not just homosexuality. There has been a naivety in the advice given by priests, pastors and ministers to people seeking help. Matching the teaching of the churches with the reality of people's lives requires an understanding of complex truths, a knowledge of human development, and a wise compassion that gives the ability to make connections between the two. Gay and lesbian people have received a raw deal from the churches for the very reason that the clergy, by and large, have been so ignorant about human development and sexuality. The lengthy chapter on modern social theory is included in order to address this ignorance. Good theology cannot be developed in isolation from understanding human beings in their psycho-cultural and socio-cultural settings. The church exists *in* the world, and must interact *with* it. Theology brings a rich dimension to all that is human because it affirms a noble dignity that is God-given. *Every* person is made in the image and likeness of God. And the theology of the churches is to recognise, enhance and celebrate a person's dignity, their *human* dignity. Theology does not attempt to make out the human as angelic; rather its task is to cultivate in each person those qualities and virtues revealed so profoundly in the person of Jesus. In other words, theology helps each person to live in love. And it does so by drawing individuals into community, so that we become a pilgrim people. In order to do that we must be constantly exploring the mystery of our humanity, as well as the mystery of God who is Love.

This is an Australian book. As will be seen, the contribution to the dialogue by Australian churches, with the exception of the Uniting Church of Australia, has been minimal. However, on many issues Australians can be said to hold the middle ground. They do not warm to extremes of the left or the right. They do not like inequality. Australia has a tradition of 'mateship' born out of the experience of Australian soldiers during World War I. There is a strong spirit among its people of providing a 'fair go' for everyone. Its strong multicultural character, present from the

European settlement of the late eighteenth to the early nineteenth centuries, has been broadened enormously since the early 1950s. There has also been a rapidly developing appreciation of the cultural traditions of Australia's indigenous people. All of this gives Australians a sense that diversity, while being difficult to deal with at first, ultimately enriches the human experience. This spirit has been reflected over a twenty-five-year period as, State by State, governments have legislated to decriminalise homosexual acts between consenting male adults in private. One exception, Tasmania, had its long-standing laws overridden by the Federal Government in 1995. Visible gay communities have formed in each of the State capital cities, and public events like queer film, cultural and summer festivals, large-scale picnics and street parties occur across the nation eliciting barely any comment. However, while the annual Sydney Gay and Lesbian Mardi Gras Parade does provoke some public comment, it is not enough to deter several hundred thousand from attending, or even more from watching it on television. Attempts to include gay and lesbian people and couples in the provisions for superannuation, health care, compassionate leave from work, and housing loans, continue to take place, not by means of a radical protest movement, but methodically and carefully through the processes of legislation and law. The Australian Government's consistent and enlightened approach to the AIDS epidemic since the early 1980s has been a model of considered judgement and practical care. The bipartisan political support has engaged the gay and lesbian community in consultation at a consistently high level. This Australian spirit creates a good climate for a mature and wise dialogue on the issue of homosexuality.

This is a confident book. Confident because it is firmly rooted in the call of the Second Vatican Council for the Catholic Church to engage itself in the widest dialogue possible in the search for truth. This call for dialogue is both a right and a responsibility. For the Catholic bishops at the Council in the 1960s wanted to see all Catholics, indeed all Christians, sharing dialogue on the issues of the day. They wanted to engage the Church with the world. Those bishops also made it clear that any fruitful dialogue had to be marked by humility, respect and charity.

The dialogue that has already been taking place has revealed an understanding of homosexuality that accepts it as *gift*. It is indeed *a remarkable gift*, because against all the odds—in the face of civil penalties, medical labels of illness, and church classification of sin—gay men and lesbian women have emerged from a gloomy and ignorant age recognising and honouring their own dignity and worth. Such people will no longer hide in some closet. They are taking their place confidently in the church and in society. They are part of the church, part of the Body of Christ, a gift to the community—bringing particular qualities and insights, not in spite of, but because of, their gayness. *Being gay and Catholic* is certainly no witch-hunt. It is bringing into the open a remarkable group of people who live in faith and with love.

Let us then explore what people are saying about homosexuality. Let us listen to the many voices that have a part in the dialogue. Let us discover a further dimension to the amazing creation of God. Let us be taken more deeply into the mystery of an inclusive church in which everyone, without exception, is a child of God.

1

OPENING THE DIALOGUE

One of the most profound moral crises of our present moment in history is the devaluing of the gift of homosexuality. The unjustifiable exclusion of gay and lesbian people from many spheres of mainstream life—especially from the church—is as perverse an offence to them as it is to God. The Christian church's continuing disregard for gay and lesbian people reinforces a culture of exclusion and violence directed at the gay community. Groups of youths indiscriminately bash gay men. Fundamentalist Christians protest at attempts to modify anti-gay laws. Parents reject gay sons and lesbian daughters. Gay activists target the church, 'outing' bishops, disrupting services and desecrating the Communion Host. The church is caught up in its own turmoil, between the forces of a long tradition condemning all homosexual acts and of a movement that seeks to comprehend evolving understandings of human sexuality.

Any reappraisal of its position on homosexuality will necessarily lead the church to reassess all of its teaching on sexuality. For while there is a rich complexity in human sexuality, virtually all forms of sexuality share a common purpose: not to alienate and isolate people, but rather to gather them together in reconciliation, unite them in friendship, and enable them to relate through commitment.

THE CATHOLIC SITUATION TODAY

There is a pressing urgency in the call for an honest and charitable dialogue about homosexuality, for the Catholic Church has confused gay men and lesbians by its mixed messages to them and its convoluted teachings about them. On the one hand it has 'done more to provoke, alienate and offend lesbians and gays' than any other church, with the possible exception of the American Christian fundamentalists. And on the other hand 'no single religion is more represented than Catholicism in the front lines of the battle against AIDS', a disease that has devastated gay communities worldwide.[1]

The core official teaching of the Catholic Church about homosexuality is contained in this one sentence:

> Although the particular inclination of the homosexual person is not a sin, it is a more or less strong tendency ordered toward an intrinsic evil; and thus the inclination itself must be seen as an objective disorder.[2]

The implications of this position are potentially both ridiculous and cruel. There is hardly a gay man or lesbian woman who would not be deeply offended by such a statement. But for those who are Catholic, the hurt cuts deeper. Catholic psychologist B. R. Simon Rosser points out that evidence indicates that 'sexuality and spirituality are profoundly linked' and that the 'markers' of homosexual orientation 'have been interpreted in other cultures as evidence of blessing, or sacred calling'. He says that 'most [homosexual men] reject their religious background and identity in total' when they experience conflict between their sexuality and religious upbringing. He points out that 'the main effect of traditional church attitudes toward homosexuality is to alienate homosexually active men from their religious tradition'.[3] As will be seen, his conclusions are even more valid in relation to lesbian women and the Christian church.

The Roman Catholic teaching on homosexuality is defined by its *Magisterium*, which in modern times has been identified with the teaching authority of the pope and bishops. However, in many ways the boundaries are set more specifically by the Vatican—the pope and the Curia consisting of an extensive network of Congregations, Tribunals and Pontifical Councils, all of which assist the pope in matters of teaching, government and discipline. Particularly since 1986, the Vatican has ridden roughshod over anyone who challenges its teaching on homosexuality. Organisations of gay and lesbian Catholics have been condemned and expelled from Church properties, liberalising legislators have been denounced, scientific research and studies ignored or ridiculed, critique of its own teaching censured, theologians silenced and outspoken priests expelled from their ministry. The Vatican arrogates to itself the position of sole authority in possession of the truth about homosexuality. It has hijacked the debate about gayness and constricted public discussion. But the discussion does take place, too often in the form of heated exchanges in which no party listens to the other.

It is difficult to avoid the conclusion that it is the Vatican that is the problem. It is the Vatican, and specifically the Congregation for the Doctrine of the Faith, that is shutting people up, and shutting people out. There are many within the gay and lesbian community who are attempting to open up serious debate, challenge repressive prejudice, and confront unloving exclusion. Theirs is not a demand for licentiousness and promiscuity, but an honest search for, and development of, ethical responsibility. It is the Vatican that makes an assumption about licentiousness and moral heterodoxy. It is gay men and lesbians who are searching for a mature moral theology. It is time for the Vatican to start listening to what the Spirit is saying through the Church's gay and lesbian members, and then to enter into a patient and loving dialogue on the issue.

Surprisingly the official Catholic teaching on homosexuality, which wields enormous influence over the lives of many people, is contained principally within only four short documents from the Congregation for the Doctrine of the Faith. There are passing references in documents from several other Vatican Congregations and Councils dealing with education, the family, the clergy and religious life, as well as in two encyclical letters and several talks by Pope John Paul II.[4]

The Vatican, attempting to formulate its teaching isolated from the ferment of new knowledge about homosexuality, presents an unbalanced image of homosexuality and distorts the truth of people's lived experiences. Part of this difficulty lies in the Vatican's opening premise about homosexuality—that it is a problem to be solved. We have seen how, in the past, shifts in initial perceptions resulted in rapid developments of thought and understanding which gave different shape to teaching, policy and action. Much of the missionary work of the sixteenth to eighteenth century was built around the belief that people of the New World were savages in need of Christianity and European culture. When their dignity was fully recognised, their rich cultures appreciated, and their ancient spiritualities honoured, missionary work took on a different spirit and practice. Following the sixteenth century Reformation the Catholic Church looked upon Protestants are being people living in error, and a great gulf of suspicion and alienation grew. Recognition of a common baptism in Christ has heralded a new, rich and energetic movement towards Christian unity. Looking at homosexuality as a problem seriously cripples discussion, distorts perceptions and stifles new thought. But when the opening concept is that homosexuality is a gift to be honoured, the discussion moves in a very different and liberating direction.

Many Christians would, no doubt, find the use of the word *gift* to describe homosexuality a shocking claim. Within their living memory it has always been understood in the most negative of ways. We need to move beyond that understanding and get to the heart of the matter. We need to view the subject with new eyes, not obscured by past experiences, but open to receive a new truth in which we discover a new *gift*.

LIMITATIONS OF THE TEACHING

Unfortunately the Vatican's teaching on homosexuality reveals seven serious limitations.

1. The teaching is *narrow* because it reduces sexuality to biological acts and fails to acknowledge the feelings, and the depth of relationship and commitment, that give meaning to the acts. It speaks of an 'innate instinct', a 'pathological constitution', which is 'incurable'. 'Homosexual relations', which others may see as analogous to marriage, are condemned because they include 'acts which lack an essential and indisputable finality'.[5] Following on from the affirmation that a homosexual orientation 'is a more or less strong tendency ordered toward an intrinsic moral evil', any such relationships, because they are 'not a complementary union able to transmit life', are called 'a materialist ideology'.[6] The teaching claims that civil legislation giving entitlements 'could actually encourage [homosexual persons] to seek a partner in order to exploit the provisions of the law'.[7]

2. The teaching is *judgemental* of gay men and lesbian women when it describes the orientation as 'essentially self-indulgent', and declares that 'a person engaging in homosexual behaviour therefore acts immorally'. It reduces same-sex relationships primarily to the using of the other person for sexual pleasure when it says that 'to choose someone of the same sex for one's sexual activity is to annul the rich symbolism and meaning, not to mention the goals, of the Creator's sexual design'.[8]

3. The teaching is *dishonest* when it declares homosexuality to be putting the nature and rights of the family 'in jeopardy'. It puts a wedge between gay and lesbian people and their families, and by implication makes them a scapegoat for some of the failures of modern family life. It labels those who speak of same-sex relationships as containing elements of 'conjugal love', as 'pressure groups' who try to 'manipulate the Church', and names them guilty of 'deceitful propaganda', reflecting 'a materialistic ideology'.[9] It claims that since 'the Church has the responsibility to promote family life', it is a legitimate form of discrimination to oppose civil legislation that might 'confer equivalent family status on homosexual unions'.[10]

4. The teaching is *unjust* when it fails to listen to the voices of gay men and lesbian women, and calls into question their faith and their 'desire to conform their lives to the teaching of Jesus', on the grounds that they question this teaching of the Church.[11] The support offered 'by prayer and sacramental grace' is given in the context of being 'called to chastity', as if this was the primary virtue for homosexual persons to attain as 'they resolutely approach Christian perfection'.[12] This perfection appears to be judged solely on their success in achieving chastity, which for the Vatican means life-long celibacy. A call to live the supreme commandment of love is missing.

5. The teaching is *insensitive* when it repeatedly labels homosexuality as a 'problem', excludes homosexual people from Church property because of their difficulty with this teaching, and denies them support at a time when they struggle in their relationship with the Church. It rejects naming the 'homosexual condition' as 'neutral',[13] although the Catholic bishops of New Zealand had earlier in 1986 called it 'morally neutral'.[14]

6. The teaching, when claiming to have a convincing biblical foundation, is *inconsistent* with developments within the Pontifical Biblical Commission, which warns of the dangers of a fundamentalist interpretation of the Scriptures in moral matters.[15] The

Congregation for the Doctrine of the Faith rejects as 'gravely erroneous' the 'new exegesis of Sacred Scripture', which says that the Bible 'has nothing to say on the subject of homosexuality', or 'somehow tacitly approves of it', or that 'moral injunctions are so cultural-bound that they are no longer applicable to contemporary life'. It claims that there is 'a clear consistency within the Scriptures themselves on the moral issue of homosexual behaviour'.[16] Tradition is presented in the *Catechism* as being based 'on Sacred Scripture, which presents homosexual acts as acts of grave depravity', although the footnote cites only four supporting texts.[17]

7. The teaching is *deficient* when it fails to remind gay men and lesbian women of the Church's teaching about freedom of conscience, which is a person's 'most secret core and sanctuary' where they are 'alone with God'.[18] In the pastoral ministry 'these homosexuals must be treated with understanding . . . [and] their culpability will be judged with prudence'.[19] It is acknowledged that 'circumstances may exist, or may have existed in the past, which would reduce or remove the culpability of the individual in a given instance; or other circumstances may increase it'.[20] But in none of the Vatican documents dealing with homosexuality is the conscience of the individual acknowledged. In the eyes of the Vatican, if a judgement is to be made, it is to be made by the Church or its ministers, and not by the individual homosexual person.

Still, we should not be surprised by the Vatican teaching on homosexuality, because throughout human history there has been a mixed understanding of homosexual acts. Gayle Rubin points out: 'Homosexual behavior is always present among humans. But in different societies and epochs it may be rewarded or punished, required or forbidden, a temporary experience or a life-long vocation'.[21]

However, we are understandably disappointed that the Vatican has so effectively closed itself off from the wealth of new knowledge that is informing us about homosexuality. William Doty holds that 'the development of a gay affirmative, anti-homophobic scholarship has been one of the impressive academic developments of the period between 1970 and 1990'.[22] And this momentum of reflection and debate has also been taking place across the whole spectrum of the Christian church, with an extensive and impressive contribution from gay and lesbian Christians themselves.

To critique an official teaching of the Catholic Church is a daunting exercise. In 1979 Pope John Paul II warned: 'Nobody, therefore, can make a theology as if it were a simple collection of his own personal ideas, but everybody must be aware of being in close union with the mission of the teaching truth for which the Church is responsible'.[23] Ideas do emerge and they need to be clarified and refined, shared and debated, critiqued and evaluated in order that their truth be discovered and honoured. The *Catechism* acknowledges that the teaching of Christian morality evolves through the participation of the whole Church community: 'The Church needs the dedication of pastors, the knowledge of all Christians and men of goodwill'. Indeed, the *Catechism* affirms that 'the Holy Spirit can use the humblest to enlighten the learned and those in the highest position'.[24]

CALLED TO DIALOGUE

This work does not seek to be an exercise in Vatican bashing, but as has already been shown, a critique of its teaching and method of imposing it on the whole Catholic Church must take place. This then is an invitation for the whole community to engage in the dialogue. It will show how the energetic work already undertaken is bearing some fruit within the church. The task should not daunt us. The injunction to be in dialogue with the world, with scientists, with people of faith, and within the Catholic community itself at every level was one of the endearing and enduring fruits of the Second Vatican Council.

That Council was the high point of Catholic life in this twentieth century. Held in the autumn months of the years 1962 through to 1965, it had among its purposes the engagement of the Church with the world. It sought to hasten the work of Christian unity and to bring about a renewal of the Catholic Church itself. First called together by Pope John XXIII, more than two thousand Catholic bishops from almost every country participated. Pope Paul VI continued the Council after the death of Pope John in 1963. The Council was enriched by the presence of non-voting experts from within the Catholic community—only bishops can vote at an Ecumenical Council—as well as observers from other Christian churches and communities and people of other faiths.

Woven through many of the Council's sixteen documents is the theme of dialogue. The *Oxford Dictionary* defines dialogue as the 'verbal interchange of thought, discussion', as well as 'the exchange of proposals, valuable or constructive communication between different groups'.[25] The Vatican Council understood dialogue as more than that. Along with teaching and communication, it is a means for people to share what has been discovered 'in such a way that they help one another in the search for truth'.[26] Pope John Paul II sees the capacity for dialogue as rooted in the very nature and dignity of a person, and as 'an indispensable step along the path towards *human self-realization*, the self-realization both of *each individual* and of *every human community*'. So important and profound is dialogue that it 'is not simply an exchange of ideas'. In some way it is always an 'exchange of gifts'. Such dialogue must be carried out with charity and in humility because of 'the truth which comes to light', which then 'might require a review of assertions and attitudes'.[27]

DIALOGUE WITH THE WORLD

The Council reaffirmed the Church's mission to bring the good news of Jesus Christ to the world, with a special commitment to 'those who are poor or afflicted in any way'. 'The joy and hope, the grief and anguish' of such people was to find an echo in the hearts of Christians.[28] This concern for others, founded in the commandment to 'love your neighbour',[29] was further emphasised by the bishops: 'Everyone should look upon his neighbour (without any exception) as another self . . . Today there is an inescapable duty to make oneself the neighbour to every man, no matter who he is, and if we meet him, to come to his aid in a positive way'.[30]

Because of this respect, the Council rejected 'as foreign to the mind of Christ any discrimination against people, or harassment of them on the basis of their race, color, condition of life or religion', recognising that all people 'are created in God's image'.[31] Elsewhere it affirmed that all 'forms of social or cultural discrimination in basic personal rights . . . must be curbed and eradicated as incompatible with God's design'. Hence, every person, in order to live a genuinely human life has a right to, among other things, his or her 'good name, to respect, to proper knowledge, the right to act according to the dictates of conscience and to safeguard his privacy'.[32]

The role and dignity of the human conscience was strongly promoted by the bishops, who, as we have seen, called it a person's 'most secret core and sanctuary', where a person 'is alone with God whose voice echoes in his depths'. Conscience carries a heavy responsibility because each person 'is bound to follow his conscience faithfully in all his activity so that he may come to God, who is his last end. Therefore he must not be forced to act contrary to his conscience'.[33] Furthermore, 'Catholics are to be keen on collaborating with all men of goodwill in the promotion of all that is true, just, holy, all that is worthy of love (cf. Phil. 4:8). They are to enter into dialogue with them, approaching them with understanding and courtesy'.[34]

The Catholic Church, through the Council, experienced a new and profound sense of solidarity with the whole human family, and showed 'respectful affection' by entering 'into dialogue with it about all these different problems'. This dialogue 'carries the responsibility of reading the signs of the time', and so the Church 'must be aware of and understand the aspirations, the yearnings, and the often dramatic features of the world in which we live'. With faith in God, 'it tries to discern in the events, the needs, and the longings which it shares with other men of our time, what may be genuine signs of the presence and purpose of God'.[35]

The paths to truth are many and varied, and people arrive at different answers to the same questions, which the Council acknowledged 'happens rather frequently, and legitimately so'. The advice given is to 'try to guide each other by sincere dialogue in a spirit of mutual charity and with anxious interest above all in the common good'. In a world of diverse cultures, faiths and political systems, differences will always be present: 'Those also have a claim on our respect and charity who think and act differently from us in social, political, and religious matters. In fact the more deeply we come to understand their ways of thinking through kindness and love, the more easily will we be able to enter into dialogue with them'.[36] The directive is clearly given: 'all must be treated with justice and humanity'.[37]

In the modern period science and religion have often been in conflict. The Council took steps to heal that rift. 'Advances in biology, psychology and the social sciences not only lead man to greater self-awareness, but provide him with the technical means of moulding the lives of whole people as well'.[38]

The Church, profiting 'from the progress of the sciences, and from the riches hidden in various cultures . . . needs to step up this exchange by calling upon the help of people living in the world'.

Calling this 'a new age of human history', brought about by 'the tremendous expansion of the natural and human sciences (including social sciences)', the bishops went on to acknowledge that 'recent psychological advances furnish deep insights into human behavior'. Such recognition is important for this study. The Vatican Council said nothing about homosexuality. It was held several years before the Stonewall riots and the rise of the modern gay rights movement. The Church, along with society in general, had not even begun to understand or consider the needs of gay men and lesbians. However, there was an awareness of a need for an improved pastoral care of people. 'In pastoral care sufficient use should be made, not only of theological principles, but also of the findings of secular sciences, especially psychology and sociology: in this way the faithful will be brought to a purer and more mature living of the faith'. Furthermore, Church members were encouraged to 'incorporate the findings of new sciences and teachings and the understanding of the most recent discoveries with Christian morality and thought'. Modern social theory and theology are to inform each other so that people 'will succeed in evaluating and interpreting everything with an authentic Christian sense of value'.[39]

DIALOGUE WITHIN THE CHURCH

Addressing the needs of the world, the bishops wished to involve the whole Church in the search for truth. 'The whole people of God' were called upon 'to listen to and distinguish the many voices of our times and to interpret them in the light of the divine Word' so that 'revealed truth may be more deeply penetrated, better understood, and more suitably presented'. Importantly, everyone was to be allowed 'a lawful freedom of enquiry, of thought, and of expression, tempered by humility and courage in whatever branch of study they have specialized'. The clergy, by reason of their pastoral ministry, had a special duty to 'prepare themselves by careful study to meet and play their part in dialogue with the world and with men of all shades of opinion'. Such theological research 'should not lose contact with its own times'.[40]

At the same time the laity were directed to 'bring to their cooperation with others their own special competence, and act on their own responsibility'. Establishing their own organisations would 'enable the Church, in certain circumstances, to fulfil her mission more effectively'. They were urged to 'conduct the apostolate of like to like'.[41] The laity were also encouraged, 'indeed sometimes obliged', to share their opinions with Church leadership 'always with truth, courage and prudence and with reverence and charity'.[42] They were warned not to expect the clergy 'to have a ready answer to every problem (even every grave problem) that arises', but were urged instead 'to shoulder their responsibilities under the guidance of Christian wisdom and with eager attention to the teaching authority of the Church'.[43]

DIALOGUE WITH OTHER CHRISTIANS

Since one of the primary tasks of the Vatican Council was to seek the unity of all Christians, great emphasis was placed on respect for other churches and ecclesial communities, and on the need to strengthen dialogue with them in which 'everyone gains a truer knowledge and more just appreciation of the teaching and religious life of both communities'. The Council called for a preservation of 'proper freedom . . . even in the theological elaborations of revealed truth', saying that 'in all things let charity prevail'. Ecumenical dialogue involves a searching together 'into the divine mysteries . . . with love for the truth, with charity and with humility'. This includes recognising that within Catholic doctrine there exists a ' "hierarchy" of truths since they vary in their relation to the foundations of the Christian faith'.[44]

Special mention was made of the difficulty of agreement in moral matters since many Christians 'do not admit to the same solutions for the more difficult problems of modern society' as do Catholics, although all 'want to cling to Christ's word as the source of Christian virtue'.[45] In 1995 Pope John Paul II reinforced this point, saying that 'in this vast area there is much room for dialogue concerning the moral principles of the Gospel and their implications'.[46]

The Council said that 'the ecumenical dialogue could start with the moral application of the Gospel'. It noted that 'the Anglican Communion occupies a special place' among those communities in which Catholic tradition continues.[47] In official dialogues pursuing Christian unity 'the Anglican–Roman Catholic International Commission is the first to have directly attempted the subject of morals'. The Commission's document, *Life in Christ*, published in 1994, specifically cited the teaching of the two churches on homosexual relations as irreconcilable, 'not on the level of fundamental moral values, but on their implementation in practical judgements'.[48] Because of the special relationship between the Anglican Communion and the Roman Catholic Church in Australia and other English-speaking countries, the evolving Anglican understanding of homosexuality will be more fully explored in Chapter 3.

Pope John Paul II speaks of five characteristics of ecumenical dialogue which can be fruitfully applied to this dialogue on homosexuality: (1) prayer makes dialogue more fruitful; (2) it is a quest for truth; (3) it examines conscience; (4) it fosters conversion; and (5) it examines differences.[49] The experiences and writings of Christian gay men and lesbians constitute a strong witness to their faithfulness to these characteristics as they have sought to bring their sexuality and spirituality into harmony, and at the same time serve the wider church community with respect.

During the Vatican Council Pope Paul VI wrote an encyclical letter on the Church, *Ecclesiam Suam*, in which he described the spirit of dialogue. His words, like those of the Council itself, call us to a rich, respectful and generous dialogue.

> The dialogue is not proud; it is not offensive . . . Its authority is intrinsic to the truth it explains, to the charity it communicates, to the example it proposes. It is not a command; it is not an imposition; it is peaceful; it avoids violent methods; it is patient; it is generous . . . In the dialogue, one discovers how different are the ways which lead to the light of faith, and how it is possible to make them converge on the same goal . . . The dialogue will make us wise.[50]

A TURNING POINT

This dialogue on homosexuality is taking place at a particular time in modern human history—but it is also a time that has been greatly influenced by past events and ideas. Thirty years ago the events of one night became a turning point for the lives of all gay men and lesbians. A riot resulting from a clash between Puerto Rican drag queens and the police, following the closing of a gay bar in Greenwich Village, New York, in the early hours of 28 July 1969, was the catalyst for the birth of the modern gay rights movement. The riots, which continued over several nights, were 'the symbolic end to victim status' for gay men and lesbians.[51] But there were many earlier confrontations, breakthroughs and defining moments.

Ecclesiastical law in England in 1290 had prescribed execution, by being buried alive, for convicted sodomites. The crime was transferred to the civil courts by Henry VIII in 1533, with death by hanging as the punishment. It was not until 1861 that the death penalty was changed to life imprisonment in England and Wales.

In Germany in 1871 the Reichstag, without debate, added homosexual acts to categories of crime in a new penal code known as Paragraph 175. The intense struggle between advancing medical and social theories and old myths was decided by the Nazis who, in 1935, extended Paragraph 175 'to include kisses, embraces and even homosexual fantasies'. The old myths, firmly set in law, became the excuse for widespread cruelty and murder. Heinrich Himmler, in 1936, called for the elimination of homosexuality. Many thousands of homosexuals, who were made to wear a pink triangle for identification, were subjected to constant humiliation, hard labour, torture and death in concentration camps.[52]

While Oscar Wilde, during his trial in England in 1895 for illegal homosexual activity, could say that 'it is that deep spiritual affection that is as pure as it is perfect . . . It is beautiful, it is fine, it is the noblest form of affection . . . There is nothing unnatural about it', the trial judge, Mr Justice Wills, would state that 'people who can do these things must be dead to all sense of shame . . . It is the worst case I have ever tried'.[53] The decriminalisation of homosexual activity in England was finally enacted in 1967, following the recommendations of the 1957 *Wolfenden Report*. The new law applied to homosexual practice between consenting adults in private.

In the USA after World War II gay communities began to form in the principal cities, but during the repressive McCarthyist period of the 1950s the FBI particularly targeted homosexuals, often accusing them of being Communists. Margaret Cruikshank identifies those factors that contributed to the rise of a numerically strong and articulate gay rights movement in the 1970s and 1980s. The constant police harassment of homosexuals and the places where they gathered during the 1950s and 1960s fuelled the fires of resentment. In the context of the 'sexual revolution' of the 1960s taboos against discussing homosexuality broke down. Social changes were far reaching as the anti-Vietnam war, women's, and black civil rights protest movements rocked the nation. In the rapid growth of a gay subculture, the ground work of earlier homosexual rights movements was recognised. To these factors can be added the greater economic prosperity experienced by gay white males, as well as the higher education enjoyed by many. The combined movements of Christian fundamentalism and conservative politics, which have strongly opposed gay rights legislation, especially in the United States, achieved the effect of rallying gay men and lesbians to the gay rights cause.[54]

THE MEANING OF WORDS

The beginnings of the gay rights movement were heady days, but even simple issues like defining what *homosexuality* actually meant were still unresolved. The evolution of an appropriate word or words to describe this aspect of human sexuality, and those who were so inclined, was still taking place.

The term *homosexual* was coined by Dr Benkert, a German advocate of homosexual rights, in 1869. He formed it from the Greek *homos* meaning 'same', with the Latin *sexualis* or 'sexual'. The term was quickly taken up by the medical profession and accepted in most countries of northern Europe and in North America to describe those with an 'erotic interest in others of the same gender'. But in much of the rest of the world it was applied only to 'the sexually receptive male' so that 'the end result may be identification as a quasi-female'.[55]

The term *inversion* was also used by medical and other writers at the end of the nineteenth century, describing 'the reversal of the current of attraction for the opposite to one's own sex'.[56] It is used in some theological discussions, but has never gained widespread support.

Homophile, from the Greek words for 'same' and 'love'—lover of same—was used by the early homosexual movements in the United States as an alternative to the clinical and harsh word *homosexual*, but it also never received widespread support, although it 'had the advantage of clearly including affectional, nonsexual relations as well as sexual ones'.[57]

The term *gay* has emerged as 'a description of homosexual sub-culture and as a more positive and respectful term for someone self-identified and accepting of her/his homosexuality'.[58] This term, which 'probably antedates "homosexual" by several centuries', began to be widely used in its new sense in the 1960s. As a name chosen by the group itself it has come to encompass a whole *gay culture*, and 'designates their attitudes, values, tastes, artistic and literary works, groups and organizations, common experiences, festivals, special events, rituals and their sense of shared history'.[59]

In more recent years gay women have shown a clear preference for the term *lesbian*, which is derived from the name of the Greek island of Lesbos, where a colony of women lived under the leadership of the classical Greek poet Sappho, who lived between c. 612 BCE and 560 BCE. *Lesbian* carries a differently nuanced meaning from *gay* and is exclusively used for women.

One of the most common vernacular terms of abuse for homosexual men during the twentieth century has been *queer*. It originally conveyed a sense of strangeness, and reinforced the idea that difference was unacceptable. In recent times it has emerged again, but now as a term adopted by the more radical elements of the gay and lesbian culture itself, reflecting the increased popularity of *queer theory* as a political interpretation of homosexuality.

Human sexuality does not fall into two neat, mutually exclusive categories of heterosexuality and homosexuality, but is rather, for some people, more a continuum of feeling, desire and activity—which makes a definition more complicated. As will be seen later, there is in reality no such person as a *homosexual*, but rather a variety of *homosexualities*.

It is clear today that 'homosexuality cannot properly be understood if it is restricted to genital sexuality'. Writers from a wide range of disciplines see that sexual fantasy and affection are fundamental to any description or definition. Wayne Dynes describes homosexuality as embracing 'the entire range of same-sex relations and affections, male-male and female-female', which may 'include deep friendships that are not genitally expressed'. He points to the preference of some that sexual orientation 'should be altered to *affectional* orientation, to indicate a broader concern with the whole person, rather than overtly expressed erotic or genital acts'.[60]

Fr Robert Nugent, co-founder of New Ways Ministry in the United States, says that 'sexual orientation is not fundamentally or even primarily a tendency towards *acts*, but a psychosexual attraction (erotic, emotional, and affective) towards particular individual *persons*'.[61]

For the purpose of this work, I stipulate the following as a working definition:

> Homosexuality describes that form of sexuality belonging to men and women whose sexual fantasies are exclusively or predominantly aroused by and/or directed towards people of the same sex. As an integral part of personality it draws them to others in affection and desire, and when understood and accepted may be a foundation for deep friendship and commitment, which bonding can also be expressed in sexual acts of intimacy. Homosexuality may also be the underlying motivation for sexual activity with people of the same sex without the qualities of friendship, affection and love. Homosexuality is distinguished from a same-sex attraction and/or activity that results from exceptional circumstances (e.g. incarceration in prisons), or mere human curiosity. Such attraction is usually of a temporary nature.

2

A GAY AND CHRISTIAN IDENTITY

In recent years an impressive and maturing collection of writings has emerged from the gay and lesbian community giving witness to a confident integration of sexuality with spirituality and with the Christian faith in particular. Increasingly people are not content to regard gay identity and Christian beliefs as enemies of one another. It has been a courageous step for gay men and lesbians to identify as Christian, because they have been subjected to ridicule and misunderstanding by both sides. Yet they are the people who are beginning to build a bridge between the two. Their place in the dialogue is essential, indeed crucial.

The sixteenth century Spanish mystic, reformer and saint, Teresa of Avila, saw that a knowing of God required a knowing and a valuing of oneself.

> The journey to God is also a journey to the self. It is an inward journey to God which is at the same time a movement into self knowledge. Union with God at the center involves the fullest possible possession of your own life.[1]

THE JOURNEY TO SELF

For too long gay men and lesbians have had to endure the judgements of others, and too often have allowed their self-perception be coloured and shaped by the ignorance and prejudice of others.

In 1966, *Time* magazine had described homosexuality as 'a pathetic little second rate substitute for reality, a pitiable flight from life', calling it 'a pernicious sickness'.[2] And certainly many lesbians and gay men, in recognising the nature of their sexuality, have felt burdened with a terrible handicap.

'I concluded that I was an aberration, one of a kind, an emotional eunuch with a heart of stone',[3] was one response, while another saw before himself 'a long life of continual and unavoidable sin and so of hopeless guilt', and asked 'why were some people singled out for this special burden?'[4]

Adrian's story: childhood fear of sex

When I was in grade one, the nun teaching me said 'Once a Catholic always a Catholic'. And those words gave me a feeling that I was trapped forever.

Adrian was born in 1928, the only child of a traditional Catholic family, in rural Victoria. His first sexual feelings of pleasure occurred before he began school. At the age of six he had a 'crush' on a teenage friend of the family. *I used to fantasise about being tied up by him. The lives of native people who lived off the land and wore no clothes fascinated me.* When Adrian was eight a Redemptorist priest gave a ten-day mission in the parish. *During it we were herded off to Confession, and this priest—I can still remember his name and see his face—grilled me. He questioned and questioned and questioned me, trying to get me to admit to some sort of sexual matter, but I did not know what to say. He just put fear into me.*

Later, when I was at boarding school, we had an annual retreat. I remember vividly being told on one that having sex with men was the biggest sexual sin, which brought the punishment of death, even in this life. And we were told that masturbation was the next most serious sin. As a young adult I was masturbating regularly and so had to endure a telling off by the priest every time I went to Confession, which was once a month in those days. I felt defeated. Everything about sex was wrong. But I wanted to have children. I saw this as the salvation to my loneliness.

Louisa's story: fear of the Church

Born of Italian parents, Louisa and her brothers were brought up as staunch Catholics. All talk about sex was taboo. Around the age of twelve Louisa was involved in some flirtation with boys, but nothing more than a few stolen kisses. When she started work at seventeen Louisa was going through an extremely religious stage, being very involved in the then flourishing Catholic charismatic movement.

At work she became close to one of the women. *I was infatuated with her, but could not name my feeling. Then after about a year of friendship with her she 'came out' to me. I had never imagined two women being intimate together. I was totally intrigued. I remember wondering if maybe this is what I had been feeling for her.* Then Louisa felt a conflict with her religious beliefs and practices. *When I accepted that I was a lesbian I could not see how lesbianism and religion could mix. I did not feel threatened by my sexuality, but I did by my religion. Around this time I heard a sermon at Mass on the subject of homosexuality in which the priest called homosexuals 'perverse people'. This was shattering stuff for me. I felt that I could no longer go to Mass. I was sure that the Church was going to cave in on me.*

Damian's story: fear of his homosexuality

Damian, at the age of six, found the senior boys at school very attractive, but did not know what it was about them that infatuated him. *But I knew that it was not right. At church I was always looking at the handsome men. Around puberty there was some experimentation of mutual masturbation with kids in the neighbourhood. At that time a priest gave us a retreat at school. And one day he called each boy in the class outside and told us that we had to say three Hail*

Marys every day for holy purity. We were warned against doing things alone which would shock our mothers if they saw us. In religion classes it was impressed upon us that we had to keep our bodies as temples of the Holy Spirit.

There was nothing spectacular or traumatic about Damian's upbringing. Life was secure and happy. Except for this secret attraction toward men.

As I moved to adulthood I had the belief that I would one day meet the right woman, she would kiss me, and I would become a heterosexual. When I was at university I did begin a sexual relationship with a woman which lasted for six years. But I did not turn into a heterosexual, because at the same time I was having a sexual relationship with another male student from university. We both thought that it was just a phase we were going through, or at least that is what I wanted to believe.

A teacher exchange programme took Damian to the United States for a year. *A married couple befriended me and after a couple of months Joan said to me, 'You're gay!'. I then admitted it to myself and that brought a great sense of relief. I no longer had to put on a front. My being gay was not an issue for them. They just accepted me for who I was. While I had no sexual encounters in America, I was envious of gay men who were in a relationship.*

The tension between homosexuality and Christianity can be so strong for some that death seems to be the only escape. Bobby was twenty when he violently committed suicide, throwing himself from a bridge into the path of a tractor trailer. His struggle with homosexuality—seeking a 'cure', under family pressure, in religion and therapy—is documented in his diary. 'I really hate being damned. It's always for the same reason, my sexuality', he wrote when aged only seventeen. His final entry, a month before his death, reads: 'I think God must get a certain amount of self-satisfaction by watching people deal with the obstacles he throws in their path . . . Well I hate God for this and my shitty existence'.[5]

Jesse's story: pushed to the limit

It was hard to imagine that nineteen-year-old Jesse, with his short blond-tipped hair, who was full of excitement about a job interview as a model that afternoon, had been, several years earlier, on the verge of suicide. *I wanted to kill myself. I could not handle the pressure of being harassed at school. I was called 'poofter', 'faggot', whatever you can think of. Even when I was only six others would say, 'You're a bit like a girl'. I did not fit into the rest of the class in the Catholic college I attended. I became friends with one other classmate. We seemed to have a lot in common, and so spent a lot of time together. We were just friends, but the others assumed that we were both gay. They gave us hell. The funny thing was that I was in love with another student, and when I told him how I felt he just ran away. I was so depressed. I thought that suicide was the only answer. So I began thinking how I might do it. The constant harassment had worn me down to breaking point.*

While too many have been overwhelmed by despair, John McNeill chose 'to trust that life is good and our gayness is a gift and not a curse'. He felt 'a marvellous liberating feeling of peace' when in prayer he was 'suddenly inundated with an intense feeling of being loved just as I am, a gay man and a gay priest'.[6] One man perceived that his homosexuality 'was an essential part' of who he was, that it was 'natural to me', and that 'it was inextricably linked to the most true and good and beautiful emotions that I'd ever experienced'. He 'knew instinctively' that he had to accept his sexuality 'as a matter of honor, a matter of being true to myself, a matter of being at peace with the world'.[7] Another man found his peace when, with his partner, he was 'lying in bed and I looked into his eyes and saw a love and acceptance so deep that I felt forgiven for the fear, shame, anxiety and confusion I had constructed around being gay'. Understanding that 'being gay has less to do with sex than with an expression of love', he 'could accept being gay in a way I never had before'.[8] A priest came to self-acceptance shortly after his mother's death, when in a state of distress and anxiety 'I looked up at the moonlit sky and shook my fist at

God', and saw in that event 'a birthing experience, a new awareness of myself, of my sexual identity and sexual desires, my skin hunger and craving for intimate relationship'.[9]

For lesbian women, the acceptance of the true self also became the moment of liberation. 'I decided it was SIN for me to continue to put myself through such anguish and to reject and try to change the way God made me', wrote one woman, and another said, 'I discovered that God loves us more for being honest than for trying to conceal the simple truth and be something we aren't'.[10]

Much of the pain associated with coming to terms with homosexuality is not in the nature of the sexuality itself, but comes more from the attitudes of society and Church. A priest–psychologist told a religious brother: 'Homosexuality is not your problem . . . Your problem is to learn to cope with the attitudes of society towards homosexuality, including those of your Church'.[11] The experience of self-acceptance certainly confronts the gay and lesbian Catholic with having to work out his or her relationship with the Church. Brian McNaught claims that 'Catholic gays want to stay within the Church . . . they love their cultural heritage and the guiding challenge of the Faith'.[12] But Andrew Holleran is not so optimistic. 'The attempt of gay men to merge their Catholicism with homosexuality has always seemed to me touching but doomed'.[13] One such man said that he did not go to church because, 'I'm too angry and resentful', but add poignantly, 'I'm also a guilty Catholic'.[14]

Lesbian women seem to carry the pain of this separation from Church with a great intensity. They see for themselves 'no room within the rigid, homophobic, sexist structure' of 'institutional Catholicism'. Being 'a Catholic lesbian feminist' is 'to live with an intolerable degree of contradiction'. Rather than say that she fell away from the Church, one lesbian said that she 'experienced the Church falling away from me', and another said that the Church 'affords no mercy for well-meaning Catholic lesbians'.[15] Several lesbians who were former nuns 'rejected it [the Church] altogether' having 'decided it was all a bunch of baloney', and another was 'filled with a rage so great that I left the Catholic Church never to return'.[16] Perceiving the Church's attitude as one telling her that she 'was bad, a sinner and damned to hell', another religious said that 'with the brains God gave me, I instinctively knew better'.[17]

This journey to self involves 'coming out', which is the 'complex, emotional, psychological and sexual experience of naming oneself lesbian or gay', and is 'better understood as a *process* rather than a single event'. It involves 'changing one's self-concept, reinterpreting past emotional history and changing relations with others'.[18] John McNeill says that 'to refuse this passage, to turn back because of the terror of this transition is to fail in a fundamental way in your trust of God'.[19] This terror can be real because 'homosexuality proves to be the chief exception to the rule of Christian love'. It generates a prejudice that people feel 'morally justified in retaining'. 'Yet more and more people—gay and straight alike—realize that the perpetuation of the closet is harmful not only to homosexuals but to society at large'.[20] The process of 'coming out' is not a self-indulgent one for lesbians and gay men, but rather 'in so doing their life and vocation become a public witness of homosexual and Christian maturing and a gift for the next generation'.[21]

Jesse: coming out

Jesse came out first to his mother. He was in Year Ten at high school. *I cried and cried and cried. It was such an unbelievable sense of relief. It was the first time that I had told anyone about my feelings. I felt the most relaxed I had ever felt in my life. And my mother said that she knew I was gay. She said that she knew that I had this big thing in my chest.*

THE JOURNEY TO GOD

When lesbian women and gay men accept themselves, when they make Saint Teresa's 'journey to the self' and come to possess their own truth, they must face, confront and explore again their relationship with God and the Church. More often than not they discover a peace with God. But with the Church it is often a different story.

Louisa: rediscovering the Church

When Louisa entered a relationship with her partner Deidre, she stopped going to Sunday Mass. *But I never stopped my relationship with God. I was still searching for peace. Then I saw an advertisement in a gay newspaper announcing the start of a new group called Acceptance—specially established for gay Catholics. I thought 'fancy those two words together'. I was then aged about twenty-three. Feeling more mature and comfortable with my sexuality by this stage, I thought that it was time that I dealt with my religion since it really was an important part of who I was.*

I went to my first Acceptance Mass and I started to feel that I was a child of God. That I was loved by God. It was then that I started to go to Mass again on Sundays—much to the joy of my parents who had no idea of the issues that I had been dealing with. Then there came an opportunity for Louisa to take part in a Church leadership programme. By now she was on the committee of Acceptance and was a Special Minister of the Eucharist in her parish. *The leadership programme was wonderful. It took me into the wider Church. I was exposed to new thoughts and ideas. I began to see how inclusive the Church really could be. I built up wonderful relationships with some of the participants. During that first year I 'came out' to members of my support team. I felt OK. I was not embarrassed. They were so accepting of me. I felt myself growing so much during that first year.*

Louisa moved interstate because of her work, and so no longer had direct responsibility for her parents. This affected her spiritual life. *There is a fall off in prayer which I regret. I don't make regular time for prayer any more. In my six-year relationship, although my partner was not particularly religious, I seemed to have had more freedom to grow. My religion was part of all that. Now I'm on my own and I've lost some of that direction. It is easy to sleep in on Sundays—although I still feel some guilt about that.*

Adrian: finding God in his gayness

Adrian married at twenty-seven. His bride, Bernadette, was twenty-two. Marriage became a business, because life was always busy with their six children. *It took some time before I accepted the fact that I was using homosexual fantasies in order to function sexually within my marriage. At age forty-five I realised that this was a problem for me and so I started to discreetly read about the subject—not that there was much useful material around in the early 1970s.*

On our twenty-fifth wedding anniversary Bernadette said, 'It's the best it's ever been'. I was shattered. It was the pits for me. The breakthrough came for me in 1986 when I read the book Why am I afraid to love? *It opened my understanding to God's love. I had been taught to be miserable and that there was no point in looking for happiness in this life. Now I understood that we were meant to be happy—now, not just later. And I asked myself the question 'How would I like God to love me? To come down from heaven to hug me and to get into bed with me'. What I wanted was a gay God. I realised then that I was gay.*

All my gay encounters are like leading to the Absolute, to God. Each man I meet reflects a bit of God. I have come to believe that monogamy is to do with fertility and children. I find that sex is pretty good, but it is only an introduction to the person. I look more for the human touch, the being close together, the comfort of skin against skin. I am still scared about dying—it is so hard to throw off that fear which was poured into me when I was a child. I'd be more comfortable if I could say that I had given up all gay sexual activity. But if I was dying there is no way that I could deny my sexuality and life. I could not ask God to change me from being gay. I don't want to change because this is who I am. Being gay has helped shape the kind of person I am. This is how God made me.

Jesse: always believing

Religion and faith have been important in Jesse's life. But now he is at a cross-roads. *I feel that I am not accepted. The Church might accept gay people, but it does not accept what goes with it—relationships. I was born like this. I am one of God's creatures. If that is what I am, why would I be condemned to hell? I feel that the Catholic Church is telling me that. I cannot accept it when people say that homosexuality is a sin. I do have faith and I do believe in Jesus. I do believe in the basics of the Catholic Church. But I don't believe in the man-made extras that come with it.* On prayer, Jesse says: *I still pray a lot. I pray to Mary—she's cool. Mary is my 'fag hag'. She is my 'religious fag hag'. I pray for my safety all the time. I pray that everyone I know is kept safe. I am constantly praying that I be forgiven my sins, but I don't know what my sins are.* On being gay: *I still feel that there is something wrong with being gay. Yet I feel that this is the way I was made. My defence is in the Bible where it says that it is not good for man to be alone. I had one relationship for six weeks. I never felt so healthy. I felt really good. I felt good about myself. I accept being gay, but find the stuff that comes with it really difficult—the harassment, people's negative attitudes, the judgements of others. I don't have much to do with the gay scene. I am not attracted to those who are over the top. The key problem for me is that I fall in love with the people I can't have.* And the future: *I want to be successful. I would absolutely like to settle into a permanent relationship. I'm that kind of person. God's image is for two people to be in love and together. I want to have a strong faith, and be comfortable with who I am.*

GAY SPIRITUALITY

Spirituality is the experience in life that draws people into relationship with God. It is about the communion of our spirit with the Spirit of God. It can be said that most, if not all, people do have an experience of spirituality, although the manner in which it is thought about and expressed is revealed in a great variety of ways. A person's spirituality has often, in the past, been equated with their religious affiliation and practice. This has changed considerably in Western societies in recent times. Christianity holds within itself a treasure-trove of spiritualities as people discover God and themselves in an extraordinary range of life situations and chosen life-styles: from the hermit to the married couple; from the contemplative in community to the advocate for the poor; from the charismatic to the minister among the sick; from the worker to the invalid.

Today we read about an emerging *gay spirituality:* a relationship with God that is bound up with a person's acceptance and respect for their own gay identity. Carl Jung recognised that the 'homosexual is endowed with a wealth of religious feelings, which help him to bring the *ecclesia spiritualis* into reality, and a spirituality which makes him responsive to revelation'.[22] John McNeill holds that 'a healthy spiritual life must be holistic; it cannot be based on a denial and rejection of the body and its feelings, especially its sexual feelings. There is a necessary sexual component in our search for intimacy with God'.[23] Gay spirituality initially sprang from the experience of suffering, alienation, of being on the fringe of society and church community. Theologian Edward Schillebeeckx describes this type of spirituality as a 'listening obedience to the suffering of human beings', and so 'the *kairos* [propitious moment] of the moment of grace of a particular time'.[24] John Struzzo calls gay and lesbian people 'the sexual anawin [the humble, lowly ones], the sexual poor; the oppressed whom God calls to special favor'. However, he goes on to point out that 'the fundamental challenge for gays and lesbians is to appreciate and celebrate the basic goodness of all creation including their sexuality, without becoming possessive and addictive'.[25] But some now reject this imagery as fundamentally negative and harmful. 'To withdraw or to be pushed to the place defined as "outside" is to accept another's definition of the centre and in so doing to accept another's definition of oneself'.[26]

In the transition from possessing negative attitudes about self because of sexuality to achieving a sense 'that here is a gift', the turning point comes through the experience of being loved by, and then invited to return love to, another. Opening oneself to the loving touch of another is an authentic journey to the God of love. Without this human love a person's 'relationship with God remains largely one of obedience, respect and will, but one that ultimately lacks passion, heart and love'.[27] John McNeill writes: 'To know God, you must love. If you never let yourself love with a gay love, you will never (baring a miracle of God's grace) know God intimately in this life'.[28] One young man found in his first love affair a 'religious dimension' impossible to avoid. 'I felt blessed, graced, smiled upon with divine permission to love this man . . . Rather than guilt, I had found God'.[29] Another, struggling with his gayness, came to the conclusion while on retreat 'Isn't that what my gift of gayness is? Is it not God's love for me?', and he realised that his healing would come in sleeping with another man—'this is not about sexuality or celibacy, but breathing life into a dying body'.[30] One man confessed to his priest 'that I had not accepted my sexual orientation as a gift from God and I needed to confess my ungratefulness'.[31] One lesbian woman, saddened by the 'anti-Catholic bias of the gay press', because of her respect for many gays and lesbians who are devoutly Catholic, felt within herself 'stirrings of spiritual renewal that I associate with Catholicism . . . because my Catholic self, shadowy as it is, is fundamentally my spiritual self'.[32] An Episcopalian lesbian describes her journey: 'It has been a long and roundabout journey and if I have come to know anything at all about God, it is a God who is a fellow traveller, a God who has led me, followed me, and sometimes merely staggered with me through the impossible and barren desert places'.[33]

Dominican priest Richard Woods, working with the gay community in Chicago in the 1970s came 'to recognize and appreciate their courage, humanity and tenacious fidelity to the church as well as their great capacity for laughter, love and sacrifice'.[34] These are sentiments just as valid twenty years later.

GAY MINISTRY

If spirituality is the life of the Divine Spirit within each person, then it is also the realisation of the presence of a gift *for* others. St Paul reminded his friend and co-worker Timothy: 'God's gift was not a spirit of timidity, but the Spirit of power, and love and self-control'.[35] Earlier, Jesus had proclaimed that in the power of the Spirit he had been sent 'to bring good news to the poor, to proclaim liberty to captives, and to the blind new sight, to set the downtrodden free'.[36]

As for the gay Christian, 'they need not forsake the gay world any more than any Christian need forsake the world in order to be saved'. True, they are 'not *of* it—that is, not its creature', but are '*for* the gay world'.[37] Organisations established for, and by, gay and lesbian Christians within the various churches began to appear from the time of the Stonewall riots. They are found extensively throughout Western society, and in most mainstream churches; sometimes they exist with approval, or are silently accepted or tolerated—or sometimes they exist in the face of enduring strong opposition. They fulfil a double function: 'to witness to their Christian faith and experience within the lesbian and gay community', as well as to take their experience into the church.[38] Within the Catholic community in English-speaking countries we find the organisations Dignity (United States and Canada), Quest (Great Britain), Acceptance (Australia), and Assent (New Zealand). The achievement of this gay Christian movement 'has been to bring a sense of personal dignity to thousands of gay Christians'.[39] The *1986 Letter* called on the bishops to expel from Church property those organisations that were 'ambiguous' or 'neglect entirely' the teaching that homosexuality was 'a disorder', and such acts were 'intrinsically evil'.[40] After experiencing expulsion from churches across the United States Dignity, at its 1987 National Convention said, with maturity, that 'faced with this alienation [from the Church leaders] we have devoted ourselves to a ministry of reconciliation'.[41]

The characteristics of a true Christian community are seen in such organisations. They are places where *koinonia* (community of believers), *diakonia* (service to the world), *kerygma* (proclamation of the Good News), and *eucharistica* (thanksgiving and praise) are present, and so 'offer an otherwise neglected group of Catholics an alternative experience of Christ's on-going saving work in the world'.[42] National Co-ordinator of Acceptance-Australia, Len Schmidt, said that 'our primary aim is to help people come to terms with their sexuality and to grow in their relationship with Christ'.[43] These organisations have worked at laying foundations for a sexual ethic for gay Christians within the broader spirituality of the Church. In shaping this ethic there is an appeal to Church leadership 'that we engage in some creative listening, sketch some general directions and leave the rest up to the good sense of faithful people'.[44] According to Fenton Johnson, gay men and lesbians, by allowing themselves 'to be defined not by how we make love but by how we have sex' had cut themselves off from the wisdom of the churches, but the same writer saw the earliest stages of a community being created in which 'a stable set of values against which we may measure and reward or correct our conduct'[45] was taking shape. These movements within the Catholic Church have been founded and developed primarily by the laity exercising their baptismal right to 'freely establish and direct associations which serve charitable or pious purposes or which foster the Christian vocation in the world'.[46] They fulfil the Vatican Council exhortation that the laity 'conduct the apostolate of like to like'.[47]

Within the United States Protestant tradition, which recognises that 'homosexuality is probably the most divisive issue since slavery split the Church,'[48] parish congregations have started to openly welcome gay and lesbian members through movements promoting reconciliation, affirmation and acceptance.[49] Pentecostal minister Troy Perry began the Metropolitan Community Church in Los Angeles in 1968, not just for gays and lesbians, but also for those who found themselves estranged from, or not welcomed into, their own churches.

Although Episcopalian priest Malcolm Boyd sees that the 'relationship between gay people and organized religion has long been an ambiguous, even tortured one',[50] John McNeill holds that 'we also need straight churches which have a public policy of being inclusive'. He sees that by 'coming out' within such a secure community, 'our self-love and self-esteem are strengthened and our interiorized homophobia overcome'.[51] John McNeill says that 'those familiar with gay and lesbian history are aware that spiritual leadership has always come in great part from the gay community in every culture and time'. He sees that in this present moment in history 'God is calling many of us to a public witness of being lesbian or gay and religious persons of deep faith'.[52] That witness is clearly visible in the gay Christian movements, and also in the lives of individuals. If gay people do have a particular sensitivity towards spirituality and service, it is not surprising that they are attracted towards the priesthood, religious life and other forms of Christian ministry where they 'are an important and vital part of the Body of Christ'.[53] Research among Anglican clergy in England showed that they were 'surprisingly satisfied with their jobs', and 'extremely sure about their religious convictions'.[54] It is asserted however, that 'gay [Catholic] priests are considered an embarrassment and a problem, a problem which some in the Church would like to eradicate'.[55]

One woman saw that lesbianism aligned her and others with the marginalised, and from that interaction arose 'the special charisms of our community . . . honesty, courage, openness and freedom'. A gay man came to the realisation: 'This is *my* church, damn it, and no one is going to take it away from me!'; while another said that he was amazed 'that God's powerful grace is so palpable' in 'the courage and willingness to go to the floor on the issues that count, to speak the truth when it hurts'—yet the hierarchy denies this and responds with 'oppression and contempt. . . . I call it the "sacrament of irony" '.[56] A spiritual director told one priest, who was living with AIDS, that while he himself had not realised that he was gay when he was ordained, 'God knew. And God called you to priesthood . . . then your gayness must be part of your ministry and you had better find ways to use it to proclaim God's love'.[57] Lesbian women who remain in religious life value their sexuality 'as a strong deep current flowing out of God through our lives, renewing our creative powers, enlivening our ministry'. They see themselves as women who 'are more loving, more kind, more giving of themselves',[58] bringing the 'treasured gifts' of sensitivity and tenderness to the world that needs 'to be held, healed and hallowed'.[59] Malcolm Boyd laments: 'I have never seen such bitterness, vindictiveness and cruelty as I have on the part of closeted gay priests'. Having chosen to 'live a lie' these men 'have paid a high price—a price of happiness and freedom'.[60]

GAY RELATIONSHIPS OF LOVE

Constantly accused of being anti-family, Christian gay men and lesbians take heart from the example of Jesus, who radically redefined family in teaching his disciples to pray 'Our Father', and who declared that 'anyone who does the will of my Father in heaven is my brother and sister and mother'.[61] The Christian family is to be marked by inclusiveness. Gay and lesbian people all belong to families. They do not destroy family by their sexuality; rather, the forces of homophobia separate many families by fear, distrust and bitterness.

The desire for relationship is of the human heart and so a gay person also 'yearns to have one's relationship respected'. The exclusion of gay men and lesbian women from 'such a union is arbitrary, harmful, cruel and therefore sinful'.[62] In the civil arena debate about 'same-sex marriages' is gaining momentum. Historian John Boswell has claimed that 'such unions in various forms, were widespread in the ancient world'. From his more recent research on same-sex unions in medieval Europe, about which there has been considerable debate, he concluded:

> Recognizing that many—probably most—earlier Western societies institutionalized some form of romantic same-sex unions gives us

> a much more accurate view of the immense variety of human romantic relationships and social responses to them than does the prudish pretence that such 'unmentionable' things never happened.[63]

Even so, some gay men and lesbians do feel themselves called to celibacy in a positive way.

Helen: a journey to celibacy

Few people have had such a turbulent time in bringing sexuality and spirituality into harmony as has Helen. Born forty years ago with a Methodist, then Baptist, upbringing, she became a Catholic with her mother at the age of twelve, with a strong longing to be a nun. Later she joined the Metropolitan Community Church, returned to Catholicism, was accepted by a contemplative religious order, then lived in a non-sectarian community, became involved in the Rajneesh movement, moved into goddess worship, and finally returned to her Catholic faith. Woven through this spiritual journey was a complex sexual life. *My first sexual awareness was towards other females with my first love at twelve. Around fifteen I was attracted towards men as well, and I felt a great conflict in this double sexual attraction. I realised that when I was with a man I felt possessed by him, but when I was with a woman it felt the most natural thing. As a teenager I felt a great conflict between a strong libido and the yearning to be a nun.*

In 1980 Helen married Michael. *The day I got married I knew that I was not doing the right thing. But I tried to make the marriage work. After the birth of our son James, I went into postnatal depression for a short time. During our four years of marriage we moved across three States. I had thought that marriage would be the cure-all of my lesbianism.* On 1 December 1992 Helen attended a Mass to mark World AIDS Day. *It allowed me to deal with some of the grieving process for my friend who had died from AIDS in Sydney. More importantly I heard the Gospel preached in a way relevant to life as it really is. I had finally come home to my Catholic faith.* The earlier attraction to consecrated life remained with

Helen. *I have a strong Franciscan spirit of Gospel simplicity. There is a sense of a call to chastity which comes from Christ and is born out of my Catholic heritage. The patriarchy of the Church is such a burden, especially as it reflects power and control over women. I am much more accepting of my lesbian sexuality. Through living in chastity I am actually more appreciative of my sexuality. I find this movement to a celibate life a real gift in my life, especially considering my past. But I realise that not everyone is called to celibacy. Gay and lesbian people have the right to a full, satisfying and intimate relationship, just like heterosexuals. My life is much more settled now. My relationship with Christ is central to everything. It is particularly in and through the Eucharist that I experience this most intensely. Friendships that are spiritual and nourishing are what are important for me now. I feel called to use creatively my whole self in serving God.*

AIDS: A SHADOW AND A LIGHT ON HOMOSEXUALITY

The AIDS pandemic holds the world in its fierce grip. The human immunodeficiency virus (HIV) which leads to acquired immune deficiency syndrome (AIDS) is spreading daily. HIV/AIDS was first named 'gay-related immunodeficiency' (GRID), and a 'homosexual stamp' was fixed to the disease in the minds of many people.[64]

This disease casts both a shadow and a light over the lives of gay men. The link between sexuality and death is powerful, and has evoked strong anti-gay sentiments among Christian fundamentalists, and an increasing fear of homosexuality in some parts of the community. Some have branded AIDS as God's judgement on homosexuals, and see such men as 'literally scavenging the world . . . importing and even manufacturing new diseases in their bodies because of their world-wide promiscuity'.[65] Such an interpretation has been firmly rejected by mainstream churches: 'AIDS should not be presented as a divine judgement'.[66] It 'reduced God to the level of an enraged terrorist'.[67]

But AIDS has brought homosexuality out into the open, and has generated in many quarters a more robust and objective discussion about sexuality. For gay men infected with the virus, or living with AIDS, it has placed them at a new cross-road in their journey, as one man testified: 'Many friends of mine now searching for a spirituality have been deep in sex and drugs throughout the Eighties and are remarkably clear about what contributes to growth and what does not'.[68] While rejecting the idea that God wishes people to have AIDS, another saw that God 'does permit it as a route to our personal holiness', and that for him it has been a 'time of grace'.[69] Bernie, an Australian gay man, acknowledged that 'AIDS can be a gift', and when accepted as such can bring about changes. 'It brought me closer to my family, my friends, my church, my God and nature'.[70]

Kevin and Michael: growing in love and faith

Kevin's Irish Catholicism was both an angel at his side and a devil on his back. Growing up in a small rural village, he went off at an early age to a minor seminary. He had a genuine dream of being a priest, but the nature and intensity of his teenage sexual feelings left him confused. *It was so difficult. Sex was just not talked about at home. And in the seminary it was only spoken about in the most negative of ways. It was drummed into us how terrible a sin masturbation was. How could I admit to anyone that I felt sexually attracted to men and fantasised about them? I could not resolve my sexual feelings so I left the seminary much to my regret.* London beckoned for Kevin, and there he found an emerging gay culture. He began to see that he was not alone in his feelings. They were exciting times. *It was great to be free. In London I could be myself. And I put my faith on hold. I was having too good a time.* In the mid 1970s Kevin met Michael, who was the image of the Australian icon of the bronzed lifesaver—*tall, handsome and extremely sexy.* They fell in love and were soon living together. While Michael, also a Catholic—of a liberal variety—was open with his family about his sexuality, Kevin was definitely, and would always remain, 'in the closet'. *When in London I rarely went to Mass, but when I went back home I did. Still*

I could not bring myself to go to Communion, and that made me sad. I had one good friend who was a priest—about fifteen years older than me. He was the finest priest I ever knew. He was always kind and never judged me. We would talk about everything and nothing for hours on end. I always felt safe and at peace in his company. In the early 1980s Michael and Kevin settled in Australia. Michael's mother lived her Catholicism deep and strong, for it had a practicality about it, born out of struggle and hardship. By example she helped Kevin start to come to terms with his Catholicism and sexuality. *I started to go to Mass again but I felt that because I was living with Michael I could not go to Communion.* Michael would joke—and there was a lot of truth in his words—*Kevin will only be totally happy if the Pope tells him it's alright.* Then Michael was diagnosed with HIV, and their relationship developed and matured as never before. *Kevin has just been wonderful to me. He is so attentive. I could not ask for a better partner.* And Kevin would say, *I love him so much. I love him more than ever.* Michael's last Communion was several days before his death, and as he prayed the 'Our Father' tears rolled down his cheeks. *This is only the second time I have seen Michael cry in the sixteen years I have been with him.* Shortly after Michael's death Kevin was also diagnosed with HIV. He bore his illness with a great calm. The impact of the virus was more gradual in Kevin's case as he slowly became less and less mobile. *I just want to be with Michael. I hope that he is waiting for me.* Sexuality and faith had at last merged in harmony.

For others, in the face of this particular life-threatening disease, the spiritual journey continues in spite of the church. Peter, describing himself as 'spiritual', said: 'I would find it insulting to myself to belong to any organized religious movement'.[71] Sister Patrice Murphy, Director of St Francis Hospital in New York, sadly commented that some 'had to transcend their church in order to find their God'.[72] Mark, at the age of thirty-one, said: 'I haven't stopped looking for God, although I've stopped looking in Church'. He added: 'I feel there is still time for me to come to some sort of belief, but I feel so burned from the years of trial and failure'.[73]

While individuals living with HIV or AIDS have had to assess life in the face of a life-threatening disease, the wider gay community has been profoundly affected. Margaret Cruikshank saw that AIDS 'created a "new basis of community among gay men" based on caring and different from the past in that it did not depend on either the search for a sexual partner or the desire for social change'.[74] However, Keri, a gay man, saw the experience of AIDS quite differently. Pointing out that youth with terminal illness was 'very sad', went on, 'I don't care what people say about AIDS being a chance for gay men to form mature commitments or grow up—that's bullshit'.[75]

AIDS has also impacted on the wider church community and forced many Christians to reassess their personal attitudes towards homosexuality, and gay men in particular. 'The inclusiveness of Jesus' ministry . . . stands before the church as an example' because it 'declared that all people are acceptable to God'.[76] Hospital chaplain Anglican Sister Hilda says that 'AIDS challenges our perception of sexuality', and she asks, 'what value is the church signalling acceptance—provided they remain celibate?'[77] Anglican priest and sociologist Gary Bouma emphasises that both people living with AIDS and gay men and lesbians must be included in the Church 'as they are, as full members'. He holds that 'the community of faith diminishes itself when it imposes categorical exclusions', because the development of theology comes from 'communities of faith wrestling with the meaning of their faith in the face of the ambiguities of life'.[78]

CONTRIBUTING TO THE DIALOGUE

It is obvious that any dialogue about homosexuality within the Catholic, and wider Christian, community is going to need the active involvement of its gay and lesbian members. They are the ones who can best, from their own experiences, inform the community about this too often misunderstood and ridiculed aspect of human sexuality. Their contribution will shape a 'gracious theology',[79] a theology that is warm and humane and accessible, a theology that breathes the love of God into human hearts and lives.

While the gay and lesbian experience most often begins in the pain and confusion of adolescence with its self-doubt and anxiety about the body, when perseverance becomes a discipline, the transition from feeling a victim to one possessing a gift is the start of ministry to others. Against the common image of a gay culture that is flamboyant, self-indulgent and irresponsible (and those elements *are* there at times), many show the deeper, more mature, and self-assured nature of gay men and lesbians, for whom faith is intrinsically and indispensably woven into their sexuality and personhood.

The contribution of the gay and lesbian community to the ministries of the church is beginning to be acknowledged and valued. The broader fruitfulness of gay lives is impressive—and highlighted by their heroic commitment and sacrifice in the midst of the AIDS epidemic, at a time when government, church and society for so long remained silent because they were 'confused and ignorant'.[80] Ironically, in the midst of so much heartache, gay and lesbian people, as communities and individuals, have come into their own, and revealed to other people their true, compassionate, practical and creative qualities. Recent years have seen the emergence of an impressive collection of literature detailing gay men and lesbians understanding their own sexuality. Their mature reflection, combined with commanding self-assurance, deep faith in God, and a critical analysis of church attitudes and teaching, make for a vibrant dialogue on homosexuality. *A gay and lesbian theology* cannot be developed in clerical circles of academia and authority alone, because its underpinning strengths lie in a spirituality and ministry that can only emerge from gay and lesbian Christians themselves. The inclusiveness that gay and lesbian people demand from the church has its foundation in Jesus, who chose not to call his disciples 'servants', but said 'I call you friends'.[81] In this friendship can be found the key to all human friendships because:

> In friendship are joined
> honour and charm
> truth and joy
> sweetness and goodwill
> affection and action.[82]

3

A CLASH OF LOYALTIES

Peter Coleman, Anglican Bishop of Crediton, England, accurately describes the churches' struggle with homosexuality as 'a clash of loyalties'. This clash is seen on two levels: firstly, that between faithfulness to traditional teaching founded upon the Bible, and the call to show solidarity with those in need, especially when they experience oppression or discrimination; and secondly, the clash between an understanding 'that homosexual genital acts are sinful', and the recognition today 'that sexuality is about relationship'. Coleman sees in the traditional teaching a negative attitude towards the human body and suspicion about sexual passion, influenced strongly by the emphasis on procreation.[1]

All the churches are confronted with the enormous task of facing the significant changes in the attitude of science and society towards sexuality that have taken place throughout this twentieth century. The increased visibility of gay people in society and in the church from the early 1970s has highlighted the inadequacies of the churches' theology and pastoral care, as well as the way the churches have contributed to discrimination. A renewed energy to work for justice has also propelled the churches into the homosexual issue, while theological scholarship has challenged traditional teaching. Gay men and lesbians, deeply offended by church statements, have not only distanced themselves from, but developed hostile attitudes towards, organised religion. 'Coming out *in* the church has meant coming out *of* the church.'[2]

The Protestant Reformation of the sixteenth century did little to change sexual ethics apart from abandoning compulsory celibacy for the clergy. While not a major concern, homosexual acts were condemned by the Reformers with traditional severity. Calvin saw them as a crime that was 'the most abominable of all',[3] and Luther rejected them as an 'idolatrous distortion instilled by the devil'.[4]

FIRST STEPS TOWARDS CHANGE

These attitudes remained unchallenged until 1953, when Derrick Sherwin Bailey in *Homosexuality and the Western Christian Tradition* gave a new interpretation to the passages of the Bible most often used to condemn homosexuality and homosexuals. This was at a time when British anxiety over homosexuality was high, it being especially perceived as a threat to national security at the start of the Cold War. Bailey pointed the church towards the emerging contemporary scientific knowledge about homosexual orientation. He held that 'the bible and Christian tradition know nothing of *homosexuality*; both are concerned solely with the commission of homosexual *acts*'.[5] While some of Bailey's argumentation has been critically challenged, he opened up the issue for scholarly debate, and influenced subsequent studies.

In 1954 the Church of England Moral Welfare Council issued an interim report, *The Problem of Homosexuality*, calling for an enquiry into the criminal law and its relation to male homosexual activity. This led to the British Parliament establishing the Wolfenden Committee to pave the way for law reform which eventually came into effect in 1967. In 1963 a group from the Society of Friends in England published *Towards a Quaker View of Sex*. Their task was to develop a pastoral response to those 'who found that society strongly condemned their sexual feeling'. Respectful of 'the need to preserve marriage and family life', throughout the work, the group said that 'the Christian standard of chastity should not be measured by a physical act, but should be a standard of human relationship, applicable within marriage as well as outside it'.[6] This small unofficial document had a significant influence on the rethinking that was just beginning to take place within some churches. It was remarkable in its insights about and sensitivity to the issue, especially concerning the situation gay men and women found themselves in with regard to their churches. The rise, several years later, of the gay rights movement, and the witness of gay Christians from within the churches, gave further impetus to the study of homosexuality by biblical and theological scholars.

THE SCRIPTURE TEXTS

Six texts in the Bible speak about sexual activity between people of the same sex. These need to be studied in their literary, historical, cultural and theological contexts. The two accounts in the Book of Genesis of the creation of man and woman have also had an important influence on our understanding of these texts.

Christian theology holds that human sexuality is a precious gift from God, and since 'we are made for communion, not for isolation', it moves people 'out of themselves to seek relationships with others'.[7] The churches have understood that the only human relationships in which there can be sexual intimacy are those between a man and a woman united in marriage.

Drawing on the creation stories of *Genesis*, Lance Pierson holds that 'God's original design is heterosexual', and understands that homosexuality is 'a distortion' and so for homosexual people 'God's ideal is to develop their sexuality into heterosexual relating'.[8] Max Stackhouse adds that homosexuality is contrary to the intentions of creation because of 'the structure of the sex organs', of which one of the 'real and undeniable purpose[s]' is human reproduction, 'a purpose not capable of being fulfilled homosexually'.[9]

On the other hand, Victor Furnish observes that the two *Genesis* creation stories from different traditions hold complementary theological truths. Written within a patriarchal culture, there is in these stories the 'presumption that "heterosexual" desire is universal'; however, they 'do not command it'. He says that 'they [the creation stories] are not about God's will for individual members of the species, but only about what is typical of the species as a whole'. The Israelites, surrounded by hostile nations, needed an increased population for the maintenance of their army and emerging agrarian life-style. 'Their views of sex were profoundly conditioned by the patriarchalism that pervaded ancient society. In addition [the laws] were formulated without any knowledge of the complex origins of one's sexual identity and sexual orientation'.[10] Similarly, Richard Siker concludes: 'Heterosexuality may be the dominant form of sexuality but it does not follow that it is the only form of appropriate sexuality'.[11]

The story of Sodom

In *Genesis*[12] we read that God sent two angels to destroy two cities because, as he told Abraham, 'How great is the outcry against Sodom and Gomorrah and very grave their sin!'(18:20). Upon arriving in Sodom, the angels, disguised as men, accepted the hospitality of Lot, but 'the men of Sodom, both young and old, all the people to the last man, surrounded the house' (19:4), demanding of Lot: 'bring them [the two men] out to us, so that we may know them' (19:5). Lot refused, and offered his two virgin daughters to them, saying 'do to them as you please' (19:8). The two angels struck all the men with blindness, and next day forced Lot and his family out of the city before its destruction and that of Gomorrah.

The sin of the two cities, as explained in other biblical references, is a lack of justice (*Isaiah* 1:10 and 3:90); adultery, lies and wickedness (*Jeremiah* 23:14); pride and failure to aid the poor and needy (*Ezekiel* 16:49); folly (*Wisdom* 10:8); inhospitality (*Wisdom* 19:14); and arrogance (*Sirach* 16:8). In the Gospels Jesus declared that on judgement day it would not go as hard for Sodom as for the cities of his own time that had failed to welcome or listen to his disciples, or failed to recognise the deeds of power (*Matthew* 10:14–15 and 11:23–24; *Luke* 10:12 and 17:20). Unclear interpretations of the sin of Sodom are given in two late New Testament books: sexual immorality and pursued unnatural lust (*Jude* 6–7); and ungodliness and licentiousness of the lawless (*2 Peter* 2:4, 6–10).

Christianity has traditionally interpreted the story as God's condemnation of homosexuality, following the *Jewish* inter-testament writings which saw homosexual acts as the reason for God's condemnation. Most modern scholars understand the primary sin as a lack of hospitality. God had already decided to destroy Sodom before the incident between the men of the town and the two angels. What is clearly condemned in the story is an attempted gang rape.

Leviticus

The holiness code of *Leviticus* took its written form around the sixth century BCE. Its purpose was 'to establish the distinctiveness of the Jewish cult over against all foreign cults'.[13] The verses read:

> You shall not lie with a male as with a woman; it is an abomination. (18:22)
>
> If a man lies with a male as with a woman, both of them have committed an abomination; they shall be put to death; their blood is upon them. (20:13)

In this section of *Leviticus* many things were condemned: incest and bestiality; child sacrifice; and sexual intercourse during menstruation; while some foods were declared unclean. No one with a blemish, scab or crushed testicles, who was blind or lame, who had a broken foot or hand, or who was a hunchback or dwarf was permitted to approach the altar with sacrificial offerings. Furnish says that the holiness code reflects a concern for purity. 'To be "pure" meant to be an unblemished specimen of one's kind, unmixed with any other kind.' He points out that when two males engage in sexual activity together, one is required 'as the Hebrew literally says—to "lie the lyings of a woman" ', and therefore 'that partner's maleness has been compromised; he is no longer an unblemished specimen of his kind'.[14] Part of the concern was about the 'seed of life' rather than the sexual activity between two men. It was believed that human life came solely from the man, and a woman's role was to be the place where that life could be nurtured. The other concern of the Israelites was that the worship of other deities, especially in the Canaanite fertility cults, involved temple prostitution with both women and men. Any activity that might be seen as resembling such false worship was understood to be an abomination. William Countryman says that Israel saw its purity system as 'a gift . . . affirming its separation from other nations and its unique relationship to God'.[15]

Robin Scroggs makes the point:

> These two verses are the only legal traditions about homosexuality in the Hebrew Bible. Furthermore, no other biblical passage refers to this prohibition, nor is there any story showing the law being applied in a concrete situation. All that can be said is that late in Israelite history a single law appears (although it may have had an earlier existence) prohibiting male homosexuality.[16]

The world of the New Testament

Before looking at the three New Testament texts from St Paul relating to same-sex activity, it is important to understand the world in which he lived, worked and wrote. Most writings emerging from the ancient Greco-Roman world were written by a privileged group of upper-class men about subjects that interested them. We know little about women and the lower classes. Within that male group we know about a particular form of homosexuality called pederasty, literally the 'love of boys'. Four kinds of pederasty are identified: a sublimated, non-sexual relationship, often seen between teacher and student; a voluntary sexual encounter with an emphasis on the physical; slave prostitution, in the home or in brothels; and paid sexual relations with effeminate call-boys, free youths who sold themselves in order to 'provide sexual gratification'. While there were laws to protect people from forced abuse and sexual harassment, there were none against pederasty per se, and none against male prostitution. In this same Greco-Roman world two Jewish cultures emerged. Palestinian Judaism, which was particularly hostile towards the Gentile world, saw these same-sex activities as a Gentile sin. The culture of Hellenistic Judaism exercised more influence on Paul's writings. Its principal writers, Philo, the Alexandrian theologian, and Josephus, the apologist and historian of the Jewish people, were most scornful of the effeminate call-boy, whom Philo dubbed 'a counterfeit coin'.[17]

The Pauline Letters

In Paul's *First Letter to the Corinthians* he addressed some specific issues of concern: a man living with his father's former wife, church members taking their complaints against each other to the civil courts for judgement and church members patronising female prostitutes. He then gives one of his typical lists of wrongdoers.

> Do you know that wrongdoers will not inherit the kingdom of God? Do not be deceived! Fornicators, idolaters, adulterers, *malokai*, *arsenokoitai*, thieves, the greedy, drunkards, revilers, robbers—none of these will inherit the kingdom of God. And this is what you used to be. But you were washed, you were sanctified, you were justified in the name of the Lord Jesus Christ and in the Spirit of our God.[18]

The meaning of the two Greek words above have been a problem for translators. Some modern examples are:

- Jerusalem Bible—*catamites and sodomites*
- New Jerusalem—*the self-indulgent and sodomites*
- New American—*boy prostitutes and practising homosexuals*

- Revised English—*sexual perverts*
- Revised Standard—*homosexuals*
- New Revised Standard—*male prostitutes and sodomites*
- Today's English Version—*homosexual perverts*

Furnish and Scroggs agree that the root meaning of *malokai* is 'soft' or 'weak' and by extension 'effeminate' or 'call-boy'. It 'is not a technical term to describe people or practices that are pederastic'.[19] This position is supported by the more recent scholarship of Dale Martin who shows that the word can refer to many things that have a soft or weak element to them: fabrics, food delicacies, light breezes. When used in a moral context it also refers to things considered 'soft', and to 'laziness, degeneracy, decadence, lack of courage, or to sum up all these vices in one ancient category, the feminine'. He points out that 'the word *malakos* refers to the entire ancient complex devaluation of the feminine . . . *Malakos* means "effeminate" '.[20]

The word *arsenokoitai* is more difficult because it has no prior history that would give a clear understanding of how the term was used by Paul. Furnish suggests 'those who go to bed with males', and so translates the two words as 'nor effeminate males, nor men who have sex with them'.[21] Coming from the words *arsen* = male, and *koite* = bed, Scroggs proposes that it could mean 'lying (with) a male', or 'one who lies with a male'. He concludes:

> If the *malakos* points to the effeminate call-boy, then the *arsenokoites* in this context must be the active partner who keeps the *malakos* as a 'mistress' or who hires him on occasion to satisfy his sexual desires. A very specific dimension of pederasty is being denounced with these two terms. Seen in this way, the list shares the disapproval of this form of pederasty in agreement with the entire literature of the Greco-Roman world on the topic.[22]

Martin is more cautious in unravelling the mystery of the word, saying that definitions of the word derived from the meaning of its components 'are naive and indefensible'. Looking at the word in other contexts indicates that 'it seems to have referred to some kind of economic exploitation by means of sex, perhaps, but not necessarily homosexual sex'. He does not claim to know what the word means, but rather 'I am claiming that *no one* knows what it meant'.[23] Countryman and John Gaden both conclude that we cannot know 'clearly or definitively what the terms meant to Paul', but that the context suggests that they are males whose sexual activity either exploits others, or departs from a monogamous heterosexual norm.[24] Soards also recognises that 'these words have sorely vexed interpreters and translators'.[25] It is important to note that neither of these words refers to female homosexuality.

Early in the *First Letter to Timothy*, Paul points out that the law is meant for the 'lawless', and here he gives us another list of such people:

> Now we know that the law is good, if one uses it legitimately. This means understanding that the law is laid down not for the innocent but for the lawless and disobedient, for the godless and sinful, for the unholy and profane, for those who kill their father or mother, for murderers, *pornoi*, *arsenokoitai*, *andrapodistai*, liars, perjurers, and whatever is contrary to the sound teaching that conforms to the glorious gospel of the blessed God, which he entrusted to me.[26]

Again we see how the Greek words are variously translated:

- Jerusalem Bible—*for those who are immoral with women, or with boys or with men*
- New Jerusalem—*the promiscuous, homosexuals, kidnappers*
- New American—*the unchaste, practising homosexuals, kidnappers*
- Revised English—*fornicators, perverts, kidnappers*
- Revised Standard—*immoral persons, sodomites, kidnappers*
- New Revised Standard—*fornicators, sodomites, slave traders*
- Today's English Version—*for the immoral, for sexual perverts, for kidnappers*

There is general agreement across the board that Paul has modelled this list on the Ten Commandments, and that words are grouped together 'in some recognizable relationship'.[27] Seeing these two lists by Paul illustrating unacceptable pre-Christian practices and actions contrary to the Gospel, Soards concludes that 'the primary intention of these verses is not to teach about homosexuality'. They only indirectly give us information about it.[28]

The longest and most important reference to homosexual acts in the Bible (and the only one concerned with women) is in Paul's *Letter to the Romans*.

> For this reason God gave them up to degrading passions. Their women exchanged natural intercourse for unnatural, and in the same way also the men, giving up natural intercourse with women, were consumed with passion for one another. Men committed

> shameless acts with men and received in their own persons the due penalty for their error.[29]

This passage is within the context of Paul showing that the entire world, of both Gentiles and Jews, is guilty of sin and so falls short of the glory of God. Salvation is God's gift and extends now to Jew and Gentile alike. The reference to homosexual acts illustrates the consequences of idolatry among the Gentiles and is described in the tradition of a Hellenistic Jewish judgement on homosexuality. The inclusion of women reflects the patriarchal view of sexuality of the time when men were dominant and in control. Furnish claims that homosexual intercourse is mentioned as one of those typical Gentile practices. It is regarded not as one of the 'sins' of the Gentiles, but as one of the *consequences* of their root sin of refusing to let the one true God be *their* God.[30] Countryman points out that Paul 'did not apply the language of sin' to homosexual acts—'instead he treated homosexual behavior as an integral, if unpleasingly dirty aspect of Gentile culture'.[31]

Giving a more rigid interpretation to the text, and recognising that 'Paul's real criticism is aimed at Gentile idolatry', Marion Soards says that Paul, along with Jewish thinkers of his time, saw that homosexual acts 'were sinful actions of unbridled lust'.[32] Lance Pierson claims that Paul mentions homosexuality as the first example of immoral behaviour 'because it was *the* immorality associated with pagan idolatry'.[33] When Paul talks of 'natural' and 'unnatural', David Field says that he has in mind the pattern of God's creation, which 'he clearly understands to be heterosexual . . . when set in the context of creation, all homosexual relations are "unnatural relations" '.[34] Gaden, Thatcher and Soards all agree that Paul had no concept of homosexual orientation.[35]

Conclusions from the Bible

James Nelson points out that the Bible speaks of homosexual acts and that 'there is no clear scriptural message about homosexuality as a psychosexual orientation, [which is a] distinct modern concept, foreign to the biblical writers'.[36] Reading the texts, Scroggs understands that 'one would assume a homosexual encounter to be only for purposes of sexual gratification'.[37]

These scattered biblical texts were written over a period of nearly one thousand years and reflect, quite naturally, varying eras and attitudes. It is just not possible to read them as a well-developed teaching about homosexuality. Scroggs reaches the conclusion: '*Biblical judgements against homosexuality are not relevant to today's debate.* They should no longer be used in denominational discussions about homosexuality . . . *not because the Bible is not authoritative*, but simply because it does not address the issues involved'.[38]

The prophets made no reference to homosexual acts, nor did Jesus himself. Ruth Barnhouse, while acknowledging that 'this is a significant silence', goes on to claim that 'in numerous places' the Bible forbids homosexual acts. Field asserts that the New Testament teaching on homosexuality 'takes on an impressive unity'. In the kingdom of God 'homosexuality has no place'.[39] Marva Dawn judges homosexual behaviour as 'an addiction'. There are two choices for the homosexual: 'to rebel against their Creator . . . or to submit to his will for sexual celibacy'. Since their behaviour is 'a violation of God's intention for humanity' they 'need recovery, not respectability'.[40] Pierson describes homosexual people as 'psychological orphans', their condition as 'arrested development', and although 'healing is a glorious possibility for gay people', 'where spirits are involved you may need to call on further deliverance ministry'. If healing is not achieved, then 'exclusion from [church] membership must take place'.[41]

THE UNCHANGING TEACHING

In many churches discussions about homosexuality have been brief. Accepting the Bible as the only authority for passing judgement on moral issues, church leaders consistently condemn all homosexual acts as sinful. Often these churches fail to make the distinction between persons, orientation and acts, and their statements lack both justice and charity. Some are hard hitting and uncompromising in their brevity. The most radical stance comes from the Christian Identity Church: 'Homosexuality is an abomination before God and should be punished by death'. The theme of homosexuality deserving negative judgement is strongly expressed in other statements. Some examples are:

- Evangelical Free Church of America (1978): 'homosexual practice . . . cried out to Him [God] for judgement upon society'.
- Assemblies of God (1979): 'homosexuality . . . will come under the judgement of God'.

- The Salvation Army (1980): homosexuality is 'a deviant behavior'.
- Church of the Nazarene (1985): 'such acts are sinful and subject to the wrath of God'.
- Free Methodist Church (1985): 'persons with homosexual inclinations are accountable to God for their behavior'.
- Greek Orthodox Archdiocese of North and South America (undated): homosexuality is 'intrinsically promiscuous and breeds promiscuity'.

The largest Protestant Church in the United States is the Southern Baptist Convention, with 43 million members. From 1976 until 1992 it addressed the issue of homosexuality seven times, affirming 'commitment to biblical truth' (1976); 'opposing legal, social and religious acceptance' (1977); deploring 'the proliferation of all homosexual practices' (1980); and reaffirming 'that all such practices are sin' (1985). This Church also affirmed that the Bible 'teaches forgiveness and transformation' (1985), and as early as 1977 urged members to 'show compassion for every person . . . and pray for the redemption of all persons'.[42]

Throughout the 1980s the television evangelists experienced a groundswell of support in the United States, as they focused their attention on issues of family values, abortion and homosexuality. Their public stand meant that the lines between Christian fundamentalism and right wing politics became blurred. 'As gay people became more forthright and more successful, their opponents would be more open and more hostile as well'.[43] These fundamentalists stirred up fears. Jerry Falwell, founder of the Moral Majority, claimed that lesbians and gay men were intent upon the 'complete elimination of God and Christianity from American society'.[44]

ENTERING INTO DIALOGUE

Other churches have embarked on a serious study of the issue of homosexuality and initiated open dialogue within their congregations, especially with lesbian and gay members. Many have maintained traditional teaching, but nuanced it with a more sensitive attitude to the dilemma facing lesbian and gay Christians.

Three Lutheran Churches merged in 1988 to become the Evangelical Lutheran Church in America. In 1970 one branch held that 'homosexuality is viewed as a departure from the heterosexual structure of God's creation'; while another in 1977 held that 'homosexual behavior is a sin, a form of idolatry, a breaking of the natural order'. But by 1981 changing attitudes began to appear. The Missouri Synod, in a statement on human sexuality, recognised that 'we are created not for a life of isolation, but for community'. It advised that homosexuals should 'abstain from homosexual acts' but concluded that 'we should not overlook the burden of loneliness which this places upon the homosexual'.[45] The Lutheran Church, like others, commissioned studies of the issue which, while not the official position of the Church, reflect the shifts in people's perception and understanding. They are tools to encourage and enable fruitful dialogue. Reflecting on the role of Scripture, a study within the Evangelical Lutheran Church in 1991 said that 'even if we conclude that Paul's judgement [in Romans] on same-sex acts, is clearly negative, this does not necessarily determine the significance of this text for us today . . . the few passages that refer to same-sex activity (with a much different social meaning than today) do not settle the issue'. This same statement highlighted the core Gospel values and commitments including the call to love one's neighbour, Jesus' affirmation of the dignity of all people, the compassionate character of the community, and the shared Christian calling to 'care for one another to live responsibly'.[46]

The first draft of a study document on sexuality, published in 1993, recommends more openness on the part of the Church to lesbians and gay men, even support for gay and lesbian relationships that are committed, mutual and loving, even if such relationships are seen as imperfect before God.[47]

The Lutheran Church in Australia has not been so open to rethinking the issue. Its President, Dr Lance Steike, said in 1995 that 'Scripture makes it clear that homosexual behaviour is sin. It's a form of idolatry. It invites the anger of God'.[48] This reflects the earlier *Statement on Homosexuality* adopted by the General Synod at the Church's 1975 Convention:

> Homosexuality is part of the mysterious disturbance and distortion that has entered God's creation and His created social structures. Like disease, it must be seen in the context of the Fall and the resultant intrusion of disruptive and abnormal forces which have upset and perverted God's original design.

The *Statement* directs Christian homosexuals to accept their situation 'in obedience to God', to resist 'the strong temptation of rebelling and murmuring against God', and to seek 'professional help and pastoral aid'. The Church on its part 'must exhibit understanding and sympathy', and 'proclaim . . . above all the forgiveness of sin for Christ's sake'.[49]

One of the first churches in America to engage in dialogue about homosexuality was the United Church of Christ which in 1969 supported the decriminalisation of homosexual acts between consenting adults in some American States. In 1983, its Fourteenth General Synod declared that:

> [O]ur present knowledge about the bases of sexual orientation and behavior is incomplete, and that psycho-social and ethical issues surrounding the rightfulness or wrongfulness of various forms of sexual expression and embodiment are still being debated within the United Church of Christ.

Many issues have been addressed by this Church: the violation of civil rights of gay and bisexual persons (1977); an equal employment opportunity policy for the Church was developed (1980); and homophobia within the Church itself was confronted (1983). This institutional homophobia 'fosters emotional strain, alienation, a lack of self worth, and in some cases a life where suicide appears to be the only option'. As early as 1969 this Church was re-evaluating the biblical texts. 'Modern Biblical scholarship suggests that, while homosexuality is condemned in the Old and New Testaments, its seriousness has been exaggerated by wrenching scriptural verses out of context.'[50]

The Uniting Church in Australia has been the one church most involved in discussions about homosexuality in that country. Controversy has raged around the issue of the acceptance for lay and ordained ministry of openly gay men and women. An Assembly Committee was established and reported to the 1985 General Synod, making it clear that it spoke *to* the Church and not *for* it. In the Preface the situation was summed up.

> The church around the world is divided at the present in its understanding of homosexuality . . . We can rejoice that God never abandons his people to their disagreements. He continues to enter into the ambiguity and pain of our human existence always leading us on towards new hope for our life together.[51]

In its response to the *Report* the Social Justice Commission of South Australia pointed out that: 'for many homosexual people recognition of their own sexual orientation is also the painful recognition that they themselves are the very people that they have learned to hate and despise. Thus they undergo an agony of self-hate, shame and fear'.[52] In 1987 the Assembly Standing Committee affirmed that regardless of sexual orientation, all the baptised belong to Christ's church. It noted that 'there is a range of deeply held convictions within the Uniting Church' and encouraged 'church members to explore more fully their understanding of the issues'. Those seeking ordination were expected to 'adhere to the standards of celibacy in singleness and faithfulness in marriage'.[53]

The 1991 National Assembly established a Task Group on Sexuality as 'a further attempt to engage the church in dialogue'. It published an *Interim Report* in 1996, calling for responses leading to a final report in mid-1997. Recognising that 'the historical distance between our times and biblical times means we cannot simply translate the writers' conclusions about sexuality into our own', the *Interim Report* sought to maintain 'the primary authority of the Scriptures'. It acknowledged that 'perhaps more than most issues, that of homosexuality arouses very deep emotional fears in people'. It saw 'no legitimate reason for rejecting homosexuality or homosexual relationships per se', but acknowledged that there were widely diverse opinions 'over whether same sex relationships should be blessed and celebrated'. It nonetheless reached the conclusion: 'The Task Group believes that the Church needs to seriously engage in further discussion about the issue. Such relationships should be recognised and affirmed and work begun on appropriate liturgical resources'.[54]

THE ANGLICAN COMMUNION

Archbishop Fischer of Canterbury gave support in the House of Lords to the principles of the recommendations of the *Wolfenden Report* in 1957. A resolution at the 1978 Lambeth Conference of Anglican Bishops admitted that 'homosexuality has rarely received understanding either in the church or in society', and that an adequate understanding and response would require Christians to 'approach the subject compassionately and without prejudice'.[55] After spending almost five years preparing it, the General Synod Board for Social Responsibility published *Homosexual Relationships* in 1979, which examined the theological, social, pastoral and legal aspects of the issue. With reference to the biblical texts it stated that 'we need to take account of knowledge not available to biblical writers', and pointed out that 'many moral and ethical precepts which in the Bible are presented as the direct commands of God have been re-interpreted in the course of Christian history, and even in some cases abandoned as guides or standards'. It recognised that some individuals 'may justifiably choose to enter a relationship' in order to enjoy companionship, and to sexually express their love.[56]

In 1988, at the Lambeth Conference, attended by most of the bishops of the worldwide Anglican Communion, a resolution was passed calling for 'a deep and dispassionate study of the question of homosexuality, which would take seriously both the teaching of Scripture and the results of scientific and medical research'. To assist this study, the House of Bishops of the General Synod of the Church of England published the statement *Issues in Human Sexuality* in 1991. This is a critically important document both because of its source, and because of the quality of its scholarship. Evaluating the scriptural evidence, the bishops saw that marriage in ancient times was bound up in the perceived need for sons. The early Christians were also anxious about the sexual licence of the Gentile world. Homosexual activity of the time was seen as being even more complex. Recognising that 'at the same time the Bible has a positive approach to the possibilities of affection in same-sex relationships', the bishops cited the examples of David and Jonathan, Ruth and Naomi, and Jesus and his disciples. They said that 'friendship is undervalued in the present age', holding that 'celibacy cannot be proscribed for anyone' and that 'the single should live in a form of chastity appropriate to their situation'. Speaking specifically about homosexual relationships, the bishops recognised that 'there are those who grow steadily in fidelity and in mutual caring, understanding and support', and acknowledged partnerships that are a blessing to the world and that 'achieve great, even heroic sacrifice and devotion'. However, they made the critically important, but not necessarily insurmountable, point that 'deliberate genital contact [between homosexuals] does nevertheless represent the crossing of a significant boundary'. They make the important distinction between lust and erotic feelings. Such erotic feelings for a homosexual are not sinful and should not lead a person to regard themselves as evil.

Looking to the story of creation they see Adam finding 'himself in lonely isolation'. 'Only the creation of another who is bone of his bone and flesh of his flesh overcomes this loneliness', this being the 'fundamental reason why a man leaves his parents in order to attach himself to his wife'. The Christian community should be a welcoming place for those homosexuals 'who follow the way of abstinence', in addition to 'those who are conscientiously convinced that a faithful, sexually active relationship with one other person, aimed at helping both partners to grow in discipleship, is the way of life God wills for them'. Concerning homosexual clergy, the bishops hold that they 'cannot claim the liberty to enter into sexually active homophile relationships'. In making this judgement, they saw that they were being inconsistent in their demands. They concluded:

> In making our response we have tried never to forget our two principal duties as bishops: to be guardians of the Christian faith and way of life; yet equally to be pastors who not only respond in love to those who cry out of any pain of injustice or distress, but also seek to discern when love is summoning the church to rethink its existing perception of the truth.[57]

Within the 120 dioceses of the Episcopal Church in the United States, the debate on homosexuality and the place of homosexuals within the Church and its ordained ministry has been vigorous. The 1976 General Convention affirmed 'that homosexual persons are children of God', while the House of Bishops at the 1979 General Convention acknowledged that it was 'most difficult to arrive at comprehensive and agreed upon statements in these matters'. At the same time celibate gay priests were affirmed in their ministry.[58]

A minority of twenty bishops dissented from the 1979 decision not to ordain sexually active homosexuals, basing their position 'on the total witness of Holy Scripture'. They held that modern exegesis and interpretation, along with enhanced understanding of the original languages and cultural context, gives 'no certain basis for a total and absolute condemnation either of homosexual persons or homosexual activities in all cases'. Speaking specifically of homosexual clergy in relationships, they saw in many of them 'no less a sign to the world of God's love' than that seen in Christian marriage. 'From such relationships we cannot believe God to be absent.' A further thirty bishops signed this statement in 1988.[59]

The most liberal position on homosexuality in the Episcopal Church, and indeed in the worldwide Anglican Communion, is found in the Diocese of Newark, which received, 'with great appreciation' a report from the Task Force on *Changing Patterns of Sexuality and Family Life* at its 113th Convention in 1987. The

Report said: 'Ideally homosexual couples would find within the community of the congregation the same recognition and affirmation which nurtures and sustains heterosexual couples in their relationship including, where appropriate, liturgies which recognize and bless such relationships'.[60]

In 1988 the General Convention condemned violence against homosexual persons and expressed deep concern for 'the tragic suffering of gay and lesbian youth' through suicide, committing the church to increased 'pastoral care of troubled youth, including exploration of the root causes' of these suicides.[61]

Since the late 1980s the division among Episcopal bishops on the issue of homosexuality has become more pronounced, especially concerning the ordination of homosexual men and women. This was highlighted in 1996 when ten bishops brought a charge of heresy against retired Bishop Walter Righter for ordaining a non-celibate gay man, even though forty other bishops had ordained some 140 gay men and women who lived in committed relationships. The Episcopal Church court eventually ruled 'that there is no core doctrine prohibiting' such ordinations, and Bishop Righter was absolved of the charge of heresy.[62]

The Anglican Church in Australia has given little time to the issue of homosexuality. The Diocese of Sydney, through its Ethics and Social Questions Committee, prepared a *Report on Homosexuality* in 1973 which stated:

> Homosexual behaviour represents a most prominent instance of disorder in creation in the area of human relationships. It threatens the whole understanding of sex and the family . . .The homosexual who feels that he cannot express his sexuality in any other way (the so called 'invert') [is] called upon to repent and seek renewal.[63]

The *Report* was overwhelmingly accepted by the Synod, when Archbishop Marcus Loane said: 'He [the homosexual] will not expect to be received [by the Church] if he does not intend to abide by God's Word and stop his homosexual acts, and seek to achieve with God's help such sexual re-orientation as may be open to him'.[64]

The Diocese of Melbourne Synod, through its Social Questions Committee, addressed the issue of homosexuality in 1971 and again in 1985. The first time was to urge for the removal of penalties in civil law in relation to homosexual activity between consenting adults. In its short discussion of theological considerations it acknowledged that 'contemporary theology is trying to come to terms with emerging sociological and psychological facts about homosexuality'. Even here the moral issue was not about homosexuality itself, but whether in holding that homosexual acts were wrong one could also hold that 'homosexual acts . . . need not be criminal merely because they do not accord with Christian values'. The Synod concluded that the distinction could be made.[65] The Committee's 1985 report, *The Church, Homosexuality and the AIDS Crisis*, was written from within a very different context, 'as a contribution to the ongoing debate on the subject'. Acknowledging that 'there is no consensus on the issue', it stated that 'it is undeniable that the clear words of Scripture . . . condemn homosexual acts'. After analysing the two opposing positions—homosexual acts are legitimate expressions of human sexuality; and that such acts are to be condemned as sinful—the *Report* concluded: 'No case has been demonstrated convincingly enough to overturn the traditional Christian view that the Scriptures condemn homosexual acts as sinful because they are unnatural in the sense that they are unnatural to humanity as created male and female in the image of God'.[66]

A discussion paper on sexuality was prepared by the General Synod Office of the Anglican Church in Australia in 1989, and published by the General Synod Doctrine Commission in 1992 in the collection *A Theology of the Human Person*. The paper reflected on the biblical passages about homosexual acts, and concluded that 'the apostle [Paul] speaks of homosexual activity rather than homosexual orientation'. It showed sensitivity to the situation homosexual people find themselves in, and placed an emphasis on friendships reflecting love of neighbour. It is noteworthy that the paper spoke of 'homosexuals and homosexualities'.[67] Even so, compared with the level of scholarship in the English and American debate on the subject, the Australian contributions have been superficial.

CONFLICTING CHRISTIAN RESPONSES

Many American-based evangelical Christian churches support ministries designed to convert homosexuals to heterosexuality. These groups, which have spread to other parts of the world, include Sexaholics Anonymous, Be Whole Ministries, Homosexuals Anonymous, Love in Action, Metanoia, Desert Stream, and the most influential, Exodus International. Based on the view that the Bible condemns all homosexual acts as sin, these Christian organisations see homosexuality as 'a sexual neurosis;' as 'a relational addiction'. The healing by God comes through deliverance that 'rids one of the dominating pervasive power of lust' and is accompanied by 'genuine repentance, the willingness to turn to Jesus'.[68]

Hostility towards lesbians and gay men from within the churches led to the formation of the Universal Fellowship of the Metropolitan Community Church in 1968. The founder, thirty-year-old ordained Southern Pentecostal minister Troy Perry, held his first service with twelve people in Los Angeles. By 1992, 27 000 members met in 264 churches in sixteen countries.[69] Anti-gay violence was directed against this fledging Church through arson of buildings, and the murder of members.[70] In its *Statement of Doctrine, Sacraments and Rites* the Metropolitan Community Church places itself within mainstream Protestantism, basing its faith 'upon the principles outlined in the historic creeds: Apostles and Nicene', and celebrating the two Sacraments of Baptism and Holy Communion. Among the other Rites of the Church are those of Holy Union and of Matrimony. In the debate about 'gay marriages' it is helpful to note the clear distinction this Church makes between Marriage and Holy Union. Although orthodox in its Protestant Confession of Faith, this Church has never been accepted into membership of the World Council of Churches, or any similar national body.[71]

FINDING A NEW DIRECTION

Churches of Protestant tradition are faced with a serious dilemma. They inherited from the Reformation a rejection of compulsory celibacy which while recognised as 'a venerable Christian tradition' was to be 'voluntarily chosen for positive rather than negative reasons'.[72] Yet at the same time they demand a celibate life from gay men and women. Countryman says that denying a whole group of people 'the right peaceably and without hurting others to pursue the kind of sexuality that corresponds to their nature is a perversion of the gospel'.[73]

People across the whole spectrum of theological thought recognise that the Christian teaching on homosexual acts, and the communication of that teaching, has alienated many lesbians and gay men from the church. Nelson says that it is 'naive and cruel' to tell such people 'your sexual orientation is still unnatural and a perversion, but this is no judgement upon you as a person'.[74] Pierson holds that 'church membership often adds to the misery of being gay, with fear of condemnation and isolation'.[75]

We have seen here a sample of the official positions taken by Christian churches on homosexuality, with polarisation similar to that observed among their theologians. This 'clash of loyalties' that besets the churches is nonetheless being handled with maturity. In most mainstream churches, leadership has encouraged an open dialogue, especially with lesbian and gay members. Such debate and dialogue is vigorous and the affirmation from within the Uniting Church in Australia 'that God never abandons his people in their disagreements' is particularly pertinent.

While some Protestant theology emerges from a biblical fundamentalism, new scholarship is pioneering a re-evaluation of the Scriptures as they relate to twentieth century concepts and experiences of homosexuality. A sexual ethic has emerged that puts emphasis on the quality of relationship rather than on individual acts. In an era of theological ferment, creative thought is bringing critical analysis to traditional formulas of faith and moral values. Understanding theology as a living and dynamic science, theologians search for a fuller truth about human sexuality.

Within both Anglican and Protestant Churches there is diversity of teaching about homosexuality by theologians, and there are signs that this is leading some to dogmatism rather than dialogue. Consideration of the possibility of same-sex relationships being respected and blessed within the Church community is a radical departure from the past. But this has been possible because Protestant theology has not held procreation as fundamental to every sexual act in the same way as Catholic theology. These developments must be tested throughout the Christian church, now involved in a wider 'dialogue of love' which, as Pope John Paul says, 'has become an outright necessity, one of the Church's priorities'. Homosexuality cannot be ignored as unimportant or too difficult an issue for the church. The area of ethics and morality demonstrates painful differences between the churches, so that 'in this vast area there is much room for dialogue concerning the moral principles of the Gospel and their implications'.[76] The contribution of Anglican and Protestant scholars and Churches is significant to the dialogue.

4

DEVELOPING CATHOLIC SEXUAL THEOLOGY

The discussion, dialogue and debate about homosexuality that have taken place within the Anglican Communion and the Protestant Churches have occurred at every level of Church membership. Synods, Assemblies, Conventions, Conferences, Standing Committees, parishes and home groups have all been caught up in the issue, showing a rich diversity of opinions and belief. The structure of the Roman Catholic Church does not allow for such open debate and discussion. In fact, in many ways it works effectively against it. Teaching authority is invested in the *Magisterium* which is the domain of the pope and bishops, who as the successors of the Apostles 'are authentic teachers, that is, teachers endowed with the authority of Christ . . . [T]he faithful for their part, are obliged to submit to their bishop's decision, made in the name of Christ, in matters of faith and morals, and to adhere to it with a ready and respectful allegiance of mind'.[1]

In the Middle Ages the term *Magisterium* had a broader meaning embracing the magisterium of the cathedral chair—the teaching authority of the bishop—and the magisterium of the professorial chair—the teaching authority of the theologian.[2] Today theologians and bishops are nonetheless called to work together, for 'while having different gifts and functions, [they] ultimately have the same goal: preserving the People of God in the truth which sets free and thereby making them "a light to the nations". This service to the ecclesiastical community brings the theologian and the Magisterium into a reciprocal relationship'.[3]

Theologian Bernard Haring explains the particular role of the *moral* theologian as bringing together the message of the Bible with the human experience of contemporary people. 'The proper ethos of the moral theologian is a grateful memory, a spirit of appreciation for what has been received from past generations and cultures, combined with a great eagerness to cultivate the spirit of discernment'.[4] The theologians have a very active role in the search for truth because sometimes in the process of discernment difficulties will be discovered in the teaching of the *Magisterium*. The theologian then 'has the duty to make known . . . the problems raised by the teaching itself, in the arguments proposed to justify it, or even in the manner in which it is presented'.[5] As students and interpreters of the Scriptures, theologians must be sensitive to the fact that here the Word of God is communicated in human language, and so must look for the meaning the writer 'intended to express and did in fact express, through the medium of a contemporary literary form'.[6] Recognising that in the biblical texts universal moral principles and particular legal and ritual purity instructions are 'mixed together', the Pontifical Biblical Commission points out that 'in many cases the response may be that no biblical text explicitly addresses the problem proposed'. It adds: 'On the most important points the moral principles of the Decalogue remain basic'. Fundamentalism is seen as dangerous because it can deceive people who 'look to the bible for ready answers to the problems of life'. It offers 'interpretations that are pious but illusory'.[7]

UNDERSTANDING THE SCRIPTURES

Study of the Scriptures, then, is trying to discover what was the intention of the sacred writer, keeping in mind the Scriptures' divine authority. The line that divides the task of interpretation and understanding no longer falls between Catholic and Protestant, but 'between those who follow a fundamentalist reading . . . and those who follow an historical-critical reading'.[8] As has been pointed out in Chapter 1, the Catholic *Magisterium* and the Vatican Congregations in particular, maintain a traditional fundamentalist interpretation of the texts believed to condemn homosexual acts. Increasingly Catholic theologians question such interpretations and they concur with many Protestant biblical scholars. Vincent Genovesi asks: 'If the people of Sodom were notorious for their homosexual behavior, why is this never clearly stated in all the other texts where Sodom's evil is detailed, and why is Sodom never mentioned in those scriptural texts which . . . do in fact make specific reference to homogenital activity?'.[9] Others point out that this event must be read in the context of the total story of Abraham. God had already decided to destroy the city long before the attempted rape of the angels sent to rescue Lot and his family.[10]

Reflecting on the *Leviticus* texts, Daniel Helminiak points out that the Hebrew word *toevah*, translated as abomination, means uncleanness, impurity, dirtiness. The author avoided *zimah* which refers to something that is wrong in itself, an injustice, a sin. Even when the Hebrew Scriptures were first translated into Greek, *toevah* was rendered as *bdelygma*, meaning ritual impurity, and not *anomia*, meaning a violation of law, a wrong, a sin. Helminiak goes on to show that the concern was 'to keep Israel from taking part in Gentile practices', especially where such same-sex activities were associated with idolatry.[11] Dick Westley holds that 'Scripture calls homosexuality an abomination only when it is a violation of the first commandment: I am the Lord your God, you shall not have strange gods before me'.[12] Vincent Genovesi says that 'such activity is prohibited because of its association with idolatry'.[13]

In the New Testament only Paul speaks about homosexual acts. Catholic scholars have faced the same problems as their Protestant colleagues in translating the words *malokai* and *arsenokoitai* in First Corinthians, and *pornoi*, *arsenokoitai* and *andrapodistai* in First Timothy as 'there is no real certainty about what these texts mean'.[14]

In his most significant text regarding homosexual acts, Paul shows that the whole world is guilty of sin, and so God's grace is his gift for all people, Jew and Gentile alike. Australian Jesuit Brendan Byrne points out that the *Letter to the Romans* is a plea for tolerance among the Christians of Rome, between those of Jewish origin and the Gentiles. After first condemning the sinfulness and alienation of the Gentile world, Paul turns on his Christian–Jewish readers, and describes their sinfulness after asking 'you who judge others, why do you do the same?'.[15] Anthony Kosnik and others remind us that Paul 'as an Hellenistic Jew was both conditioned by the Levitical legislation of the Old Testament and appalled at the depravity of the age', and so 'understandably rejected homosexual perversion whether by men or women'.[16] This passage has usually been cited as the only one referring to lesbianism, but Daniel Helminiak questions that interpretation, showing that the words *para physin*, usually translated as unnatural, may refer 'to female sexual relations that are "beyond the ordinary" . . . anything that would not be considered the standard way of having sex'. He observes that the two words used by Paul to describe sexual acts between men, and translated as degrading passions and shameless acts, do not have an ethical connotation, because Paul writes in the spirit of the Levitical purity codes. He 'calls their sexual deeds degrading, shameful, dishonourable . . . [and] their other deeds wickedness, evil and malice'.[17]

Genovesi shows that Paul clearly condemns rape, female and male prostitution, and any sexual relationship 'which is essentially lacking in mutuality and equality'. He goes on:

> What seems overdrawn, however, is any conclusion that Paul's teaching must remain as a condemnation of all homogenital activity, even that which occurs between two committed people whom we would describe today as being constitutively or permanently homosexually orientated. . .The thought thus suggests itself that, at least under certain conditions, the homogenital behavior of true homosexuals might not stand under Paul's negative judgement, or that of Scripture in general.[18]

Brendan Byrne draws this conclusion:

> The ancient world in general and Paul in particular made no distinction between being of homosexual disposition as an *abiding* personal psychological orientation, the cause of which remains mysterious still to modern science, and freely choosing to indulge in homosexual relations. This gap between ancient and modern thinking must clearly be taken into consideration in any modern moral assessment in which Scripture plays a part.[19]

BUILDING ON TRADITION

The Sodom story profoundly influenced early Christian teaching on homosexual acts. St Augustine taught: 'These shameful acts against nature, such as were condemned in Sodom, ought everywhere and always to be detested and punished'.[20] St Thomas Aquinas, in the thirteenth century, shifted the basis of condemnation from Scripture to the natural law. He regarded masturbation, sodomy and bestiality as being against nature, and from that standpoint, more serious than fornication, incest and adultery. In his *Summa Theologica* he wrote: 'Sins of abuse are more serious than sins of omission . . . The gravest, however, is bestiality which does not even involve the same species . . . After bestiality, sodomy is the worst because the wrong sex is involved'.[21]

Until the late 1960s, this teaching was rarely, if ever, challenged. In his moral theology textbook, popular in English-speaking seminaries, Bernard Haring held:

> One of the commonest forms of sexual deviation is *homosexuality* which St Paul calls a punishment exposing the perversity of those who refuse to adore God . . . Homosexuality is frequently the result of seduction and utter loss of sexual control . . . The deviates are frequently crippled by a misguided, undisciplined life or psychic defects in their moral freedom and responsibility, but their psychic condition as such does not exonerate them any more than natural passion excuses fornicators.[22]

Fr John Harvey, who for almost forty years has worked in pastoral care among homosexual people in New York city, has been one of the most significant English-speaking theologians explaining traditional teaching. He founded Courage as a support organisation for homosexuals who accept the celibate life as their only moral choice. Writing in the *New Catholic Encyclopedia* in 1967 he explained:

> The homosexual act by its essence excludes all possibility of transmission of life; such an act cannot fulfil the procreative purpose of the sexual faculty and is, therefore, an inordinate use of that faculty. Since it runs contrary to a very important goal of human nature, it is a grave transgression of the divine will.[23]

In 1977 he wrote that since 'homosexual acts do exclude all possibility of the procreation of life, they do not fulfil an essential purpose of human sexuality'.[24] And in 1987 he continued to hold that 'there is no way one can justify homosexual acts. The homosexual lifestyle cannot be reconciled with a truly Christian way of life'. Harvey firmly bases his teaching within the biblical theology of creation, saying that 'sexual activity ought to be heterosexual and marital'. Harvey claims that 'in thirty-two years of counselling homosexual persons, I have yet to meet a practising homosexual person who could be called "gay" in the sense of joyful'. He goes on to say that 'in many homosexual persons there is also a terrible sense of inferiority'.[25] He sees that the physical, psychological and spiritual complementarity between man and woman in marriage can never be realised in same-sex relationships.[26]

Other theologians, while also holding that homosexual acts are immoral and advocating a life of celibacy, nevertheless accept that some form of stable loving relationship is to be preferred to promiscuity. **Edward Malloy**, believing that 'the stable couple is not the typical arrangement in the homosexual way of life', teaches that 'the celibate option for the Christian homosexual' should be upheld. Rejecting any rite of marriage for such people, he does go on to say that 'homosexual couples committed to a permanent and exclusive relationship offer the best hope for the preservation of Christian values by active homosexuals'.[27]

Lisa Sowle Cahill concludes from her study of Scripture, human experience, natural law, tradition and the Christian community that 'these sources together point unavoidably toward a heterosexual norm for human sexuality'. Understanding homosexual orientation as 'a less than fully human and Christian form of sexual preference', does not necessarily lead to 'a corollary prohibition of those genital acts' by which committed homosexual relationships are strengthened.[28] **Ronald Lawler** sees 'a frustrating sterility in homosexual liaisons' because procreation and the unitive good are impossible. He concludes: 'Homosexual life is a bitter form of life, for it is founded on actions which pursue not the real goods of human persons but only the mere appearances of these goods. The unhappiness of many homosexuals is a sign that their lives are not properly oriented toward what is truly good'.[29]

RETHINKING THE SITUATION

The more visible and vocal presence of lesbians and gay men in the Church, and the developments taking place in modern social theory moved other Catholic theologians to test the traditional teaching. And they found it wanting. The particular focus of their concern has been love that expresses itself within stable, faithful and committed same-sex relationships. They have not sought to make acceptable those acts that involve violence or coercion, promiscuity or anonymity, or the seduction of the young. The years 1976–1977 saw the publication of three ground-breaking works in the United States. *The Church and the Homosexual* by **John McNeill**, a Jesuit priest with extensive psychotherapy experience in the gay community, was the first work in English to deal comprehensively with the issue from within the Catholic Church. A controversial book even before it was published, it led to John McNeill being silenced by the Vatican, and following his public response to the Vatican's *1986 Letter* he was expelled from the Jesuits and the priesthood. McNeill seeks to put the relevant biblical texts in their cultural and religious context and concludes:

> Once all the cultural and historical circumstances are kept in mind, the only condemnation of homosexual activity to be found with certainty in Scripture is a condemnation of perverse homosexual activity indulged in by otherwise truly heterosexual individuals as an expression of contempt or self-centred lust and usually associated with some form of idol worship.[30]

In considering tradition, McNeill notes that 'one of the most remarkable of these anomalies [of tradition] is the almost complete disregard of lesbianism in the various documents'. A false belief 'that the male semen at emission was almost human' dominated sexual theory until advances in biology began in the sixteenth century. Studying the link between human nature and homosexuality, McNeill writes:

> The call of the Gospel is not one of conforming passively to biological givens; rather, that call is to transform and humanize the natural order through the power of love . . . Homosexual love, although incapable of procreation, is certainly not doomed to fruitlessness . . . it is certain that by means of a homosexual love, many humans have been liberated to a truly spiritual fertility.

Seeing the debate rage on the origin of homosexuality—was it nature or nurture?—he proposes a different, more urgent, 'fruitful question' which 'is not "from whence" homosexuals came, but where they are going—or better, to what purpose do they exist?' On the discovery of this answer depend two important consequences. Firstly, the ability of the homosexual to accept himself or herself with true self-love and understanding. And secondly, the ability of the heterosexual society to accept a homosexual minority, not just as objects of pity and tolerance at best, but as equals capable of collaborating in the mutual task of building a more humane society.[31] McNeill would later describe this first work as a 'quest for intellectual freedom from the homophobic thought patterns of the past and as a positive effort to arrive at an understanding of homosexuality as a gift from God'.[32]

The second significant work at this time was a report on human sexuality, *Human Sexuality: New Directions in American Catholic Thought*, commissioned by the **Board of Directors of the Catholic Theological Society of America** and written by **Anthony Kosnik**. The Board voted to 'receive' and publish the report in order to provide 'some helpful and illuminating guidelines in the present confusion'. The report explores the then more recent findings of the social sciences, as well as current biblical and theological positions, and developes its pastoral guidelines from the starting point that 'justice to homosexuals demand[s] an unbiased critical analysis of the question'. It sees 'the silence and neglect' of theologians and pastoral workers, and the attitudes of the Church in general, as contributing to 'the alienation, loneliness and discrimination suffered by homosexuals'.

With a view of sex as 'more than genitality, and the purpose of sexuality—creativity and integration—as broader than biological procreation and physical union', the report dismantles the stereotyped images of homosexual persons saying that 'homosexuals have the same rights to friendship, association and community as heterosexuals'. Pastors are urged to assist the homosexual to:

> make a moral judgement upon his or her relationships and actions in terms of whether or not they are self-liberating, other-enriching, honest, faithful, life-serving and joyous. Like everyone else, homosexuals are bound to avoid depersonalization, selfishness, dishonesty, promiscuity, harm to society and demoralization.

Since the Church has failed to support homosexual friendships and relationships, promiscuity has inadvertently been promoted for that precise reason. Therefore, 'pastors may recommend close, stable friendships between homosexuals, not simply as a lesser of two evils but as a positive good'. While not accepting the term 'marriage' for same-sex unions, the report raises the possibility of communal prayer for 'people striving to live Christian lives' in such a union. Calling for respect for the conscience of the individual, the point is made that 'no one is ever bound to the morally impossible'. The concluding pastoral guideline is important:

> It bears repeating that there is much that is uncertain and provisional about the subject of homosexuality. Much research needs yet to be done, much pastoral experience yet to be accumulated before more than tentative pastoral guidelines can be formulated. It bears repeating, however, without provision, that where there

> is sincere affection, responsibility, and the germ of authentic human relationship—in other words, where there is love—God is surely present.[33]

Church authorities published observations expressing disagreements with the report and took disciplinary action against Anthony Kosnik.[34]

The third work of importance, published in 1977, was *Sexual Morality: A Catholic Perspective* by **Philip Keane**. While acknowledging that the Scriptures give great priority to the man–woman relationship in marriage and show 'that homosexual activity always involves evil', he warns that 'we may have to very sensitively define just what this evil means in particular cases'. He believes that 'the one who can make a genuine option for perfect chastity ought morally to take this option. For some homosexuals perfect chastity might be a very good choice'. About those unable to choose perfect chastity, he says:

> This homosexual wishes to live a responsible homosexual life-style involving as far as possible a stable relationship with another homosexual, a relationship in which the sexual acts contribute to the growth and development of both parties. The experience of homosexuals is that this sort of homosexual relationship strengthens the homosexual couple's sense of self-worth and enables them to contribute more effectively to the good of society.

Keane holds 'that there is a priority or normativity to heterosexual acts and relationships that cannot be dismissed in any theology of homosexuality'. Because homosexual relationships and acts cannot be open to procreation and the man–woman relationship, they 'always involve a significant degree of ontic evil'. He goes on to say that 'these acts are ontically evil in what they lack, but not morally evil in the actual concrete totality in which they exist'. He explains: 'For the human race as a whole, heterosexual marital sex acts will alway have a priority in such a way that the human race can never be fully comfortable about homosexual acts, even in the cases in which homosexual acts are judged as moral due to their special circumstances'. While rejecting the notion of homosexual marriages, he says that 'the Church and society should be open to finding other ways of supporting stable homosexual union'.[35] The Vatican required Archbishop Hunthausen of Seattle to withdraw his imprimatur from Philip Keane's book.

CHARLES CURRAN

One of the most outstanding moral theologians of the twentieth century has been **Charles Curran**. Professor at the Catholic University of America (1965–91), he was president of the Catholic Theological Society of America, the Society of Christian Ethics and the American Theological Society. Curran has been a prolific writer on sexual ethics. From the beginning he recognised the limitation of the Scriptures in the areas of morality because they 'do not have a monopoly on ethical wisdom and thus do not constitute the sole way into the ethic problem for the Christian ethicist'. At the same time he warned that though the 'theological ethician must be in constant dialogue with (contemporary) sciences', such 'morality cannot be totally identified with psychology and psychiatry'.[36] To arrive at truth Curran saw six streams of knowledge needing to be drawn together: Scripture and its relationship to the issue in hand; Christian tradition and its application to the present situation; the teaching of the Church *Magisterium*; human ethical reasoning; the data of the modern social sciences; and the lived experience of people. In 1979 he pointed out:

> The moral theologian must be open to the data of all the sciences but cannot be an expert in most of the empirical sciences . . . Part of the contemporary crisis of culture comes from the fact that all of us human beings must make decisions in the midst of great complexity and of some uncertainty about which approach is best. The ethicist or moral theologian who studies the morality of human acts faces the same problem.[37]

Curran used the example of how the Catholic understanding of religious liberty as contained in the Vatican Council documents began with people's experience 'and only later was the theory developed'.[38]

As early as 1970 Curran wrote: 'I believe that homosexual actions are wrong'. He was however prepared to acknowledge that there might be some justification for allowing a theology of compromise in the case of a homosexual person who could not be helped by modern medical science. 'Compromise maintains that because of the existence of sin in the world a person might be forced to accept some behavior which under ordinary circumstances he would not want to choose.'[39] He saw that the meaning of human sexuality and marriage was found in the union of love and procreation. While marriage was the ideal, he recognised that the homosexual was 'not responsible for his condition'. He called for a dialogue with 'the homophile movement', and admitted in 1972 that:

> Celibacy and sublimation are not always possible or even desirable for the homosexual. There are many somewhat stable homosexual unions which afford their partners some human fulfilment and contentment. Obviously such unions are better than homosexual promiscuity . . . Homosexuality can never become an ideal.[40]

In 1977, while continuing to hold that the 'ideal meaning of human sexual relations is in terms of the male and female', Curran took another step in his revised theology. 'For an irreversible or constitutional homosexual, homosexual acts in the context of a loving relationship striving for permanency can be and are morally good'. He then introduced the concept of a psychic structure in the homosexual person different from that of the heterosexual person:

> The Catholic ethical tradition has characteristically insisted on an ontological or metaphysical basis for morality. *Agere sequitur esse*—morality follows from our being. We should act in accord with who and what we are. In this case the invert has a different psychic structure and a different sexual humanity; consequently the invert's action can and should correspond to this different being. Homosexual acts are grounded in the homosexual psychic structure of the invert.

To explain this psychic structure, Curran attributes it to what he calls 'sin in the world'. This sin must be clearly distinguished from personal sin and guilt. Curran distinguishes between the absolute natural law that existed in the state of paradise before the fall, and the relative natural law that exists now after the fall. While the Christian is called to struggle against sin, and have a heart open to conversion, ready to improve the conditions of our world, 'one must admit that in our imperfect world, in which the fullness of grace is not yet here, there will always remain some aspects of the sin of the world in our life'. For the true homosexual:

> The psychic structure of the irreversible invert constitutes such a manifestation of sin in the world . . . Since it is irreversible, it cannot and should not be changed. The individual person bears no personal moral guilt for this condition . . . At the same time this is not the ideal, and those who are not irreversible homosexuals have a moral obligation to strive for a loving heterosexual union.[41]

In 1984 Curran reaffirmed that 'the ideal meaning of human sexual relationships is in term[s] of male and female', but 'that for the irreversible, constitutional or genuine homosexual, homosexual acts in the context of a loving relationship striving for permanency are objectively morally good'. While Catholic moral theology has condemned artificial contraception because it interferes in the procreative nature of the sexual act in marriage, Curran points out that some separation between sexuality and procreation is accepted. Sterile people may marry. Husband and wife can, in the planning of their family, 'intend that their sexual relations not be procreative', choosing sexual intercourse at known infertile times. 'There is some relationship between sexuality and procreation, but that relationship is very difficult to define and very difficult to use as a criterion for absolute condemnations'.[42] Charles Curran's understanding of the morality of homosexual acts and homosexuality itself had considerably developed over a fourteen-year period of research and teaching.

In 1986, after a seven-year investigation, the Congregation for the Doctrine of the Faith declared that Charles Curran was ineligible to teach Catholic theology because of his 'nuanced dissent from hierarchical teachings on a variety of sexual issues including . . . homosexuality'.[43]

BRAVE NEW THOUGHT

The American priest–sociologist Andrew Greeley describes the moral theologian **Richard McCormick** as one who 'continues to be a voice of rationality, sanity, balance and intelligence in a discipline that is rent by controversy, ideology and reaction'.[44] In his opening reflections on homosexuality in *The Critical Calling: Reflections on Moral Dilemmas Since Vatican II*, McCormick says that 'there is nothing shameworthy in making a mistake. In a pilgrim church we all do. There is everything wrong in not risking it'. He saw that 'pastoral adaptations' needed to be made for those for whom conforming their sexuality to the heterosexual relationship of marriage was impossible, and 'what those adaptations might be seemed to be the heart of the question'.

After he reviewed the position of leading American theologians and the *Magisterium*, McCormick developed what he called his own 'modest proposal'. Recognising that sin holds power, even in the redeemed world, he believes that 'Christ is the liberator supreme'. Those who follow Christ will find the meaning of their lives in their capacity to love others 'for we learn to love by being loved'. The power of sin can be present in human sexuality, 'in exploitative self-destructive *actions* and patterns of behavior', as well as 'in the underlying personality *configurations* which are not totally of our own making e.g., narcissism, impotence, deviation of instinct'. The Church's conviction is 'that the sexual expression of interpersonal love offers us the best chance for our growth and humanization . . . if it is structured within the man–woman relationship of covenanted (permanent and exclusive) friendship', and so invites all to reach for this ideal. But McCormick remains concerned for those who are incapable of sexual intimacy within such a heterosexual relationship—'irreversibly homosexual'—and who at the same time are 'not called to celibacy for the Kingdom'. In such a situation the Church and its ministers must continue to be 'a liberating presence' for the homosexual. This can happen:

> (a) by inviting him to appropriate the qualities of the covenanted man–woman relationship through fidelity and exclusiveness; (b) by aiding the individual to develop those healthy, outgoing attitudes and emotional responses that make this possible; (c) by extending the full sacramental and social supports of the Church to his striving; (d) by condemning and combating all social, legal and ecclesial discrimination against and oppression of the homosexual.

Concerning the judgements—irreversibly homosexual, and not called to celibacy—McCormick holds that these 'are the *responsibility of the individual before God*'. He goes on to say: 'The Church does not "justify" such a decision for the simple reason that she cannot. It is the individual's responsibility. But the Church can respect it'.[45]

British Dominican theologian **Gareth Moore** makes the point in his consideration of homosexuality that the fruitfulness of human relationships and sexuality 'was not to be limited to procreation'. 'We should no doubt be ready to criticize sexual activity of any kind that is incompatible with love . . . Yet persistently Christians have refused to think about this subject [homosexuality] in terms of the love commandment, in contravention of the explicit and central demands of the Gospel.' In responding to the criticism that homosexual acts are unnatural, Moore points out: 'Nature is not something to which we have to conform. Much of our energy is devoted to manipulating natural forces or averting them . . . Inventiveness, adaptability and the manipulation of the natural world are part of our nature'. Moore also addresses the point raised in the *1975 Declaration* that homosexual people have an 'inability to fit into society'. He reminds us that homosexuals, Jews and gypsies did not fit into Nazi society, and that this was not the fault of those people, but of the Nazi society itself. ' "Society" is not a given, unalterable structure, but consists of people who are capable of either accepting or rejecting others'. He then stresses that 'the desire to exclude is a radically anti-Christian desire. Here we should remember that Christianity was first a religion designed for the excluded and that it first flourished among those who counted for nothing'.

When any group is marginalised by society, it forms its own group identity, which often rejects the values of the society that rejected the group. This Moore sees as one reason behind the flamboyant public image of gay culture. He is critical of the term 'homosexual condition' used in Vatican documents, saying that 'the concept of homosexuality as a condition serves only to introduce more obscurity into an already difficult subject'. The use of the medical model adds confusion. 'Any suffering on the part of a homosexual stems not from the homosexuality itself but from other people's reaction to it . . . The fact is that, if I am a gay man, my homosexuality does not itself cause me distress; but it may distress other people and then it is they who call it a disease.' Moore sees a danger in setting heterosexuality against homosexuality, so that if the first is understood as good, the second must necessarily be bad.

> Even if it can be shown that what happens in heterosexual intercourse is better than what happens in homosexual intercourse, homosexual intercourse may still be good; it may indeed be very good. All that will have been shown is that it is not as good. If heterosexual sex is the best, still we have no licence to make the best the enemy of the good. If we establish that homosexual sex is inferior sex, that is not, prima facie, any reason why it should be discouraged, let alone combated.[46]

Lay theologians are now bringing new insights to the issue. Husband and wife team **James and Evelyn Whitehead**, combine the disciplines of pastoral theology and developmental psychology in their writings. Understanding the need for 'every adult to come to self-acceptance and a life of self-giving that is mature and fulfilling', they have long called on the Church to assist gay people with appropriate 'rites of passage' blessings. For as long as the

Church refuses such possibilities, they hold that it denies 'the larger community the benefits of the religious gifts and insights with which its gay members have been graced'.[47] Assessing the traditional connection between sexuality and procreation they hold that 'human sexuality has more to do with fruitfulness than fertility'. They reject the notion that the 'spontaneous impulses of arousal and affection (the "inclination" of the [1986] Vatican document)' of lesbians and gay men are unnatural, and rather see in them 'the energetic roots of human love'. Indeed, they say, 'it is part of the gift of creation, a sign of God's delight in our bodies'.[48] For the dialogue between theology and the social sciences to be fruitful it must include 'the testimony of mature Christians in the variety of lifestyles that constitute the community of faith'. They cite Cardinal Newman's description of the 'sense of the faithful' as 'a sort of instinct . . . deep in the bosom of the mystical body', as that which 'must sometimes safeguard aspects of genuine belief that are being overlooked or neglected by religious officials'. The Whiteheads continue to lament that there is no place or form in the Church where lesbians and gay men can 'protect the promises that their love generates'. The Church's enforced singleness suggests 'that commitment and fidelity are unachievable for gay and lesbian adults'. For them 'the choice of celibacy must be a decision not *against* but *for* something. The person must choose not just to avoid, but to engage'.[49]

British theologian **Elizabeth Stuart** has responded to the desire of the Whiteheads and edited a prayer book that celebrates the rites of passage for lesbians and gay men.[50] Her gay and lesbian theology of relationships draws on the often neglected, but rich tradition of friendship found in the Church:

> In Christ, traditional concepts of family are dissolved to be replaced by the kinship of friendship. Lesbian, gay and bisexual people have an important insight into the reality of experiencing something like a universal family/kingdom. It is the ethic of friendship that is the true 'family value'; and the Church should be supporting all those who exist in the bonds of friendship, not simply the 'nuclear family'.

Stuart is concerned that marriage 'seems to be above criticism' in the Church, that in many ways 'it has become an idol'. The expectation is that if you cannot live up to the ideal of marriage you must remain celibate. She sees friendship that emerges as relationship among lesbians and gay male couples as possessing 'mutual and equal acceptance, respect and delight'. While the Church must continue to bless heterosexual marriage, it should no longer withhold its blessing from lesbian and gay people.[51]

PURSUING DIALOGUE

Theology is a living science, a dynamic and robust quest for truth as revealed by God. Sexuality is a vibrant part of the human personality, shaping a person's ability to relate to other people. Across the centuries Christian theology has pondered the mystery of human sexuality. At times it became lost in the conflict of tension between body and spirit. In the evolution of marriage it so focused on procreation that love and relationship and mutuality were sacrificed. And the heritage of patriarchy made it suspicious of and hostile towards new thought.

The discussion about homosexuality in Catholic theology has, for a long time, portrayed it as the enemy of marriage and the man–woman relationship because its nature is seen to be so different. While there is a new emphasis on relationship and covenant in the marriage bond, homosexuality is still too often reduced to a consideration of specific acts divorced from the people who share them. Like the early psychoanalysts who came to an understanding of homosexuality through their disturbed patients (whose problems were often not caused by their sexuality), so some theologians have hardened their position of opposition through their pastoral interaction with distressed and disturbed people. Their observation of the public, flamboyant and confrontational expression of homosexuality in the gay and lesbian culture has further alienated these theologians from dialogue.

The new thought arises among Catholic theologians where there has been dialogue with a more articulate lesbian and gay membership of the Church. Their experience of harmonising sexuality and spirituality has been taken seriously, and has led to a re-evaluation of Scripture and tradition. The torch of new theology is being passed on from the clerical theologians (many of whom have experienced the disciplinary action of the Vatican) to those among the laity who often bring to the issue a broader knowledge of the progress of contemporary social theory. All theologians, clerical and lay, are called to the service of the Church, and to work with the *Magisterium* in discovering, understanding and teaching truth. This is, in the area of homosexuality, a tense development of theology, but one demanded by justice. It cannot fruitfully take place unless there is freedom of enquiry and the opportunity for dialogue marked by charity and humility.

5

UNCERTAIN BISHOPS STRUGGLE AS TEACHERS AND PASTORS

Bishops in the Catholic Church exercise their office within their own territory 'in their own right', and at the same time are 'in communion with one another and with the Roman Pontiff in a bond of unity, charity and peace'.[1] While a primitive curia supported the pope from the sixth century, its present formal and complex organised form dates back only to 1588 and Pope Sixtus V. This sophisticated bureaucracy of some sixty-five Congregations, Tribunals, Councils, Offices, Commissions, Committees and Institutions—the Roman Curia—assists the pope in his responsibilities of governing the universal Church.[2] Within the Curia the Congregation for the Doctrine of the Faith, responsible for safeguarding Catholic faith and morals, has both shaped and controlled the official teaching of the Catholic Church on homosexuality since early in the 1970s. This intense centralising of Church authority and teaching, which undermines the collegial ministry of bishops and pope, has hampered the efforts of individual bishops to help shape a better understanding of homosexuality in the Church.

The recent explanations of teaching on homosexuality are to be seen against the background of the Christian understanding of sexuality and marriage that placed a strong emphasis on procreation. St Augustine, in 400 AD, taught that intercourse, for procreation only, and not for pleasure, 'belongs to marriage'.[3] By the eighteenth century St Alphonsus Liguori permitted intercourse for pleasure, as long as procreation was not excluded.[4] The 1917 *Code of Canon Law* decreed: 'The primary end of marriage is the procreation and education of children; its secondary end is mutual help and the allaying of concupiscence'.[5]

The Second Vatican Council departed from the notion of primary and secondary ends, and described marriage as 'the human act by which the partners mutually surrender themselves to each other for the good of the partners, of the children, and of society'.[6] This teaching was expanded by Pope Paul VI in 1968. 'That teaching, often set forth by the magisterium, is founded upon the inseparable connection, willed by God and unable to be broken by man on his own initiative, between the two meanings of the conjugal act: the unitive meaning and the procreative meaning'.[7] More recently, the *Catechism of the Catholic Church* speaking about sexuality said that 'physical, moral and spiritual *differences* and *complementarity* are orientated toward the goods of marriage and the flourishing of family life'. It added that 'The spouses' union achieves the twofold end of marriage: the good of the spouses themselves and the transmission of life'. These two values 'cannot be separated' without compromising marriage, the family and the spiritual life of the couple.[8]

THE VATICAN TEACHING ON HOMOSEXUALITY

The Second Vatican Council (1962–1965) made no mention of the subject of homosexuality. It had been held before the Stonewall riots, the gay rights movement and the impact of AIDS on the world.

In 1975 the Congregation for the Doctrine of the Faith published the *Declaration on Certain Questions Concerning Sexual Ethics* because of 'the corruption of morals' caused by 'the unbridled exaltation of sex'. It addressed itself to those who 'have begun to judge indulgently, and to even excuse completely, homosexual relations between certain people'. Using medical language, the *Declaration* spoke of 'homosexuals who are definitively such because of some kind of innate instinct or a pathological constitution judged to be incurable', and of those who experienced their tendency as 'transitory or at least not incurable'. Furthermore, 'homosexual relations' that were sometimes described as being 'within a sincere communion of life and love' were rejected as not being 'analogous to marriage'. St Paul's *Letter to the Romans* was cited as proof 'that homosexual acts are intrinsically disordered and can in no case be approved of'. At the same time the 'judgement of Scripture does not of course permit us to conclude that all those who suffer from this anomaly are personally responsible for it'.[9] This teaching was supported by the Congregation for Catholic Education, which in giving educational guidelines for human love, said that 'homosexual relations are acts deprived of their essential and indispensable rule'.[10]

Fearful that 'an overly benign interpretation' was being 'given to the homosexual condition itself', Cardinal Ratzinger, Prefect of the Congregation, addressed a letter on the pastoral care of homosexual persons to the bishops of the Catholic Church in 1986. In it the distinction was made 'between the homosexual condition or tendency and individual homosexual actions'. The homosexual *orientation* is described thus:

> Although the particular inclination of the homosexual person is not a sin, it is a more or less strong tendency ordered toward an intrinsic moral evil; and thus the inclination itself must be seen as an objective disorder.

Furthermore, since it is only in marriage 'that the use of the sexual faculty can be morally good', the *1986 Letter* holds that 'a person engaging in homosexual behaviour . . . acts immorally'. The *1986 Letter*, by its own admission, is not an exhaustive treatment of the issue, but has nevertheless profoundly shaped the *Magisterium* teaching ever since, even if its language is somewhat softened in the *Catechism of the Catholic Church*.

The Vatican, in 1986, was nervous about the issue of homosexuality. Bishops as individuals and in groups had been addressing the topic through pastoral statements in many countries. Movements of gay Catholics were becoming increasingly visible around the world, seeking, indeed demanding, that the Church change its teaching on the subject. The *1986 Letter* reaffirmed the traditional biblical foundation for its teaching. It recognised the dignity belonging to every person, and laid down the principles to be used when judging the culpability of a person's homosexual activity. Encouraging bishops to provide pastoral care 'in full accord with the teaching of the Church', it took a hard line on those organisations that challenged, or were ambiguous about, the Church's teaching, and demanded that bishops withdraw their support from them. It counselled against describing people simply in terms of their sexual orientation. It denounced as 'deplorable' any 'violent malice in speech or in action' directed towards homosexual persons, but when 'civil legislation is introduced to protect behaviour to which no one has any conceivable right' no one should be surprised if 'irrational and violent reactions increase'. Civil legislation was to be assessed in the light of defending and promoting family life. The generosity and self-giving of homosexual persons were acknowledged, and they were called to a life of chastity.[11]

The following year Pope John Paul II, meeting with the American bishops in Los Angeles, encouraged them in the pastoral care they gave to homosexual persons. He said that 'they are always worthy of the Church's love and Christ's truth'.[12]

Responding—or reacting—to changes in legislation throughout the United States concerning the civil rights of lesbians and gay men, the Congregation for the Doctrine of the Faith in 1992 issued guidelines to the American bishops 'offering discreet assistance to those who may be confronted with the task of evaluating draft legislation regarding non-discrimination on the basis of sexual orientation'.[13] While holding that homosexual persons 'have the same rights as all persons', the *1992 Considerations* said that the rights to work and housing were 'not absolute', and it could be 'obligatory' to limit them 'for objectively disordered external conduct'. When considering 'the placement of children for adoption or foster care, in employment of teachers or athletics coaches and in military recruitment', it was 'not unjust discrimination to take sexual orientation into account'. Making homosexuality a basis for entitlements led to the risk of people declaring their homosexuality, or even seeking a partner. The *1992 Considerations* made the strange statement, implying that there was choice about a person's sexuality: 'There is no right to homosexuality'.[14]

The 1985 Extraordinary Synod of Bishops, held to mark the twentieth anniversary of the closing of the Second Vatican Council, called for the composition of a catechism of Catholic belief. The *Catechism of the Catholic Church*, described by Pope John Paul as 'a sure norm for teaching the faith',[15] was first published in French in 1992, and in English in 1994. It is helpful to note that a catechism does not argue a position or teaching, but sets out beliefs in an orderly manner.

Retaining the 1975 teaching that 'homosexual acts are intrinsically disordered', because of tradition based on Scripture and the natural law itself, the *Catechism* is more sensitive to the findings of modern social theory than earlier Vatican documents. It speaks of homosexuality in terms of relations, rather than simply as acts. Present in 'a great variety of forms' throughout time and cultures, 'its psychological genesis remains largely unexplained'. This 'condition' is not chosen, and therefore 'every sign of unjust discrimination' must be replaced by an acceptance with 'respect, compassion and sensitivity'. The way to chastity is through 'the virtues of self-mastery . . . the support of disinterested friendship, by prayer and sacramental grace'. Seen as the fruit of chastity, 'whether it develops between persons of the same or opposite sex, friendship represents a great good for all'. The *Catechism* had counselled that 'everyone, man and woman, should acknowledge and accept his sexual *identity*'. The *Catechism* avoids calling the homosexual orientation itself a 'disordered' one, and speaks only of the *acts* being 'disordered'. Because such acts 'close the sexual act to the gift of life', they can never be approved.[16]

In his 1993 encyclical letter, *Veritatis Splendor: On Certain Fundamental Questions of the Church's Moral Teaching*, which explored some fundamental questions of the church's moral teaching, Pope John Paul II made one reference to homosexuality. In a section examining various approaches to understanding freedom and the natural law, the pope is critical of those who hold that 'man, as a rational being, not only can but actually *must freely determine the meaning* of his behaviour'. These theologians, he says, level objections 'against the traditional conception of the *natural law*, which is accused of presenting as moral laws what are in themselves mere biological laws'. They see this happening in documents of the Church's *Magisterium*, 'particularly those dealing with the area of sexual and conjugal ethics'. They believe that 'on the basis of a naturalistic understanding of the sexual act that contraception, direct sterilisation . . . homosexual relations . . . were condemned as morally unacceptable'. The pope rejects this reasoning, explaining that 'the true meaning of the natural law' is '*the person himself in the unity of soul and body*, in the unity of his spiritual and biological inclinations and of all the other specific characteristics necessary for the pursuit of his end'.[17]

While Pope John Paul II supported some of the 1994 measures in the European Parliament to eliminate unjust discrimination towards 'people with homosexual *tendencies* . . . because every human person is worthy of respect', he saw in the legislation the danger of 'distorting the true meaning of the family'. He held that the Parliament was seeking 'to *legitimize a moral disorder*'. He held that 'what is not morally acceptable is the legal approval of homosexual *activity*'.[18]

A veiled reference to homosexual acts and the threat of HIV infection is found in the 1995 encyclical letter *Evangelium Vitae: The Gospel of Life* in which Pope John Paul defends the value and inviolability of human life. Reflecting on the biblical story of Cain's murder of his brother Abel, the pope asks: 'how can we fail to consider' sins against life caused by people? 'What of the spreading of death caused . . . by the promotion of certain kinds of sexual activity which, besides being morally unacceptable, also involve grave risks to life?' The pope does not pursue his own question in the encyclical, but proclaims the '*Gospel of life*', concentrating particularly on the issues of abortion and euthanasia in the broader context of what he calls a '*conspiracy against life*'. He sees a struggle between the 'culture of life' and the 'culture of death' brought about by '*the eclipse of the sense of God and of man*'.[19]

At the end of 1995 the Pontifical Council for the Family issued guidelines for education about human sexuality within the family. Seeing homosexuality as a 'problem', and asserting that 'this condition constitutes a trial', the Council claims that homosexuality is 'spreading more and more in urbanised societies'. It draws heavily on the *Catechism* but adds that 'when the practice of homosexual acts has not become a habit, many cases can benefit from appropriate therapy'. It also warns that the subject should not be discussed before adolescence, and when it is, only in terms of the relationship of chastity, health and sexuality to the family.[20]

THE BISHOPS OF THE UNITED STATES OF AMERICA

As the gay rights movement developed in the 1970s, gay Catholics sought greater support from their Church. A small but significant number of American bishops responded with pastoral statements. Their first collective statement on homosexuality was addressed, in 1973, to priests in their role as confessors in the sacrament of Penance. While in the light of later statements and knowledge coming from the social sciences this first statement was in many ways both naive and quaint, it was a beginning. Stating the traditional teaching that homosexual acts were 'inordinate uses of the sexual faculty', the bishops held that they were 'a grave transgression of the goals of human sexuality and of human personality'. The bishops showed a lack of understanding, claiming that 'lasting and fulfilling homosexual relationships are not found very often', believing that causes of homosexuality included 'a bad case of acne, deep shyness, the habit of stammering'. However, in their guidelines the bishops encouraged a more pastoral approach to people. They distinguished between, and encouraged appropriate support and guidance for, temporary homosexuals and apparent permanent homosexuals, as well as the married homosexual, the seminarian, religious and priest, and lesbians. Saying that 'very often freedom is diminished', they advised that 'in assessing the responsibility of the homosexual the confessor must avoid both harshness and permissiveness'.[21]

Addressing American Catholics in 1979, the bishops raised many moral and pastoral issues, including homosexuality, in *To live in Christ Jesus*. They acknowledged that while homosexual orientation was not chosen, homosexual activity 'is morally wrong', and so 'homosexuals are called to give witness to chastity'. They upheld homosexual people's right 'to respect, friendship and justice' and 'an active role in the Christian community' free from prejudice. Sensitive to the fact that marriage was unlikely for such people, they counselled that 'the Christian community should provide them with a special degree of pastoral understanding and care'.[22]

Many individual bishops, as well as State groups, addressed the issue from 1979 until 1986, when Cardinal Ratzinger's *1986 Letter* brought a sudden end to attempts to openly engage in dialogue on homosexuality. It is obvious that the bishops were struggling with the issue, calling it: a 'real and complex issue'—Archbishop Roach; a 'complex issue', and a 'highly charged and emotional issue'—Archbishop Quinn; 'highly complex'—Archbishop Weakland; 'difficult and complex'—Bishop Sullivan; 'extremely delicate and sensitive', and a 'sensitive and volatile subject'—Archbishop Hunthausen; 'enormously complex and charged with much emotion'—Archbishop (now Cardinal) Hickey; a 'complex question'—Archbishop Whealan; 'a tough issue'—Archbishop Pilarczyk; or a 'serious problem'—Bishop Brzana.[23]

Some bishops placed an emphasis on maintaining Church teaching, while others tried to develop a more pastoral approach to the needs of gay men and lesbians. All, in one way or another, included the Church's condemnation of homosexual acts. So we read of homosexual activity as: 'wrong'—Archbishop Roach; 'objectively immoral'—Cardinal Medeiros; 'seriously wrong'—Bishop Brzana; 'gravely evil'—Archbishop Hickey; objectively wrong'—the bishops of Massachusetts; 'morally wrong'—Cardinal Bernadin; 'sinful'—Archbishop Borders; 'sinful acts'—the bishops of Texas; 'immoral'—Cardinal Bevilacqua.[24]

Some statements emphasised the need for healing, counselling and reconciliation for homosexual persons. Cardinal Medeiros said that 'Christ loves and wants to heal [homosexual persons] in the light of truth through genuine love', while Archbishop Hickey said that they 'should receive adequate counselling and, when necessary, psychological help'.[25] But, in 1992, Bishop Untener of Saginaw said that he was worried about a 'drift back to severity'.[26]

However, the vast majority of statements do place emphasis on the pastoral care of homosexual persons, and often reflect a genuine understanding of the dilemma Catholic lesbians and gay men have in integrating their faith and sexuality. Archbishop Quinn of San Francisco admitted that 'some aspects of the question do not admit of easy answers'. Bishop Sullivan of Richmond said that it was not enough to simply give the official Church teaching on the subject because sometimes it 'has been presented in such a way that it has been the source or occasion of some of the pain and alienation that many homosexual Catholics experience'.[27] The American bishops, in their 1990 document, *Human Sexuality*, believed that 'the distinction between *being* homosexual and *doing* homosexual genital actions, while it is not always clear and convincing, is a helpful and important one when dealing with the complex issue of homosexuality, particularly in the educational and pastoral arena.[28]

Some bishops developed their pastoral response to lesbian and gay Catholics through wide consultation. With their support and guidance some dioceses developed policies concerning the situation and pastoral care of gay men, lesbians and their families. While not strictly part of the Catholic *Magisterium*, these documents, approved by their bishops, are significant in reflecting changing attitudes in the Catholic community. The Diocese of Baltimore, in 1981, recognised that the orientation 'is in no way held to be a sinful condition' and therefore rejected the notion that people had to try to change it. It saw chastity as increasing a person's dignity, and cautioned that 'the demands this virtue makes on us individuals depends on our particular state of life'.[29] This issue of chastity was later taken up by the Conference of Bishops. 'Chastity, for the single person, is not synonymous with an interior calling to perpetual celibacy. Controlling one's desires for sexual intimacy can be particularly difficult. Being single in a largely couples' society is not an easy calling, whether it be temporary or permanent'.[30]

The Senate of Priests of the Archdiocese of San Francisco published, with the approval of Archbishop Quinn, an extensive ministry statement in 1983. It witnesses to a significant dialogue with gay Catholics in its preparation. It dismantles many of the lesbian and gay stereotypes, and respects the *feelings* that are part of the gay experience, especially in 'being "different" from the majority of people', a difference that 'often must be a secret one', leading 'to a deeper alienation'. Drawing on the writings of popes Paul VI and John Paul II, this statement develops what is called the principle of gradualism: 'Personal integrity comes about progressively . . . [and] instant serenity is almost never the human reality'. Valuing the role of conscience, it sees that its formation 'necessitates both a learning of moral rules and a personal internalization of the Christian principles inherent in the truths that Christ revealed'.[31]

Recognising that AIDS has 'had a terrible impact on the homosexual community',[32] American bishops have more recently and with sensitivity addressed gay men. Acknowledging the gap between gay men and the Church the bishops of California made the admission: 'We regret this distance, and long to heal their wounds by offering our support and fellowship'.[33]

Nationally the bishops issued two statements on HIV/AIDS: *The Many Faces of AIDS: A Gospel Response* in 1987, and then *Called to Compassion and Responsibility: A Response to the HIV/AIDS Crisis* in 1989. The first shows that there was real dialogue on the issue, and it is marked by an understanding of the plurality of American society which 'we recognize and respect'.[34] Violence directed towards gay men in the wake of the AIDS epidemic has been repeatedly condemned by the bishops. The civil rights of gay men and lesbians have been affirmed and their deprivation of basic rights recognised as 'a result of prejudice'.[35] 'The right to be free of unjust discrimination in housing and unemployment' is upheld.[36]

However, on the issue of recognising gay relationships as legal 'domestic partnerships', there has been strong opposition. 'Legislation . . . should not seek to equate legal marriage and homosexual relationships'. Such proposed legislation is named as 'dangerous and deceptive'.[37] A dissenting voice comes from Detroit Auxiliary Bishop Gumbleton, who believes that 'we need to support gay and lesbian people in their relationships'. Speaking at a seminar on sexual minorities, he rejected homosexual orientation as objectively disordered, saying, 'I don't accept that'. Gumbleton disagrees with the *1992 Considerations* position that homosexuals should keep silence to avoid discrimination, because in that case they would have 'to pretend, hide or deny their sexuality to avoid problems in society'.[38]

The American bishops speak to lesbians

The 1973 *Principles to Guide Confessors* recognised the particular circumstances of life for lesbians, and directed that 'the confessor should become acquainted with some of the traits of the lesbian'. In 1988 the American bishops embarked on an ambitious project, namely, to write a pastoral letter on women's issues. The fact that the final draft of the document failed to get sufficient votes in the Bishops' Conference to be adopted, should not be interpreted as meaning that the document or process was of no value. The bishops did issue it as a Committee report.

The mandate of the task was 'to report the result of extensive consultations with women, to reflect on this input in the light of Christian heritage and to offer responses and recommendations, not as final conclusions, but as contributions to ongoing dialogue and appropriate action in homes, schools, parishes and dioceses'.[39] The bishops listened to 75 000 women in 140 diocesan consultations.[40] Tragically, Vatican officials rejected this consultative process saying that 'bishops are teachers, not learners; truth cannot emerge through consultation'.[41]

Five documents were produced in this consultation. Initially, lesbians were considered under the headings: 'Listening to Voices of Alienation', and 'Moral Instruction and Compassionate Assistance'. The bishops showed an openness that was significant:

> Lesbian women deserve special understanding and support from the Christian community to enable them to live a chaste and loving celibate life. At the same time we must be ready to hear,

> with pastoral solicitude and concern, what these women have to say about the particular ways in which their dignity as persons is belittled and demeaned by sexism abetted by cultural prejudices.[42]

The second draft considered lesbians under 'The Single Life' and revealed bishops who 'strove in our listening sessions to hear with pastoral solicitude and concern', what women were saying about the denial of their dignity. The bishops committed themselves 'to explore further what it means for homosexuals to commit themselves to Christ and to chaste and loving relationships'.[43]

The third draft saw the introduction of a new heading, 'Responding Pastorally to Homosexual Persons', with additional comments. The situation of homosexual persons now called 'for special consideration *and much prayer*'. The shift was made from bishops listening, to the women speaking—perhaps with some aggression: '*Lesbian women were especially outspoken* about the ways in which their dignity as persons has been belittled and demeaned by sexism, abetted by cultural prejudices'. To this the bishops added: 'We condemn such treatment totally'. They further added: 'As relational beings called to emulate this justice and mercy shown to us by our Savior, we dare not treat this responsibility as unimportant'. In the striving for 'chaste and loving relationships', the bishops reminded lesbians that this was an expectation 'rooted in Catholic teaching'. The bishops' own 'need to explore further' how lesbians might commit themselves to Christ was dropped from this third draft.[44]

The fourth draft, reducing the heading simply to 'Homosexual Persons', saw significant changes. After recognising that the situation of homosexual persons called for 'special consideration and much prayer', three new sentences, in the language of the *1986 Letter*, were introduced:

> As the church teaches, homosexuality is an objective disorder and every genital act of homosexuality is a morally grave matter. Such acts are incompatible with the Gospel of Jesus Christ. However, it is equally incompatible with the Gospel to treat persons who may have a homosexual orientation in a demeaning way, for any such action violates their dignity as human beings.

The bishops removed reference to their own need 'to emulate the justice and mercy shown to us by our Savior', and changed 'chaste and loving relationships' to 'chaste and loving *friendships*'.[45]

The fifth and final form of the document saw further changes. The condemnation of discrimination was significantly strengthened. 'However, it is equally incompatible with the Gospel to treat persons who may have a homosexual orientation in a demeaning way *or to arbitrarily discriminate against them*, for *all* [instead of *any*] such actions violate human dignity'. There was one final change. Speaking about dignity being belittled, the bishops 'condemn such treatment', but have dropped the '*totally*' of the fourth draft.[46] One is left to wonder which statement lesbian Catholics consider to best express their experiences, hopes and concerns.

Some bishops have been particularly sensitive to the need for dialogue with the lesbian and gay community. Archbishop Weakland said that they must be seen, 'not as an enemy to be battered down, but as persons worthy of respect and friendship'.[47] Bishop Walter Sullivan said that 'we cannot allow ourselves to be paralyzed by fear that prevents us from speaking and listening to each other actively'.[48] And as was recognised by the Baltimore Diocese as early as 1981: 'The Church must listen to gays and lesbians to learn what they have to teach about the saving presence of Christ among us'.[49]

THE BISHOPS OF ENGLAND AND WALES

When the British Parliament legislated to remove homosexual behaviour between consenting adults in private from the criminal code, Archbishop Godfrey of Westminster, while holding that homosexual acts were grievously sinful, raised the question: 'If the law takes cognizance of private acts of homosexuality and makes them crimes, do worse evils follow for the common good?'. In 1970 the bishops of England and Wales on the same topic said: 'We cannot expect the civil law to do our work for us'.[50]

The most extensive and highly respected document dealing with homosexuality published by these bishops (and probably by any Conference of Catholic bishops in the English-speaking world) was produced in 1979 through their Catholic Social Welfare Commission: *An Introduction to the Pastoral Care of Homosexual People*. The topic was explored within the framework of love. 'A life without love is incomplete and disappointing'. They continued: 'All human loving is a seeking after the One who is most lovable. Our human loving is all part of longing for God'. Acknowledging that Scripture and the tradition of Christianity 'make it quite clear that these [homosexual acts] are immoral', they warned that 'to limit this attraction to physical and even just sexual attraction is a misleading generalisation'. Pastors are advised that they may distinguish 'between irresponsible indiscriminate sexual activity and the permanent association between two homosexual persons who feel incapable of enduring a solitary life devoid of sexual expression'. While recognising that homosexual persons cannot find 'intimate partnerships' in marriage, their own form of 'stable union with each other' is, nonetheless, objectively 'morally unacceptable'. But 'the question is: Are such persons necessarily culpable?'.

The document concludes with an extensive list of pastoral guidelines. People cannot be classified simply by their sexuality; pastors should be helpful in the process of 'coming out'; societies for Christian homosexuals can be helpful; marriage is not the answer to the situation; people should be encouraged 'in accepting their condition positively;' 'the Church has a serious obligation to work towards the elimination of any injustices'; homosexuals, like heterosexuals, have the need for and right to the Sacraments. Finally, the bishops saw that homosexual persons 'may feel that nature in some way cheated them . . . [and] that the Church is demanding impossible standards'. 'The problem of the homosexual is part of a greater problem of the human incompleteness of a people who are on the way to God. Maturity comes when problems are acknowledged and faced'.[51]

Clarifying the Church's teaching about homosexual persons, Cardinal Basil Hume of Westminster wrote some *Observations* in July 1993. Drawing on the Vatican's *1986 Letter* and the English bishops' 1979 statement on pastoral care, he affirmed that the sexual expression of love was 'to find its place exclusively within marriage' where such love 'must always be open to the possible transmission of new life'. He then explained: 'When the church describes such [homosexual genital] acts as "intrinsically disordered" it means that these acts are not consistent with the two fundamental principles mentioned above [of love and new life]'. Cardinal Hume admitted that 'the word "disordered" is a harsh one in our English language', but explained that in traditional Catholic moral theology and philosophy 'it is meant to describe an inclination which is a departure from what is generally regarded to be the norm'. To call the inclination 'an objective disorder' referred only to the orientation towards homosexual genital acts. 'The church does not consider the whole personality and character of the individual to be thereby disordered'. The Cardinal strongly opposed discrimination, injustices and violence, pledged continuing pastoral care, and held that changes in legislation concerning homosexual persons 'must be considered case by case'.[52]

Early in 1995 Cardinal Hume issued *A Note* expanding on his *Observations*, including reflections on friendship and human love. Understanding that 'friendship is necessary for every person', the Cardinal went on to say: 'Sexual loving presupposes friendship but friendship does not require full sexual involvement'. Recalling how Jesus loved the sisters and brother Martha, Mary and Lazarus, he said that 'love between two persons, whether of the same sex or of a different sex, is to be treasured and respected'. He added:

> To love another is in fact to reach out to God who shares his lovableness with the one we love. To be loved is to receive a sign, or a share, of God's unconditional love.
>
> To love another, whether of the same sex or of a different sex, is to have entered the area of the richest human experience . . . Human loving is precarious for human nature is wounded and frail.

Knowing the ethic of sexuality to be demanding, when people fail 'the Church does not reject such people but wishes to walk with them in order to guide them'. The *Note* contains a strong rejection of 'the victimisation of homosexual men and women', as well as of 'homophobia' which 'should have no place among Catholics'. Even when homosexual people themselves 'act in a provocative or destructive manner this does not justify "homophobic" attitudes or reactions'. The Cardinal ends his *Note* calling on all people 'to work towards achieving a difficult ideal, even if this will only be achieved gradually'.[53] This *Note* is marked by great sensitivity, calm, compassion and kindness.

THE BISHOPS OF AUSTRALIA

The Catholic bishops of Australia have never collectively issued a specific statement dealing with the teaching about homosexuality and/or the pastoral care of homosexual people. Most statements have been in the contexts either of addressing proposals to decriminalise homosexual acts between consenting adults in private, or of the AIDS epidemic. Their collective statement in

August 1971 drew heavily on the earlier work of Archbishop Godfrey and the English and Welsh bishops. Accepting the nature of a pluralistic society which held different values, the bishops cautioned Catholics against hasty support for any proposed amendments. Making no distinction between orientation or activity they said that 'homosexuality objectively is immoral', and is a 'sexual aberration'. They counselled pastors to 'readily perceive factors reducing imputability', and pointed out that 'there is widespread scope for pastoral and psychological assistance for these people'.[54] Opposing, in 1984, the Australian Broadcasting Corporation's extension of spouse privileges to de facto—heterosexual and homosexual—partners, the bishops said that the policy would work against 'the stability of marriage and public morality'.[55]

South Australia, in 1972, was the first State in the Commonwealth of Australia to decriminalise homosexual activity between consenting adults in private. Archbishop Gleeson of Adelaide supported the change while also teaching 'that deliberate homosexual acts are immoral'.[56] In the early 1980s Cardinal Freeman of Sydney believed that homosexual acts should continue to be regarded as unlawful because of the educative influence of law. But he called on authorities to 'observe discretion and mercy in bringing prosecutions', especially as they affected family life.[57] In 1989, Archbishop Foley of Perth, while describing homosexuality as a 'morally reprehensible practice', nonetheless supported legislative change.[58] Auxiliary Bishop Gerry of Brisbane likewise gave support to Queensland changes in 1990 saying that 'no good purpose is served by making criminals of those who engage in homosexual practices in the privacy of their own homes'.[59] But in 1991 Archbishop D'Arcy of Hobart opposed all changes to Tasmania's criminal code.[60]

In Australia male homosexuals have consistently accounted for around 80 per cent of those infected with HIV. The Australian bishops issued two statements: *The AIDS Crisis* in 1988, and *AIDS: A challenge to love*, in 1989. Stating clearly that 'we do not condone homosexual practices', they promised to all persons an attitude 'of respect, concern and practical help'. They recognised the difficulty of infected gay men having to reveal their health situation and sexuality to their families. 'Some have faced the loss of home and work, been disowned by their families and deserted by their partners. Because of these pressures they have to struggle with depression, often with feelings of shame and guilt and even the temptation to suicide'.[61]

Their second statement was more direct. 'Homosexual acts are intrinsically wrong. These acts are immoral and cannot be condoned or approved'. They held that even the heterosexual spread of the virus 'can be traced to earlier infection of the transmitting partner through homosexual practices'.[62] Addressing the Federal Government's Third National AIDS Strategy Draft they maintained that homosexual acts 'are wrong in themselves', and called for 'the promotion of chastity, celibacy and monogamy'.[63] While since the early 1970s the bishops generally, State by State, had not stood in the way of legislative changes to decriminalise sexual activity between consenting men in private, in 1994, the bishops' Central Commission took a very different stand. They saw danger in the Federal Government's decision to legislate over Tasmania's criminal code which outlawed homosexual acts, because such action could be interpreted as promoting an 'alternative lifestyle' to the detriment of marriage and the procreation of children.[64] Sydney's annual Lesbian and Gay Mardi Gras provoked a strong response from Cardinal Clancy in 1994 when he described the homosexual condition as 'a disorder of nature' and the behaviour as 'morally indefensible'. While 'culpability does not necessarily attach', he concluded that 'the homosexual lifestyle is not, and can never be, a legitimate alternative to the heterosexual lifestyle'.[65]

On their annual Social Justice Sunday in September 1995, the bishops, through their Australian Catholic Social Justice Council, issued *Tolerance: A Christian Perspective on the International Year for Tolerance*. In it they included seven examples of 'expressions of intolerance' found in Australian society, among which they named 'intolerance to homosexual people'. Drawing on the *Catechism* they said that 'to be gay or lesbian is not a matter of choice'. Because people failed to distinguish between homosexual *acts*, 'which the Church teaches to be wrong', and the *person*, intolerance, expressed 'as discrimination, hostility or even violence', often arose. The Church rejects unjust discrimination and accepts homosexual people 'with respect, compassion and sensitivity'.[66] This is the most informed and sensitive statement on homosexuality to come from the Australian Catholic bishops. Two Dioceses have demonstrated a positive and practical pastoral response to gay and lesbian members in the Church. In 1984 Archbishop Faulkner of Adelaide appointed a chaplain to Acceptance, so that the group could be a more effective bridge to the wider church community for those who had felt the pain of separation. With the Eucharist at its centre, the group provides on-going faith formation for its members. In Brisbane, Archbishop Rush established the *Church-Acceptance Dialogue Group* in 1990 as a way of sensitively raising awareness and increasing knowledge of the issue of integrating homosexuality with Catholic faith. One of the auxiliary bishops of Brisbane is a member of the group which has the support of Archbishop Rush's successor, Archbishop Bathersby. Late in 1996 the group published a resource document, *We are the Church, Too?*, to facilitate discussion on the issues throughout the Diocese. The programme has been trialled in several parishes. These examples demonstrate a genuine willingness to draw gay and lesbian Catholics into an active role in Church life, which the *Magisterium* has called for.

THE *MAGISTERIUM* AND THE INTERPRETATION OF SCRIPTURE

No document of the Vatican gives a detailed exegesis of the scriptural passages relating to homosexual acts. The most extensive, although still brief, treatment is in the *1986 Letter*, where the 'new exegesis of Sacred Scripture' is declared to be 'gravely erroneous'. Acknowledging that the Scriptures reflect 'varied patterns of thought and expression', the *1986 Letter* maintains that there is 'a clear consistency . . . on the moral issue of homosexual behavior'. Drawing on the creation narratives, the *1986 Letter* sees that 'in the complementarity of the sexes, they are called to reflect the inner life of the Creator'. Regarding the Sodom story 'there can be no doubt of the moral judgement made against homosexual relations'. Paul in his *Letter to the Romans* speaks of 'the acute distortion of idolatry', and the *1986 Letter* claims that he 'is at a loss to find a clearer example of disharmony than homosexual relations'. In this document there is no attempt to tease out the meaning of the difficult words Paul used in his lists of sins in First Corinthians and First Timothy. Here they are understood to mean 'those who behave in a homosexual fashion', and 'those who engage in homosexual acts'.[67] The analysis of the biblical texts is completed in some four hundred words!

Likewise, very few bishops in their statements present a detailed study of the scriptural texts. Archbishop Quinn of San Francisco acknowledged that the biblical writers 'did not necessarily ask the same questions about a given ethical or moral issue which we would ask today'. Therefore the texts cannot provide immediate answers to our questions. After reflecting on each text he concluded that 'it is clear that the Scriptures, both the Old and the New Testament, reject and condemn homosexual acts'. He saw that the Scriptures 'do not explicitly deal with the question of homosexual attraction or with the issue of homosexual lifestyle'. But because 'an important element of that lifestyle, namely homosexual intercourse' is clearly condemned, Archbishop Quinn argued that 'it is beyond dispute that there is a clear basis in Scripture for the consistent rejection of a homosexual lifestyle'.[68]

Archbishop Weakland admitted that the Bible strongly condemns homosexual acts, but he also acknowledged the 'tremendous help' given by biblical scholarship in putting the texts into a total cultural context. 'All these texts do exist and cannot be taken lightly, even if our knowledge of psychology and the make-up of the human person is vastly different today from St Paul's.'[69] Archbishop Hunthausen was more open to the new biblical exegesis and said that 'no credible Catholic Scripture scholar can be content with a literal or fundamentalist approach to the interpretation of Scripture on this or any other issue'. Because of 'new developments in the human and behavioral sciences' theologians continue to re-examine the Scriptures.[70]

THE STRUGGLE TO DIALOGUE

From the American bishops' 1973 *Principles to Guide Confessors in Questions of Homosexuality*, to Cardinal Hume's 1995 *A Note on the Teaching of the Catholic Church concerning Homosexual People*, from the Vatican's 1975 *Declaration on Certain Questions Concerning Sexual Ethics*, to the 1994 *Catechism of the Catholic Church*, the *Magisterium* has demonstrated significant progress in coming to a better understanding of the extent and nature of homosexuality. But even this progress still leaves many gay and lesbian Catholics dissatisfied and frustrated. While the *Magisterium* has increasingly expressed its respect for the dignity of such people, and strongly criticised many forms of discrimination directed against them, it consistently condemns all sexual activity between same-sex couples. The *Magisterium* holds up one good expression of sexuality—the harmony of love and openness to new life within marriage—as the only good. Chastity for all other people is equated with celibacy—

either in preparation for marriage, or for life in the case of gay men and lesbians and heterosexual single people. It is a common element in magisterial teaching that homosexuality is some kind of threat to marriage and family life, although the nature of such a threat is not explained. But back in 1979 the bishops of The Netherlands approved of a statement that held that homosexual and heterosexual people 'are not in opposition to each other as if they were two separate worlds'. Understanding homosexuality was not 'an attack on the Church's evaluation of marriage and family life'.[71]

There appears to be a willingness, even eagerness, on the part of individual bishops to engage in more fruitful dialogue on the subject. They, like their Anglican counterparts, are caught in a clash of loyalties. They want to express the unity of the Church and be loyal to its traditions. But they are being shown a fuller understanding of homosexuality through the gay and lesbian members of their communities and the advances in modern social theory. Those committed to a vision of an inclusive Church, with a strong pastoral care for those who experience being on the fringe of the Church keenly feel this clash of loyalties. On the other hand, the Vatican, or Roman Curia, shows inconsistency in handling the issue. It is more content to talk *about* lesbians and gay men—although no document uses those terms—and their sexuality, rather than *with* them. With no structures to encourage, let alone allow for, dialogue, the Vatican becomes more and more isolated from the lives of gay men and lesbians, especially those who are members of the Church itself.

6

BROADENING THE DIALOGUE: THE CONTRIBUTION OF MODERN SOCIAL THEORY

While the churches have tried to come to terms with homosexuality in the last thirty years, modern social theory has been exploring its mystery for over one hundred years. Unfortunately there has been little dialogue between the two until perhaps the last fifteen years. Although the terms *homosexuality* and *homosexual* date only from the mid to late nineteenth century, same-sex interaction and relationships have been present in the histories of most, if not all cultures.

Sociologist David Greenberg, in his monumental work *The Construction of Homosexuality*, identified three broad sweeps of homosexual behaviour: transgenerational, transgenderal and egalitarian. Unfortunately most studies have focused on male homosexuality, so our knowledge of lesbianism is somewhat limited.

Transgenerational homosexuality is most often seen as part of initiation rites in which the older partner takes on an active or masculine role in order to give masculinity to the younger and passive partner. 'Often the relationship is believed to transfer a special charisma to the younger partner'.[1] The well-documented practices of the Sambia people in the Highlands of New Guinea illustrate this type of activity. Gilbert Herdt, who lived with this tribe for two years, calls these 'boy-inseminating practices'. The elders teach that semen must be consumed daily in order to achieve masculinity. 'To be effective, male initiation must convert small, puny boys, attached to their mothers, into virile, aggressive warriors, who are first erotically excited by boys and then by women'.[2] Another example is found in the Samurai tradition of Japan, where the warrior would go to battle with his favoured youth, who was often his sexual partner, a relationship accepted and seen as desirable. These relationships, marked by intense loyalty, were highly romanticised and gave rise to a genre of Samurai love poems.[3]

In transgenderal homosexuality one partner takes on the gender of the opposite sex. The best-studied example is found among North American Indians where the *berdache*—male and female—was accepted and respected in the tribes. 'Berdaches adopted the clothing, occupational specializations, mannerisms and speech patterns of the opposite gender.' It would seem that homosexuality was not the cause of the change, but a frequent consequence. Berdaches never formed relationships with each other, and were held in high esteem because it was believed that they had special shamanistic powers.[4]

Egalitarian homosexuality occurs in situations where the partners treat each other as equals, and this form is found among men and women of most cultures. To Greenberg's categories we should add same-sex interaction that appears to be based on equality, but in which, in fact, class or ethnicity or wealth dictate inequality. One example is the very macho culture of the Mexican–Latin American community. Since women are the object of male desire, a passive male is considered effeminate, and is therefore stigmatised while the active one is not.[5] In such a culture the notion of lesbianism is not even considered. While many cultures accept some form of homosexual behaviour 'it should be equally clear that simple involvement with another person of the same sex never becomes the basis for ascribing a distinctive social identity based on that involvement'.[6]

Psychotherapist and sex researcher C. A. Tripp claims that the concept of maleness within a society has a significant influence on homosexuality. 'Where male aspirations are cast in a non-competitive mould, homosexuality tends to be low, but where perhaps the very same aspirations are rated individually with a consequent emphasis on such concepts as the winner and the hero, the homosexual potential is readily activated'.[7]

When societies changed from tribes to political units resembling states some five thousand years ago, class-structured homosexuality began to emerge in which wealth bestowed sexual power. In order to protect male sexual rights, the freedom of women was restricted. The classical Greek world accepted some forms of same-sex interaction as honourable, especially between teacher and student; they were seen 'to be a transient and natural stage in the lives of both adults and youths'.[8]

For the Hebrew people, sexual behaviour between men was an abomination, especially because of the homosexual prostitution that formed part of the foreign worship of gods. Christianity followed the Hebrew tradition, but the intensity of that opposition waxed and waned through the centuries. Classed as a sin, homosexual behaviour could be forgiven—the penitent was not expelled from the church, and he was classed not as 'a homosexual', but as rather someone who had engaged in a homosexual act.[9] So the historian John Boswell argues that gay people 'were dispersed throughout the general population everywhere in Europe; they constituted a substantial minority in every age'. Early Christians did not hold a prejudice against them. He rejects the premise that Christianity was 'the *cause* of intolerance in regard to gay people'. Other forces in society and government were the first to react against homosexuality, as it was not until 1179 that a General Council of the Church—Lateran III—dealt with the matter. Civil legislation forbidding homosexual acts was only introduced in 533 by the Emperor Justinian, two centuries after Christianity had become the official religion of the Roman Empire. The development of the Penitential Books to assist the clergy in imposing appropriate penalties for sins reveal a concern for sexual sins between men, but little for those between women. Severe penalties were reserved for sodomy or anal intercourse. The literature of the Dark Ages gives little detail of homosexual activity, but the Middle Ages (1000–1300), with its economic revival in western Europe, saw the flourishing of literature again, which included both Latin and vernacular homoerotic love poems. Boswell concludes:

> Almost all historians are agreed that the late eleventh and early twelfth centuries were periods of 'openness' and tolerance in European society . . . And most historians consider that the thirteenth and fourteenth centuries were ages of less tolerance, adventurousness, acceptance—epochs in which European societies seem to have been bent on restraining, contracting, protecting,

> limiting and excluding. Few scholars, however, are in exact agreement about why this change took place.[10]

Many Western countries imposed the death penalty, not against a *type* of person, but against certain *sexual acts* shared between people of the same sex. From the time of the Industrial Revolution patterns of family living and social ordering began to change. People became more mobile, many migrated to distant lands, so that family ties were weakened. Marriage was no longer primarily an alliance between families but a free union between individuals. Women could decline a marriage proposal as love and affection between the spouses gained in importance. During this time, while male and female homosexual behaviour existed, 'there was, quite simply, no "social space" that allowed men and women to be gay'. World War II witnessed massive international movements of people and 'temporarily created a new erotic situation conducive to homosexual expression', giving people a personal identity which enabled them 'to remain outside the heterosexual family and to construct a personal life, based on attraction to one's own sex'. Paradoxically, the war which enslaved so many people, became the catalyst for others to experience a new kind of freedom for the first time. The unsettling effect of the war enabled some to create a new life far from the family, places and influences which had shaped their childhood and adolescent years. Gay men, and to a lesser extent, lesbian women, began to resettle in the large cities, seeing themselves as part of an emerging community and were able 'to organise politically on the basis of that identity'.[11] At the same time Western family life was undergoing further change as divorce rates rose and women became more economically independent. An effect of this was the casting of gay men and lesbians as scapegoats for the failure of family life, and the strengthening of anti-homosexual attitudes. Anthropologist Gayle Rubin sums up the situation thus: 'Homosexual behavior is always present among humans. But in different societies and epochs it may be rewarded or punished, required or forbidden, a temporary experience or a life-long vocation'.[12]

Two schools of interpretation grapple with that reality. Is homosexuality a construction of contemporary Western society, or is it a sexual essentialism, seen in a continuity with earlier historical periods? It is not intended to argue here for one interpretation or the other. The debate, nature versus nurture, will continue, and it is a valuable element in the dialogue about homosexuality. Historian Robert Padgug holds that:

> in order to be gay, more than individual inclinations (however we might conceive of those) or homosexual activity is required; entire ranges of social attitudes and the construction of particular cultures, subcultures, and social relations are first necessary. To 'commit' a homosexual act is one thing; to *be* a homosexual is something entirely different.[13]

Wherever the truth lies, patriarchal cultures have an understanding of gay as lacking masculinity. In most cultures the assumption is that sexual opposites attract. 'If someone is attracted to the masculine, then that person must be feminine—if not in the body, then somehow in the mind'.[14] The notion that people form two distinct species, 'one exclusively heterosexual, and the other exclusively homosexual, is of fairly recent origin', born in the eighteenth century 'and institutionalized in 19th century medicine'.[15]

SIGMUND FREUD

Sigmund Freud has been described as one of the West's great analysts of the psychodynamics of love and sexuality. He understood that there was a relationship between sexuality and spirituality. Freud was working at a time when there was a new awareness of homosexuality, but little knowledge of the sexual history of other cultures, or of biology. He believed that all people had the potential to be bisexual because sexuality itself was *wounded*. In 1915 he said that 'psycho-analytic research is most decidedly opposed to any attempt at separating off homosexuals from the rest of mankind as a group of special character . . . [I]t has been found that all human beings are capable of making a homosexual object-choice and have in fact made one in the unconscious'.[16]

While psychoanalysis could help us understand homosexuality to a certain extent, it was unable to predict or fully explain its developmental process. Freud refers to the process that causes a man's sexual desire to be directed towards other males as the 'Oedipus complex'. In the child's love for his mother, the father is seen as rival. There is a fear of castration as a punishment for the jealous sexual feelings, so such feelings are abandoned until puberty.

At that stage, by pursuing other men, the son assures the father that he will not compete with him for the mother's love, and the mother is reassured that she will not be abandoned for another woman.[17] In 1920 Freud further explained: 'What is for practical reasons called homosexuality may arise from a whole variety of psychosexual inhibitory processes; that particular process we have singled out is perhaps only one of many, and is perhaps related to only one type of "homosexuality" '. The same year Freud stated that there were 'various forms of homosexuality'.

Most of Freud's theorising about homosexuality was based on his work with male patients. He developed little understanding of female sexuality, describing it as a 'dark continent for psychology'. He rejected the notion that homosexuals should be treated as sick people, believing that 'a perverse orientation is far from being a sickness'.[18] Freud's insight into the difference between instinct and object in the ancient world compared with the world of his own time is important in today's dialogue.

> The most striking distinction between the erotic life of antiquity and our own no doubt lies in the fact that the ancients laid the stress upon the instinct itself, whereas we emphasize its object. The ancients glorified the instinct and were prepared on its account to honour even an inferior object; while we despise the instinctual activity in itself, and find excuses for it only in the merits of the object.[19]

Christianity has taken the position that, in homosexuality, because the object is inferior or not complementary, namely a person of the same rather than opposite sex, then the instinct or orientation must be intrinsically flawed or evil. Freud saw that the ancients honoured the sexual instinct that was drawn to love and tenderness towards another person. Even if that person was of the same sex, the relationship was respected, even though it fell short of what was considered the ideal of a man–woman relationship.

Perhaps Freud's attitude to male homosexuality is summed up best in his letter to an American mother in 1935.

> Homosexuality is assuredly no advantage but it is nothing to be ashamed of, no vice, no denigration, it cannot be classed as an illness; we consider it to be a variation of the sexual function produced by a certain arrest of sexual development . . . It is a great injustice to persecute homosexuality as a crime and cruelty too.[20]

SCIENCES OF THE MIND

Homosexuality was at first thought to be very rare: one 1885 book claimed that there were only thirty-five known cases in the entire world. The early analysts were able neither to determine what exactly homosexuality was, apart from a same-sex object-choice, nor to agree if such a choice was an emotional disorder. It was considered to be 'an inhibition of the heterosexual potential present in all human subjects'.[21]

Although Brill, one of the early Freudians, declared in 1913 that 'homosexuality may occur in persons just as healthy as normal heterosexual persons', the first generation of American Freudians in particular, moved away from Freud's understanding. Brill, addressing the American Medical Association in New York, claimed to 'cure his patients'. But from 1930 through to the postwar era, a major shift occurred in the psychoanalytic theory of homosexuality with greater study of childhood development, leading many to conclude that homosexuality was a perversion. So Alexander (1948) saw it as a perversion, a 'distortion in the quality of sexual strivings'. Some analysts were particularly severe in their description of the homosexual person. Silverberg (1938) claimed that since the passive homosexual was trying to bring an end to the race, 'society is justified in its violent feelings towards him and . . . in taking steps against him'. Robbins (1943) described the condition of homosexuals as 'suffering, unhappiness, limitations in functioning, severe disturbances in interpersonal relationships'. Bergler (1947) claimed that 99.9 per cent of homosexuals could be cured; in 1954 he said that 'there are no happy homosexuals' because they all 'harbor a profound *inner* guilt because of their perversion'. In 1956 he claimed that they were 'essentially disagreeable', and 'a mixture of superciliousness, false aggression and whimpering'. In the period following the first Kinsey Report (1948), while the writings on homosexuality increased, there was little new thought. Kardiner (1954) compared the homosexual's 'notorious' hatred for women with the Nazi's hatred of the Jews. Allan (1953) saw the homosexual as ill, like a dwarf is ill, 'because he has never developed'. Hamilton (1954) said that the homosexual is 'incapable of love' because he is 'hobbled in his emotional life'. Hendin (1978) held that 'criminals help produce other criminals, drug abusers other drug abusers, and homosexuals other homosexuals'.[22] Sandor

Rado said that it was 'an illness based on a fear of women, and that it could be cured'.[23]

Irving Bieber, who made studies of two hundred male homosexual and heterosexual patients in New York city, concluded that homosexuality arose from a bad family situation where the mother dominated and the father was emotionally cold. He wrote: 'We consider homosexuality to be a pathological, bio-social, psychosexual adaptation consequent to the pervasive fears surrounding the expression of heterosexual impulses'.[24]

However, there were other voices that described the situation differently. W. Brown (1964) recognised that some homosexuals were capable of 'genuine affection, friendliness and co-operation'. Pasche (1964) said that homosexual love could include 'tenderness, protectiveness and admiration'. Marmor (1975) saw as functioning responsibly both male and female homosexuals who 'live emotionally stable, mature and well-adjusted lives, psychodynamically indistinguishable from well-adjusted heterosexuals, except for their alternative sexual preferences'.[25] It was slowly being accepted by the analysts that homosexuals did not have to change the object of their desire in order to live balanced lives. The need was to accept and integrate their sexuality into the other spheres of their lives.

ELIMINATING DISEASE

In 1952 the American Psychiatric Association had formally classified homosexuality as an illness, but in 1973 removed it from its official list of mental disorders. It was decided to retain 'ego-dystonic homosexuality' on the list, because it described that form of homosexuality that 'causes distress to the individual'. In 1987 even that 'illness' was removed from the APA's *Diagnostic and Statistical Manual of Mental Disorders*.[26]

Although many psychiatrists were unconvinced by the 1973 decision, it did put the study of this aspect of human desire and behaviour into a different framework. Analysts and others could approach the issue from more positive starting points, and gain new insights into what Freud called a 'mystery'. Up until this point most writings by psychoanalysists had evolved from experience with patients whose neuroses were thought to be, but often were not, related to their homosexuality. New research began to take place among homosexuals who were not patients, many of whom were living 'normal' lives in the community.

C. A. Tripp was closely associated with Alfred Kinsey and the Institute for Sex Research before establishing his own research in New York. In 1977 Tripp published one of the most significant studies to influence our understanding of the cultural and social construction of homosexuality: *The Homosexual Matrix*. In this work he was complementing the pioneering role of Evelyn Hooker. Looking at the adolescent years of homosexuals he concluded that they often arrived at puberty early; their adolescent sexual activities were 'hardly more than explorations in erotica'; and that neither such sexual experiences, nor 'child seductivity' caused homosexuality, because 'it usually turns out that the die was already cast by then'. He discounted the myth that homosexuality and effeminacy were essentially linked. He saw among homosexual men a quality that avoided 'the sharp edge of masculine eccentricity', and produced rather 'a somewhat gentle, often gentlemanly, but still quite robust maleness'. While he recognised some 'super masculine homosexuals', he observed that they also 'appear to be remarkably affectionate, even tender, in their partner-contacts'. Tripp makes the point that:

> a larger observation is that no single element in homosexuality, no one original influence is by itself likely to be definitive. The final existence of any sexual orientation depends upon the extent to which its various parts have reinforced each other in producing a structure, a system of values, a pattern of responses.[27]

A study of almost one thousand homosexual men and women, and nearly five hundred heterosexuals, was carried out in 1978 in the San Francisco Bay area by Allan Bell and associates. The study looked particularly at the respondents' relationship with their parents, and at the influence their parents had on them, especially during childhood and adolescence. While fathers were more likely to be perceived in a relatively negative fashion by boys, this had 'little eventual influence on [the boys'] sexual orientation'. The findings corroborated those of other studies that had found prehomosexual boys 'to be less stereotypically "masculine" than preheterosexual boys'. Homosexual respondents, during adolescence, had 'a continuing sense of being different from their male peers'. The important difference was 'what [they] *felt* sexually, not what they *did* sexually'. The 'feelings of homosexual arousal and feeling sexually different' occurred years before any same-sex activities. The report concluded:

> No particular phenomenon of family life can be singled out, on the basis of our findings, as especially consequential for either homosexual or heterosexual development. You may supply your sons with footballs and your daughters with dolls, but no-one can guarantee that they will enjoy them. *What we seem to have identified . . . is a pattern of feelings and reactions within the child that cannot be traced back to a single social or psychological root.*[28]

A popular image of the homosexual male, perpetuated by film, gay pride and mardi gras parades, and by the media, is of an effeminate, flamboyant person. But Richard Isay, a clinical professor of psychiatry, saw this as a form of self-mockery, and as an 'angry recognition and flaunting of conventional cultural stereotype'. Isay believed early childhood had considerable influence on how sexuality was expressed, but 'an indiscernible influence on the sex of the love object', because he saw 'sexual orientation as immutable from birth'. Isay's work with adult gay men enabled him to see common elements in their childhood experiences. Homoerotic attraction began between ages eight and thirteen, and sometimes there was a real sense that it had 'always been present'. From as early an age as four, a sense of being 'different' was experienced; as children these men saw themselves as being more sensitive, feeling hurt more readily, and having more aesthetic interests than others. They shared a lack of enjoyment in competitive activities, and felt themselves to have been less aggressive than other children. Reflecting on the father–son relationship, Isay questions the theory of the distant father as a cause of the son's homosexuality. 'The fathers of homosexual sons may withdraw because they perceived that their sons are too closely attached and attracted to them for the father's own comfort, or because they feel that their sons are unacceptably "different"'.

Isay rejects the assertion of most psychoanalysts: that adolescence is a second chance for a youth 'to put aside his homosexuality with proper psychological guidance' and embrace heterosexuality. 'I consider this attitude clinically harmful to the gay adolescent's self esteem'. Rather, he sees this as a time when sexual identity is consolidated 'through homoerotic fantasy, masturbation with homoerotic imagery, sexual attraction to other boys, and sexual experiences'. Even so, the integration of a positive self-image is often slower for homosexual youths than heterosexual ones, because they strive 'to deny and avoid the stigma'. Therapy for gay men is to be based on two convictions: gay men can live 'well adjusted and productive lives with gratifying and stable love relationships', and 'effort to change the sexual orientation of a gay man is harmful to him'. Isay concludes: '[I have] never encountered in my practice a gay man who "chooses" to be homosexual, but it is also true that most gay men I know prefer their sexuality to heterosexuality, since what is experienced as normal and natural is usually preferred, even if such behavior is socially disadvantaged'.[29]

Adrian: accepting his gayness

Adrian, who grew up on a farm and is now in his late sixties says: *If I was offered a choice now between being homosexual and heterosexual, I could not ask to be changed. While it has been hellish and hard to come to terms with being gay after so many years of marriage and a large family, I could not change. This is who I am. My gayness is part of who I am as a person, and if I changed I would be denying who I am, and I would become a different person.*

Richard Friedman, a clinical associate professor of psychiatry at Columbia University, in 1988 agreed with Isay in recognising in the childhood of homosexual adult males an 'unmasculinity', which included avoidance of rough-and-tumble play, aversion to aggressive interaction with other boys and a fear of injury. He says that research shows 'that only subgroups of homosexual men manifest histories of severe boyhood effeminacy'. He points out that 'ten to twelve year old boys do not freely choose their sexual fantasies. Lust happens to them and they masturbate. Their sexual fantasies subsequently shape the boundaries of their lives'. The experience of having exclusively homosexual fantasies at adolescence makes a youth feel even more isolated. The disparity between those fantasies and the expected heterosexual role behaviour that it is simply assumed he will display becomes a problem. Yet Friedman concludes: 'Looking at predominantly or exclusively homosexual adolescents, one of the most striking findings is that there is no evidence at present that these young people experience persistent devastating psychopathology associated with their sexual orientation'.

Prior to sexual activity with others, many adolescents have well-consolidated erotic fantasies, which in turn 'restrict future behavioral options'. Friedman rejects Freud's 'Oedipus complex' theory. While early analysts held that neurosis stemmed from it, he asks why then it should not be epidemic among homosexual adults. The evidence indicates that this is not so. What seems likely to him is 'that homosexuality is associated with some psychological mechanism, not understood or even studied to date, that protects the individual from diverse psychiatric disorders'. Friedman points out that 'many psychoanalysts and psychotherapists see gay patients who have requested help because of impulsivity, compulsivity, and driven frantic sexuality. Often the symptomatic behavior is attributed by the analyst, and sometimes by the patient as well, to homosexuality'.[30]

These more recent researchers point to the role of sexual fantasy in helping to clarify sexual orientation. Sexual fantasies happen, and they are a natural part of the process of sexual awareness and development. The churches have been afraid of such fantasies, labelling them as 'impure thoughts', and therefore sinful. This negative attitude has in particular imposed upon young boys approaching puberty a heavy load of unnecessary guilt, which stays as a burden all through their lives.

Isay says that Evelyn Hooker's conclusions from her studies is that 'no distinguishing psychopathology or greater degree of social or psychological maladjustment was found in homosexual men'.[31] In the past the treatment of homosexuality often involved coercive therapy—lobotomy, and electric shock, even castration.[32]

Mickey: forced to change

When I worked at the telephone exchange a supervisor, Maud, took me under her wing when I was not coping with work or life. After a time I came out to her as a lesbian and she told me that I was emotionally sick and wanted me to go into an institution for wayward girls. I eventually went as a voluntary patient into a mental hospital. I stayed there for three months, and then continued psychotherapy for six years. They tried everything on me in order to change me into a heterosexual: shock treatment, LSD, aversion therapy, drug therapy, psychotherapy. It was a disturbing experience and it all failed. I had actually felt comfortable with my lesbianism since the age of thirteen. But everyone was telling me to be something else. Looking back now I realise that my relationship with Maud was an approval-seeking situation. She was a mother figure with whom I was probably in love. She was kind, but also overbearing. I allowed myself to become dependent upon her and she was always jealous and disapproving of my lesbian friends.

I came out to my family when I was seventeen. I was not living at home at the time. My whole family rejected me. I have never been allowed to have contact with my nieces or nephews or their children. Attempts to reconnect with family have always failed.

In the midst of so much emotional upheaval, Mickey became a Catholic at the age of eighteen. She was in a relationship with a Catholic woman. Even when becoming a Catholic she felt a tension between her new faith and her sexuality which would not be resolved for many years.

I eventually met two Sisters who pointed me in a new direction. One said, 'Why are you wasting your time worrying about your sexuality and your faith? Accept yourself and get on with life'. The other actually encouraged me to look for a life-partner. She talked to me a lot about my faith and prayer and this helped me become more comfortable with my faith and religion in a way I had never experienced before. I then became involved as a volunteer with the AIDS Council of South Australia, and then with Gayline, a telephone counselling service. It felt good to be working with so many other lesbians and gay men. I now felt a balance between my sexuality and my Church. I am proud to talk about both, although a lot of gay Catholic people get nervous when I do. Through my work with Gayline I met Lynette. Our friendship blossomed into a relationship which has grown in strength over the last five years. I am now sixty and look to the day when Lynette and I can enjoy travelling as we enter our twilight years. I am comfortable with the Church, recognising that it has its flaws like the rest of us. I am myself now. It has been at times a very tortured journey to this point in my life, manipulated and allowing myself to be manipulated by others and their expectations of me. But more recently other people have affirmed my dignity by accepting and loving the real me. I have now grown in independence and have a peaceful balance between my sexuality and my faith.

JUNG AND THE JUNGIANS

Carl Jung, one-time student of Sigmund Freud, moved away from his teacher's theory of the existence of two sexual currents in each person, and held that there is one current which is capable of flowing in a variety of directions. As early as 1912 he asserted homosexuality was the result of 'a disturbance in relation to women', and twenty-five years later said that 'in homosexuality the son's entire heterosexuality is tied to the mother in an unconscious form . . . In the son [a mother complex] injures the masculine instinct through an unnatural sexualization'. He saw the homosexual in that position where 'he is likely to *identify* with the anima rather than *relate* to her'. So Jung saw homosexuality as an immaturity, holding that 'in the majority of cases it is an isolated psychic deviation from the norm and cannot be regarded as pathological or degenerative'. Jung says little about same-sex love between women, saying that such relationships bind women together for political activity. These friendships involve the 'exchange of tender feelings', and 'intimate thoughts', while genital desire and activity are secondary. Such women, he says, are often 'high-spirited, intellectual, and rather masculine'.[33]

Jung's insights into the impact homosexuality has on a person's religious sensitivities are invaluable today, especially for the churches as they grapple with the dilemma of whether to ordain to the ministry, or refuse ordination to those men and women who are 'out' about their homosexuality.

> [Homosexuality] gives him a quiet capacity for friendship, which often creates ties of astonishing tenderness between men and may even rescue friendship between the sexes from the limbo of the impossible. He may have good taste and an aesthetic sense which

> are fostered by the presence of a feminine streak. Then he may be supremely gifted as a teacher because of his almost feminine insight and tact. He is likely to have a feeling for history and to be conservative in the best sense and cherish the values of the past. Often he is endowed with a wealth of religious feelings, which help to bring the *ecclesia spiritualis* into reality; and a spiritual receptivity which makes him responsive to revelation.[34]

Jungian analysts demonstrated an attitude to homosexuality different from the early American psychoanalysts. Joyande Jacobi, a long-time associate of Jung, wrote in 1969 that when faced with homosexuals who had low self-esteem, she sought to awaken their artistic capabilities, helping them 'to break away from the ruinous pattern of chance encounter in the sexual sphere' so that they could 'devote their affection to one man in a lasting and also fruitful relationship'. She did observe in 1969 that 'they are unfortunate individuals, but in most cases are highly gifted'. M. Esther Harding, another long associate of Jung and positively disposed to homosexuality, who tended to focus on female homosexuality, saw the limitation of that word. In 1970 she said that while in the mind of the public it is often linked 'with debased practices and criminality', in reality it often refers to friendship 'of a high moral and ethical quality'. She therefore warned that 'it is necessary to be cautious how we apply the term *perversion*'. While Jung's contemporaries remained reasonably close to his theories, the next generation of Jungian analysts were more open to accepting ideas and theories from other sources as well. David Walsh, writing for the Analytical Psychology Club of London, saw a hatred of sexuality rather than of homosexuality as the problem. Eugine Monick in 1987 challenged the attitude of the psychoanalysts who passed judgements on homosexuals.

THE KINSEY REPORT

In 1948 Alfred Kinsey, the American sexologist, and colleagues published *Sexual Behavior in the Human Male* and in 1953 *Sexual Behavior in the Human Female*. These fundamentally affected the nature of future discussion and research on sexuality. Kinsey saw sexuality as a continuum, not as two poles—one heterosexual, the other homosexual.

> Males do not represent two discrete populations, heterosexual and homosexual . . . Only the human mind invents categories and tries to force facts into separated pigeon-holes. The living world is a continuum in each and everyone of its aspects. The sooner we learn this concerning human sexual behavior the sooner we shall reach a sound understanding of the realities of sex.[36]

The two research projects on which the books were based involved 5,200 white American males and 5,940 white American females. The respondents were placed on a seven-point spectrum from exclusive heterosexuality to exclusive homosexuality. The findings revealed that 4 per cent of males were exclusively homosexual throughout their lives. Eighteen per cent were predominantly homosexual for at least three years between the ages of sixteen and fifty-five, while another 7 per cent had had a homosexual experience 'to the point of orgasm' at some time within the same age range.[37]

The numbers among women were much lower with 1 to 3 per cent of unmarried women 'exclusively homosexual in their psychic response and/or overt experience'. A further 2 to 6 per cent of unmarried women were more or less exclusively homosexual. The figures among married women were much less.[38]

Kinsey's research was severely criticised at first, then later accepted, but it is again being more critically analysed today. The restriction of the research to white Americans was certainly limiting. What is valuable from the research is not so much the figures, but the revelation of the fluidity of human sexuality. The research paved the way for more serious studies of what is commonly called 'bisexuality'.

Kinsey and his co-workers continued research to discover if people's sex lives changed following therapy. Where they interviewed men who had been homosexual and were now acting heterosexually, 'they found that all these men were simply suppressing homosexual behavior, that they still had an active homosexual fantasy life, and that they used homosexual fantasies to maintain potency when they attempted intercourse'.[39] This and further research cuts across earlier hopes to 'cure' homosexuality, and discredits the attempts of some church groups, like Exodus International, to change people's sexual orientation. Allan Bell, from the Kinsey Institute, said in 1976 that 'there is no such thing as homosexuality', because 'the homosexual experience is so diverse . . . the variety of its psychological, social and sexual correlates so enormous [and] its originating factors so enormous'.[40]

Shere Hite claimed that by 1994, 'almost sixty percent' of teenage males had sexual experiences with other boys, but that girls rarely learnt about sex together. Their friendships were 'intensely emotional and sometimes romantic', in which 'they create great intimacy verbally'—unlike the friendships of boys which place an emphasis on physical intimacy. Hite concludes that 'our culture has a very strong taboo against affectionate male physical contact. Many men are afraid to touch and cuddle with their sons after the early years, or even altogether. Most of society finds male affection shocking'.[41]

Hung: learning to accept

When I told my father that I was gay and that I masturbated he told me not to worry. 'Masturbation is normal', he said. 'You have a clash between your religion and who you are. Be yourself. Don't let your religious beliefs or the priests influence you too much.' My father had become a Catholic when he married my mother. While he was a good Catholic, he was more discerning about what he was told in church, unlike most people in Vietnam who believed everything the priest told them.

I was sexually aware at the age of six. I was fascinated by one of my cousins who was in his late twenties. I loved to touch him, especially his feet, but the family ridiculed me, and I thought that meant that they did not love me. When I was at school I was called 'BD' or 'Be De', a Vietnamese slang term for a transvestite. Not that I dressed up, but I was probably a fairly sensitive child and youth, was academically inclined, and hated the rough games of the boys. When I was ten I decided to become a priest because then I would not have to marry. The priests where I lived spoke of women and sexuality as if it was all 'dirty'. At the same time I discovered the pleasure of masturbation. A few years later I read in a Catholic book Everlasting Health *that masturbation was a sin. I was left in turmoil. I wanted to be a priest, but I was a terrible sinner, masturbating, wanting to touch other boys, and having fantasies about them. I thought that I was the only person like this.*

At high school Hung fell in love with another student, who had a girlfriend. Hung saw his friend every day, but his friend never shared his feelings. At this time a relative began the process of sponsoring Hung's family to Australia. Hung was devastated. Anytime he could see his friend he was happy. But if he went to Australia he would never see him again. *I was so depressed, I just wanted to die.*

I began to confide in one of my aunties. She tried to build up my self-confidence. When I shared my deepest sexual secrets with her she told me to find a girlfriend. I found one, but nothing changed. I still had the same feelings and fantasies. I asked God to change me. I asked him to help me forget my friend. I went to church twice a day, seven days a week. I began physically torturing myself in order to get rid of my feelings. And then at eighteen I entered the seminary as a part-time student. I became even more spiritual. This was when I confided in my parents. My mother just cried, 'You are just going through a phase'. I went to a Carmelite convent to ask the Mother Superior to pray for me. Her words devastated me. 'If you are gay, no seminary or monastery in the world will accept you. You will have to do something about it, like taking drugs to get rid of your sexuality.'

Hung migrated to Australia in 1992. Still troubled by his homosexual feelings (he had never had a relationship with another man) he sought advice in Confession. Again he was told that homosexuality and masturbation were terrible sins. So he contacted Gayline (a telephone counselling service) and was referred to another priest. *'Homosexuality is a gift, not a cross to bear. Make the gift valuable to yourself and to others.' I started going to Acceptance where I found the help I needed to grow in self-confidence. I have come to recognise now how beneficial the struggle has been for me. My sexuality helped me to build up a strong relationship with God, which is not superficial, but has substance. My sexuality is not a sin, but a gift from God, a ladder to climb in order to reach my spiritual potential. I do hate the institutional things about the Church. I go to Mass when I want to, about three times a month, not when other people tell me to go. I like to pray alone in the church. It gives me peace, happiness, spiritual strength and encouragement. I live my Catholicity in my heart. In the future, through my career I would like to help other youths, in particular Vietnamese youths who are gay, especially those who are without support and in need of emotional assistance. To help them come to terms with their sexuality in a constructive way and to connect their sexuality with their religious beliefs.*

BIOLOGY

At the end of the nineteenth century a group of Germans led by the philosopher and physician Magnus Hirschfeld worked to decriminalise homosexual behaviour. They were firm believers in a biological cause, and while most of their theories have been discredited, their first attempt to develop scholarship and research on homosexuality were courageous and groundbreaking. It came to a tragic end with the rise of Nazism in Germany. The 1960s saw the shift from considering it as a neurosis, to a sexual preference or orientation, but in the 1970s the idea that homosexual behaviour was biologically based gained momentum. A Dutch researcher, Richard Swaeb, in 1990 claimed that a group of cells in the suprachiasmatic nucleus in the brain was in homosexual men nearly twice the size of that in heterosexual men.[42] While criticised by many, this research led Simon LeVay, an American neurobiologist, to concentrate his research on the hypothalamus.

LeVay believes that scientific evidence supports 'a strong influence of nature, and only a modest influence of nurture'. He acknowledges that 'the brain has a structure that is intricate almost beyond belief, and functions that are complex almost beyond comprehension'. He warns that 'believing in a biological explanation for sexual orientation is not the same thing as insisting that sexual orientation is inborn or genetically determined'.[43]

LeVay's research in the early 1990s was carried out on the brains of nineteen homosexual men who had died of AIDS; sixteen heterosexual men, of whom six had died of AIDS; and six women whose orientation was unknown. His studies showed that a cell group 'derived from the third interstitial nucleus of the anterior hypothalamus'—INAH3—'was more than twice as large in the men as in the women', but that 'there was no significant difference between the volumes of INAH3 in the gay men and in the women'. The other three cell groups—INAH1, INAH2 and INAH4—showed no variation between men and women, so he concluded that 'the size of INAH3 in men may indeed influence sexual orientation'. However, he warned that 'such a causal connection is speculative at this point'.[44] Critics of LeVay have speculated that the difference in size of INAH3 in his research may have been 'caused by the hormonal abnormalities associated with AIDS'.[45] Professor Steven Rose, of Britain's Open University, says quite bluntly: 'On Simon LeVay's work . . . it is so methodologically flawed that it's not true'.[46]

Richard Pillard of Boston University spearheaded three studies of identical and non-identical twins, looking to genetic structure rather than brain structure, in order to find a biological link to sexual orientation. The percentage of identical male twins both being gay ranged from 52 per cent to 57 per cent, while among non-identical twins the range was 22 to 24 per cent. For identical female twins the figures showed that 48 to 50 per cent were both gay, while among female non-identical twins the percentage fell to 16 per cent.[47] Commenting on Pillard's studies of male twins, psychiatrist William Byne concluded that 'this result would support a genetic interpretation because identical twins share all their genes, whereas fraternal [non-identical] twins share only half theirs'. But while non-twin brothers share the same proportion of genes as non-identical twins, only 9 per cent were shown to share homosexuality. At the same time 'the incidence of homosexuality in the adopted brothers of homosexuals' was 11 per cent.[48]

Research by Dean Hamer and others of the Department of Biochemistry at the National Cancer Institute in Bethesda, tried to resolve the question: 'Is there a gene on the X chromosome that influences male sexual orientation?'. From forty pairs of gay brothers it was shown that thirty-three of them (83 per cent) 'were concordant, or the same, for a series of 5 markers in chromosome region Xq28'. The findings also showed 'that sexual orientation was *not* strongly linked to any other region of the X chromosome'. Finally, it was discovered 'that gay men have more maternal than paternal male relatives who also are gay'. The research indicated that 'it's unlikely the same version of Xq28 associated with male homosexuality also is associated with lesbianism'. The conclusion is 'that there is a gene at the tip of the X chromosome that influences sexual orientation, at least in some gay men'. Linking the research to LeVay's work on the brain, Hamer suggests that 'the most simple hypothesis would be that Xq28 makes a protein that is directly involved in the growth or death of neurons in IHAH–3'. He adds that 'only the isolation of the Xq28 gene, and further testing of LeVay's hypothesis will provide the answer'.[49]

A study of 2100 pairs of twins by the Queensland Institute of Medical Research in 1995 found that the rate of gay identical twins was almost twice as high as non-identical twins. Researcher Michael Dunn thought 'that homosexuality is less genetic in women than in men. It's consistent with some lesbian women who say that they could go "either way", while many gay men held that they were so since early childhood'.[50]

Professor Rose warns that this 'neurogenetic determinism'—a synthesis of neuroscience and new genetics—must be located 'in a more integrated understanding of the relationships between the biological, personal and social'.[51] Friedman also gives a note of warning because 'in some cases, the behavior may be strongly influenced by the individual's genetic makeup . . . In other instances, however, the environment might play a greater role, and many forms of homosexuality may not be genetically influenced at all'.[52] Byne says that perhaps 'the answers to the most salient questions in this debate lie not within the biology of human brains but rather in the cultures those brains have created'.[53] A cautious conclusion is given by John Cornwell, Director of the Science and Human Dimensions Project at Jesus College, Cambridge.

> A moral philosophy that fails to make close connections with what science tells us about our nature does not bode well for either a balanced view of human identity, or a balanced view of human rights and obligations. Clearly there is much work to be done on the borders of theology and neuroscience: the task is to explore a middle ground of reconciliation—where neurobiology is no indignity to the soul, and the soul is no indignity to neurobiology. In the meantime, the wheel of neuroscience does not stand still.[54]

Ruth Hubbard, a Harvard biologist, makes the comment that 'studies of human biology cannot explain the wide range of human behavior. Such efforts fail to acknowledge that sexual attraction depends on personal experience and cultural values and that desire is too complex, varied and interesting to be reduced to genes'.[55]

BISEXUALITY

The research of Alfred Kinsey and his Institute highlights the fluid nature of sexual attraction and activity. Sexual orientation cannot be defined simply in terms of heterosexual and homosexual. For a significant minority it cannot be limited to something that was firmly established at birth and fixed from that moment on. When people experience 'a mingling of sexual feelings, behaviours and romantic inclinations' it is usually described as *bisexuality*. It is experienced differently by men, for whom it is 'easier to have sex with other men, than to fall in love with them', and women, for whom it is 'easier to fall in love with other women than to have sex with them'. Some female participants in a study of eight hundred bisexuals in San Francisco, carried out by sociologists Martin Weinberg and associates, 'emphasized that their behavior was bi-intimate rather than bisexual'. Those whose sexuality is bisexual are often labelled as being confused, or dishonest, or in a state of transition to homosexuality. Weinberg holds with Freud that 'all individuals seem to have the potential to be sexually attracted to both sexes', and against Jung, who sees adolescent sexual experiences as 'important in directing or reinforcing the course of one's future sexual preference'.[56]

Bisexual men who marry are sexually attracted to their wives, while homosexual men who marry do not experience the attraction, but often have a genuine love for them. Michael Ross, who carried out a comparative psychological study of married homosexual men in Australia, Sweden and Finland, gives five reasons why such men marry: social pressure; attempting to remove one's homosexuality; love of partner and desire for family life and children; ignorance of one's own homosexuality; and seeking companionship (especially for older homosexuals).[57] The advice given frequently in the past by the clergy: 'Get married and these feelings will disappear'. Many did just that, only to discover that the *feelings* did not go away, and for all the love they might have for spouse and children, marriage became an emotional trap or prison. The clergy, ignorant of the basics of human sexual development, promoted a solution to the 'problem' that for many was ultimately destructive for all concerned. From a small survey of married homosexual men and women in England, Brenda Maddox concluded that 'a truly tolerant society may in reality be the one which allows gay people the freedom *not* to marry, exempting them from the traditional social obligations to produce heirs and pass on property'.[58]

Anne: diversity in sexuality

I have always been aware of being a sexual person. I was aware of it too bloody young. It has been my downfall. I thought that it was all that I had to give. Anne married for the first time at the age of nineteen. She was pregnant. Her husband was seventeen. *No one wanted us to get married, but I was determined to do so. But I never really settled into the marriage. I was too restless. During that first marriage I went to Mass every Sunday. I really struggled in my conscience for a year over the pill. When I finally decided to take it I discovered that it gave me freedom to be promiscuous because that was the way I was. That marriage lasted six years during which we had two daughters.*

But then Anne began an affair with a man at work who was twelve years her senior. Separated from his wife, he was raising two children also. Entering a de facto relationship, they moved to a large country town, and six years later were married in the Registry Office. Her daughter starting at a Catholic high school got Anne thinking about the Church again. *For a long time I did not think that I should be going to church because of my life-style. But I needed the Church. When I returned to Sunday Mass I thought that the readings from the Bible were just for me. They spoke to my heart. One of the women in the parish took me under her wing. She suggested that at Communion time I go forward and receive a blessing from the priest. The first time I did this I just cried. In fact I always cried at Communion time because I could not share in it because of my marriage situation.*

Both Anne and her second husband needed their previous marriage to be annulled in order to celebrate their marriage in the Catholic Church. Anne's annulment came after three years, but Jim was not successful. *And then I met Sarah at work. And I fell in love. I had just never considered two women in love, let alone making love before. It was the person of Sarah that attracted me, not her sexuality. I was then caught in a terrible triangle: a twenty-year marriage, a secret relationship with a woman, and a heavy involvement in Church activities. It all got to be too much. I could not live this double life. I felt that I was being hypocritical. And yet I could not understand it. So after all those years of marriage, I left Jim. I kept thinking, hoping, that somehow God would intervene. Sarah and I moved to another town and have been together for seven years. It has been hard, but it is coming together.*

Recently I returned to the town and parish where I had lived my marriage with Jim. And the priest there, who had been such a supportive friend all those years, asked me 'Anne, are you happy?'. 'Yes, I am', I replied, then asked, 'Should I be?' and he said, 'Of course you should'.

About sexuality: *Sex has always been there. I thought that if people had sex with me then that meant that they loved me. But my relationship with Sarah is not built on sex. It is more the emotional bonding in friendship and trust. I've grown up a lot.* About the Church: *I have been able to move back into the Catholic Church through Acceptance. I would love to go to Communion. But the Church says I can't because I am in a relationship with another woman. At this stage I could not go against the Church's teaching and receive Communion.* About faith: *My faith in God is always there. You would wonder how in all the things I've done I would still believe. Yet I do. Prayer has always been part of my journey.* And the future: *I would hope that I would always be with Sarah. At some stage or other I hope that the sex will cease and then I could go to Communion.*

LESBIANISM

In this chapter there have been only passing references made to lesbianism. This is largely due to the limited research that has been carried out on the sexuality of women, compared with that on male sexuality. This is not a modern phenomenon, for throughout human history the lives, and especially the sexuality, of women have been largely neglected. In religious literature there are some isolated references to sexual sins committed between women, but church penalties were much less severe than for sexual activities between men. There is little evidence of church or society persecuting women involved together sexually in medieval Europe.[59]

The development of lesbianism, according to Bell, is related less to 'paternal relationships, traits, or identification', to the number of siblings, or a woman's place in the family, 'to rape, sexual molestation, parental punishments, or other traumatic experiences', but, rather, more to 'one's covert sexual feelings'.[60] Increasingly, distinctions are being made:

> For some, lesbianism remains a state of awareness of self experienced at an early age . . . for them, there was no choice: they were lesbians and they had to follow their inclination. For others, lesbianism is a personal choice, a conscious rejection of the patriarchy, of traditional roles of women, of limitations placed on women's control of their own lives.

Dolores Maggiore goes on to point out that women's liberation and feminism, coming out of the 1960s political experience of civil rights and anti-war movements, gave women a group consciousness, which 'supplied the philosophical base to lesbianism'.[61]

Christine Downing agrees with this distinction, seeing that some lesbians accept 'their rejection of a heterosexual, male-dominated environment' as more central, while others 'turn to women because of the sexual and emotional fulfilment they find women giving one another'.[62] Friedman and Downing also recognise those who are 'primary lesbians', who from an early age (six to twelve) have experienced homoerotic feelings, and those who have arrived at 'a lesbian identity in middle age'. This second group find that men, while able to arouse them sexually, cannot sustain intimacy. From another woman they gain 'empathy, intimacy, connectedness and caring'. Friedman and Downing also identify 'political lesbianism' which has no true parallel in men. Shared political ideals and values influence their erotic experience.[63]

Today people are questioning whether it is appropriate to put the experiences and desires of lesbian women and gay men together under the one banner of *homosexuality*. When this happens, which is usual, the differences of women's love of women and men's love of men are lost because the focus is most often on behaviours 'rather than on what the behaviors *mean* to the actors'. '[E]quating sex with genitality and orgasm' disassociates 'sexual from sensual contact'. At the same time there are some powerful similarities because some men 'insist that the term *homosexual* radically distorts what their love of men means to them'. As they attempt to articulate what love means, they 'clearly echo the testimony of their lesbian sisters'.[64]

Friedman and Downing, along with Andy Metcalf, support a rethink of the use of the term *homosexuality*:

> In a general sense it seems to us to be useful to conceptualize lesbianism as a subset of female behavior, and homosexuality as a subset of male behavior.[65]
>
> There has been a growing recognition that gay sexuality has to be seen not as a completely distinct form of sexuality, but as a part of male sexuality as a whole, illuminating it from its particular viewpoint. The gay perspective has a way of seeing through the rhetoric of masculinity and exposing the hollowness of the image.[66]

FROM HOMOSEXUAL TO GAY TO QUEER

The 'gay and lesbian community', which is increasingly better educated, wealthier, more visible and more articulate in Western societies, has challenged traditional concepts of masculinity, gender roles, and the nature of family. This community has become a new political force. It confronts homophobia and patriarchy. Psychologists George Lough and John Sanford recognise the needs of men, who are too often taught to see one another as competitors not to be trusted. Men lack intimacy with each other, fearing that by being affectionate they will be labelled as homosexual. 'Strangely, men show their love for each other by putting each other down. This is because our culture won't permit them to do it honestly in words of affection and praise, unless, of course they are drunk.'[67]

Homosexuality and gayness are not the same thing. 'Homosexuals became GAY when they rejected the notion that they were sick, or sinful', and in banding together 'created a subculture'. 'Membership [of the gay subculture] is chosen rather than automatic.'[68] George Weinberg sees homosexuality as in no way making a person less masculine than other men, or less feminine than other women. He says:

> A homosexual person is gay when he regards himself as happily gifted with whatever capacity he has to see people as romantically beautiful. It is to be free of shame, guilt, regret over the fact that one is homosexual . . . To be gay is to view one's sexuality as the healthy heterosexual views his. To be gay is to be free of the need for ongoing self inquisition.[69]

Recent developments in postmodernist social theory have challenged the static understandings of sexuality in general, and of homosexuality in particular. This understanding of homosexuality emerges from the writings of the French philosopher Michel Foucault. In the 1960s he set about challenging the notion of 'sexuality' that had its origin at the beginning of the nineteenth century, arising out of a threefold connection. Firstly, in the development of diverse fields of knowledge, especially in the biology of reproduction. Secondly, in 'the establishment of a set of rules and norms—in part traditional, in part new—which found support in religious, judicial, pedagogical, and medical institutions'. And thirdly, 'in the way individuals were led to assign meaning and value to their conduct, their duties, their pleasures, their feelings and sensations, their dreams'. All this 'caused individuals to recognize themselves as subjects of a "sexuality" '.[70] This led to the development of *queer theory*, which attempts to reject the role of compliant victim–client status that gay men and lesbian women accepted when their sexuality was for so long misrepresented and devalued. While 'the sodomite had been a temporary aberration', by the eighteenth century 'the homosexual was now a species'.[71]

Queer theory argues that sexuality is complex and constantly changing and that there is never a fixed or irrevocable identity for anyone. This reflects the postmodern condition which 'is a site of constant mobility and change, but no clear direction of development'.[72] Historian Gertrude Himmelfarb says that 'modernism tolerates relativism, postmodernism celebrates it'. Modernism 'makes a strenuous effort to attain as much objectivity and unbiased truth as possible', but 'postmodernism takes the rejection of absolute truth as a deliverance from all truth and from the obligation to maintain any degree of objectivity'.[73] Elizabeth Grosz says that 'most queer politics . . . are precisely about making one's sexual practices the political truth about one's life'.[74]

This queer theory puts a great emphasis on being a rebel at the margins of society and expresses itself in confronting and shocking political, cultural and religious establishments. Borrowing ideas from queer theory, a new movement began within the lesbian and gay community in 1990, called Queer Nation. It grew as a response to the slowness of legislative changes in the United States to give civil rights to gay and lesbian people, and to attempts in some States to repeal gay rights laws. It was also a response to the increase of violence against lesbians and gays, including murders. Part of its

Manifesto reads: 'In this culture, being queer means you've been condemned to death; appreciate our power and our bond; realize that whenever one of us is hurt we all suffer; know that we have to fight for ourselves because no one else will'. The anger within such a movement is seen in its slogans and statements: 'I hate straights', and 'Bash back . . . Let yourself be angry . . . that there is no place in this country where we are safe'.[75] In Australia the rage of this movement has had little impact, but the use of the word *queer* has increased within the gay community; although in a more benign way, often as an outrageous or provocative substitute for the cumbersome 'lesbian and gay' title, especially in cultural settings like various queer film festivals across the nation.

A new gay intelligentsia, among whom Bruce Bawer and Andrew Sullivan are articulate members, are challenging queer theory, assessing it to be 'ultimately selfish and immature'. They see themselves as second-generation activists who have the task of educating wider society about the true nature of homosexuality, a role that 'requires discipline, commitment, responsibility'. To them the 'images of raw sexuality—images that variously amuse, titillate, shock and offend'—of the post-Stonewall activists have revealed 'nothing important about who most people really are'.[76]

CONTRIBUTING TO THE DIALOGUE

So we see that understanding of the diverse nature of human sexuality, and homosexuality in particular, has undergone enormous shifts in the past century through the intricate workings of the social sciences and modern social theory. Today there is perhaps a certain preoccupation, especially in the sciences related to biology, with finding a cause for homosexuality. The debate around nature versus nurture will continue for a long time. Among the valuable new knowledge gained—and of particular reassurance for lesbians and gay men—is that while history has most often been forthright about 'homosexual acts', there is a new valuing of the dynamics of same-sex attraction and relationships. This minority variation in sexuality has influenced our understanding of people, and of the complementary nature of the masculine and feminine in all people. We now know that people do not choose their sexual orientation; the choice lies in deciding responsibly how to respond to the forces of fantasy and attraction and the desire for relationship within each person.

But the need for dialogue is urgent. It is not just about theories. It is not just an intellectual exercise. It is about life itself. For all the progress that the various sciences have made in helping us understand and appreciate the rich variety of human sexuality, because of prevailing attitudes homosexuality remains a burden for adolescents. In 1989 the US Department of Health and Human Services published a *Secretary's Report* on youth suicide. It began with the claim: 'Suicide is the leading cause of death among gay male, lesbian and transsexual youth. They are part of two populations at serious risk of suicide: sexual minorities and the young'. Religion depicting homosexuality as sin impacts on gay youth so that they 'may feel wicked and condemned to hell and attempt suicide in despair of ever obtaining redemption'. Sobering advice was offered to the churches. 'Religion needs to reassess homosexuality in a positive context within their belief systems . . . Faiths that condemn homosexuality should recognize how they contribute to the rejection of gay youth by their families and suicide among lesbian and gay male youth'.[77] And the contribution of modern social theory can release people from ignorance which leads to fear, prejudice and discrimination, and despair. Tripp's question of twenty years ago seems devastating in its simplicity. 'In the final analysis, what does it all mean?—or does homosexuality have any special meaning? Probably not. It is a fact of life; the rest is interpretation and consequence.'[78]

7

FINDING A NEW DIRECTION THROUGH DIALOGUE

Movements to abandon old prejudices and ignorance and to progress towards new understandings of friendships and love between people of the same gender have been taking place, even if some are tentative. We can now see how ill-conceived and plainly wrong were many long-held beliefs about homosexuality. The new knowledge has touched and affected the attitude of the Catholic Church towards gay men and lesbian women, especially at the pastoral level. However there is no shift in the core belief of the *Magisterium* that homosexual acts are always intrinsically evil, and that the inclination or orientation is a moral disorder.

THE MANY VOICES OF DIALOGUE

By now we can hear many voices contributing to the dialogue, and they represent a wide range of insights, ideas, theories and opinions. The churches have spent less than thirty years in serious exploration of the issue, whereas the social sciences have been engaged in it for well over a century. Almost all of what was held as true one hundred years ago has had to be abandoned as new knowledge has come to light through research and interdisciplinary sharing of knowledge. This is an important lesson for the churches to learn. Patience is needed, openness to others' discoveries is to be encouraged, as is the humility to admit the inappropriateness of some old beliefs.

Christianity *has* shown a remarkable ability to adapt its teaching in the light of new developments and knowledge. Perhaps the classic example is the issue of slavery. Both apostles, Peter—'slaves, accept the authority of your masters with all deference, not only those who are kind and gentle but also those who are harsh' (*1 Peter* 2:18 NRSV)—and Paul—'slaves, obey your earthly masters in everything' (*Colossians* 3:22 NRSV)—accepted slavery as part of life. But today, any act or enterprise 'that for any reason . . . leads to the *enslavement of human beings*, is condemned'.[1] Catholics prayed for 'the perfidious Jews' every Good Friday until 1962, yet just three years later the Vatican Council taught that the Church 'deplores all hatreds, persecutions, displays of antisemitism levelled at any time or from any source against the Jews'.[2] The Hebrew Bible abounds in wars fought in the name of God, and Catholic popes have raised armies to defend their territories and initiate aggression towards enemies. Today the Church urges prayer that God 'may free us from the ancient bondage of war', and teaches that 'every act of war directed to the indiscriminate destruction of whole cities or vast areas with their inhabitants is a crime against God and man, which merits firm and unequivocal condemnation'.[3] In 1832 Pope Gregory XVI denounced freedom of conscience in his encyclical *Mirari vos*, but the Second Vatican Council affirmed conscience as a person's 'most secret core and sanctuary'.

Throughout its history the Christian church has developed its moral teaching in the light of new knowledge and reflection. It has always been part of the dynamism of Christianity to cross significant boundaries. Even the first generation of Jewish-Christians had to cross a significant boundary of religious, cultural and ethnic exclusions in order to accept Gentiles into their community. Immediately, another significant boundary presented itself. Did the new Gentile-Christians have to accept the law of Moses with its prescription for circumcision, dietary laws and cultural traditions? And to resolve the matter Peter and Paul had to settle a disagreement. As Paul himself testified: 'I opposed him to his face, since he was manifestly wrong'.[4] The crossing of new significant boundaries is woven through the history of the Christian church. If the issue of homosexuality and the morality of same-sex relationships is 'another significant boundary' in the life of the church, as we have heard the Anglican bishops in England express it, then past crossings of boundaries should help us today. Dialogue helps us all to see and understand truth more clearly. And the characteristics of such dialogue have also been spelt out. The Vatican Council insists that it be conducted with charity and humility. Pope Paul VI says that it is to be marked by peacefulness, patience and generosity. Pope John Paul II claims it to be an exchange of gifts.

It is clear that on the issue of homosexuality the *Magisterium* of the Catholic Church is in crisis. The Vatican controls the teaching and insists that its teaching on the issue *must* be the prevailing Catholic position. The decade from the mid 1970s to 1986 was a fertile period for the development of a pastoral theology relating to homosexual people by bishops in many countries. This initiative, which demonstrated that the bishops were listening to their gay brothers and lesbian sisters, was brought to an abrupt end by Cardinal Ratzinger's *1986 Letter*. The disciplining of bishops and theologians who move away from or question the Vatican's position is disturbing. The right to 'a lawful freedom of enquiry', guaranteed by the Second Vatican Council, is disregarded. The Vatican makes dialogue about homosexuality within Catholic circles very difficult, and many gay and lesbian people themselves are so disillusioned that they consider it to be impossible in the light of how Catholic teaching is presently articulated.

Truth is not arrived at by a majority vote, nor is it honoured by retaining at all costs a teaching that is seriously and respectfully challenged from many quarters. It is transparently obvious that there is a need for dialogue on the issue within the Catholic community. The Vatican needs to show leadership, *not by imposing* its teaching, but *by encouraging dialogue* throughout the Church and with people of appropriate experience, knowledge and understanding.

If the dialogue we construct is seen in terms of contrary factions, and we view its end result in terms of winners and losers, then the whole dialogue is doomed to failure. However, if we can construct the dialogue as people coming together for an 'exchange of gifts', then we lay a foundation of respect, charity and humility. If the goal of the dialogue is 'that they help one another in the search for truth', then we have diffused the adversarial element. If the dialogue is a promotion of 'all that is true, just, holy, all that is worthy of love', then it will be a conversion experience for all. For the truth that will emerge from this dialogue 'might require a review of assertions and attitudes', by all involved.[5] The dialogue will make us all wise.

This work shows that the dialogue will not be easy. But it is a morally compelling right, not a dispensation, because through it all we must 'try to guide each other . . . in a spirit of mutual charity and with anxious interest above all in the common good'. This common good 'is the sum total of social conditions, which allow people, either as groups or as individuals, to reach their fulfilment more fully and more easily'. The development of the social order, which requires ongoing improvement, 'must constantly yield to the good of the person'. Furthermore, 'it must be founded in truth, built on justice, and enlivened by love: it should grow in freedom toward a more humane equilibrium' and will include 'a renewal of attitudes and far-reaching social changes'.[6]

THE DIGNITY OF GAY AND LESBIAN PEOPLE

Sometimes we might be forgiven for misunderstanding much of what the churches say about homosexuality because of the way they present their message. Often it is spoken about in some abstract way, as impersonal as a mathematical formula. At other times it is presented on the assumption that all homosexual people are some form of alien monster intent upon corruption and destruction. *We are talking about people*. They have the same human dignity, rights and responsibilities as all other people. And the stories that emerge from their lives are to be respected and honoured—indeed, as are those of other people, who are to be allowed 'a lawful freedom of enquiry, of thought, and of expression, tempered by humility and courage'.[7]

We have seen a growing confidence among Christian and spiritual gay people in articulating their experience and self-awareness *as homosexual persons*. They value their sexuality as a gift. In this gift they are discovering a new dimension of spirituality because their sexuality is fundamental to their ability to relate to others in love. Increasingly gay men and lesbian women reject the idea that their sexuality is a 'disorder', that they are victims of some unfortunate quirk of nature. They understand the truth that people cannot live without love. They realise that if a person 'does not encounter love . . . does not experience it and make it his own . . . does not participate intimately in it', then life is 'incomprehensible' and 'senseless'.[8]

This experience, this knowledge, cannot be dismissed as some sort of an illusion. Their sexual orientation, in its essence, is not a compulsion towards selfish, indulgent acts (although they do occur, as they do within heterosexual contexts), but is a propensity towards affection, commitment and love. It is not simply about *having sex*, but about *relating* to another. This propensity towards affection is sadly discredited by the Vatican when it claims that homosexual acts 'do not proceed from a genuine affective and sexual complementarity'.[9] The integrity of gay men in particular, has been tested in the crucible of AIDS, where they have regularly revealed themselves as people of creative compassion with a profound sense of loyalty to their suffering brothers and sisters.

Gay and lesbian Christians experience their spirituality as a response to what the biologist and theologian Charles Birch calls God's 'compassionate, persuasive love'. Usually finding only limited support from within the Christian community, they witness to a trust in God's providence which is 'a creative and saving possibility in every situation which cannot be destroyed by any event'. Gay and lesbian Christians well know that '*created goods* . . . [are] often obliterated by the wickedness of human beings', and so they must rely on God 'the *creative good* . . . [who] works against obstacles and evils of all sorts'.[10]

WHY HOMOSEXUALITY?

Gay and lesbian people turn their attention not so much to the causes of their sexuality, but rather to its purpose, its unique value, its bestowal as a gift. Their contribution to society and church is expressed thoughtfully.

For John McNeill, the 'interpersonal love between equals' in a gay or lesbian relationship challenges 'the role playing determined by tradition' that often shapes heterosexual marriages. The gay experience of equality can act 'as the foundation for the marriage relationship' at a time in human history when marriage is under unprecedented pressure.[11]

Malcolm Boyd sees gay people making 'a significant contribution' to society by highlighting 'the awareness that virtually everybody occupies some kind of closet'. He points out that 'everyone knows what it means to hide the experience of loneliness, refusing or being unable to share and explain deep feelings and truths'.[12] He sees in the gay experience God's gifts: 'the capacity to love, the capacity for a deep sensitivity, the capacity for service'.[13]

American Catholic writer and activist Richard Cleaver sees that gay men help dismantle the damage done to other men through homophobia and heterosexism. 'Men in our culture have been kept from learning to care for one another.' Gay men themselves have been forced to unlearn homophobia 'in order to love one another', and so are in a position to help all men make that transition from fear to love.[14]

Paul Monette, American gay novelist and eloquent writer about the impact of AIDS on his generation, sees that gay men and lesbians, having 'fought through self-hatred and their self-recriminations have a capacity for empathy that is glorious'. He sees 'a kind of flagrant joy about us that goes very deep and is not available to most people'. The capacity to laugh 'is like praising God'.[15]

Episcopalian lesbian M. R. Ritley, whose spiritual journey took her through non-Western spiritual traditions as well as the Society of Friends, believes that 'gay is a spiritual quality'. This confers on people a separation which she understands as 'right'. This gift also confers a certain spirit of commitment to a task, as well as detachment at its completion, as she expresses in a poem:

> Go where you are sent.
> Wait till you are shown what to do.
> Do it with the whole self.
> Remain till you have done what you were sent to do.
> Walk away with empty hands.[16]

Fenton Johnson, novelist and essayist, and raised a Catholic, sees 'that gay men and lesbians may have some special access to understanding the nature and importance of love'. The reason for this insight is 'because no one knows the value of something better than those who have struggled to achieve it'.[17]

Mel White, former writer for various television evangelists and conservative American politicians, and now a pastor within the Metropolitan Community Church, sees gay people being able to call the church to a new honesty. Having experienced first hand the use of Scripture to condemn gays and lesbians, he asks: 'Is it too much to say that those who condemn gay and lesbian people and chase us out of our churches are the true Sodomites, for they refuse to obey God with acts of justice and hospitality?'.[18]

Episcopalian layman John Fortunato sees that 'to be gay and Christian, integrating both into the wholeness we deep down know ourselves to be, [is] to embrace them both as gifts of God'. But by living authentic lives and rejoicing in uniqueness is actually 'to place ourselves on the outskirts of the community we most care about'.[19]

Catholic pastoral psychotherapist Lorna Hochstein has a special interest in the interaction between lesbian spirituality and organised religion. She sees lesbians as being able to bring to the Catholic community a 'minority report' about the nature of God. Accepting 'that God created us lesbian' leads to a deeper spirituality. Love between women 'is a dramatic sign that God's presence is possible anywhere, anytime, and that hopelessness is not ever justified'. She rejects the temptation 'to cease struggling for truthfulness in our relationships'.[20]

Presbyterian minister Chris Glaser sees that 'one of our special graces as lesbians and gays is that, in the midst of unwelcoming environments, we have created homes'. He explains this as 'making the world safe for diversity—perhaps that is ultimately our call: to be peacemakers'. This would involve 'creating a church and world which *has* to take everyone in, which *wants* to take us all in: fragile, human, strangers, who also happen to be children of God'.[21]

English gay Catholic Andrew Sullivan, former editor of the *New Republic* in Washington, says that since 'there is no institutional model, gay relationships are often sustained more powerfully by genuine commitment', and since they 'often incorporate the virtues of friendship more effectively than traditional marriages', are able to 'help strengthen and inform many heterosexual bonds'. The impact of AIDS on gay men's lives has highlighted a difference between them and their heterosexual brothers because 'the perspectives of those who have stared death in the face in their twenties are bound to be different than those who have stared into cribs'. Yet he sees such gay men involved in another form of procreation—'in a society's cultural regeneration, its entrepreneurial or intellectual rejuvenation, its religious ministry, or its professional education'. Homosexuals, he says, have learned differently about life, because 'there are parts of it that cannot be understood, let alone solved; that some things lead nowhere and mean nothing . . . that problems are more sanely enjoyed than solved; that there is reason in mystery; that there is beauty in the wild flowers that grow randomly among our wheat'.[22]

THE FRUITFULNESS OF LOVE

The Catholic Church declares homosexual acts to be a disorder because they can never achieve what is held to be one of the essential purposes of human sexuality: the procreation of children. Such acts will always be frustrated. But this is also true of heterosexual acts of intercourse, even within marriage, because of infertility and sterility.

Pope John Paul II spoke words of hope and encouragement to married couples who experienced physical infertility by addressing 'the spiritual fecundity of the family'. Such fecundity or fruitfulness is 'a marvellous fruit of the Spirit of God who opens the eyes of the heart to discover new needs and sufferings in our society and gives courage for accepting them and responding to them'. This, the pope says, 'broadens enormously the horizons of the parenthood of Christian families'. The qualities of married and family life he proposes include 'forming a community of persons', 'serving life', 'participating in the development of society', and 'sharing in the life and mission of the church'.[23]

Many Christian gay and lesbian couples live out those same qualities in their relationships. The response of the gay community to the AIDS epidemic has shown remarkable compassion and generosity towards a new area of need and suffering in our society. The inability to achieve a physical fruitfulness does not render gay and lesbian relationships sterile. They are a witness to a rich fruitfulness of spiritual, emotional and societal dimensions.

The Vatican, supported by various bishops, has strongly rejected the concept of family as including gay couples. This was made clear by the Vatican delegation at the United Nations Women's Conference in Beijing in 1995, when it 'objected to the use of the word *families* in a way that could imply any group of two or more individuals could be considered a family, including a gay couple'.[24] This is in contrast to the Australian Catholic bishops who saw 'many different types of families living in Australia' and described them 'as those intimate communities within society whose members are committed to each other in love'. They developed what they called 'an inclusive approach' in discussing them during the United Nations International Year of the Family.[25]

FUNDAMENTAL QUESTIONS FOR DIALOGUE

Christian gay and lesbian people, and those who are Catholic in particular, want to enter into dialogue within the church about six crucially important questions:

1. Since intention, commitment and fidelity help shape the morality of heterosexual intercourse, even in marriage, on what grounds then can it be held that *every* sexual act between people of the same sex is *always* an intrinsic moral evil?
2. Since the homosexual orientation is integral to the nature and personhood of gay men and lesbian women, on what grounds can such orientation be declared an objective disorder?
3. Since celibacy is treasured as a gift for the sake of the Kingdom when freely chosen in priesthood or consecrated life, on what grounds can it be imposed as being always obligatory for gay men and lesbian women?
4. Since the complementarity of heterosexuality is reflected in the physical, spiritual and emotional dimensions of the male and female, why is the complementarity of gay and lesbian relationships judged solely on the limitation of the physical, with no consideration given to the spiritual and emotional dimensions?
5. Since the Bible condemns certain homosexual acts, on what grounds can this be extended to include the orientation of homosexuality about which the biblical writers knew nothing?
6. Since tradition, with limited access to knowledge about human development and sexuality, has constantly taught that homosexual acts are sinful, on what grounds can the new developments in biblical scholarship and modern social theory continue to be significantly excluded from the development of moral theology?

HOPE FOR DIALOGUE

It was said earlier that this is not an exercise in Vatican bashing. In Chapter 1, seven limitations in the teaching of the *Magisterium*, and especially that of the Vatican, were highlighted. It is possible now to point to seven grounds upon which the same teaching makes the beginning of a new dialogue not only possible, but essential.

1. It *acknowledges* that it is 'in a position to learn from scientific discovery' while claiming that its more global vision of 'the rich reality of the human person in his spiritual and physical dimensions', does 'greater justice to the rich reality of the human person'. It claims that 'the Catholic moral perspective . . . finds support in the more secure findings of the natural sciences', which it acknowledges 'have their own legitimate and proper methodology and field of inquiry'. However, this openness to modern social theory is heavily qualified in the *1986 Letter*.[26]
2. It *condemns* 'violent malice in speech [and] in action', because of the dignity of each person, and calls for 'respect, compassion, and sensitivity' towards homosexual persons.[27] However, the *1992 Considerations* were not so generous in this matter and counselled the restriction of rights in relation to employment, housing and health benefits. 'These rights are not absolute', because 'there is no right to homosexuality'.[28]
3. It *rejects* reducing homosexual behaviour to being 'always and totally compulsive', and respects as essential 'the fundamental liberty which characterizes the human person and gives him his dignity'.[29]
4. It *invites* the homosexual person to faith in the crucified Christ and 'to carry the cross', which is also 'the way to eternal life for *all* who follow Christ'. This 'conformity of the self-denial of homosexual men and women with the sacrifice of the Lord will constitute for them a source of self-giving' through which they will be saved from a way of life 'which constantly threatens to destroy them'. This union with Christ will enable them to produce in their lives the fruits of the Spirit: 'love, joy, peace, patience, kindness, goodness, trustfulness, gentleness and self-control (*Galatians* 5:22)'.[30] However, the focus on the sacrifice of Christ, and the anticipation that homosexual people will be destroyed by their way of life, does echo the negative attitudes of the early psychoanalysts.
5. It *refuses* to define people primarily by their sexuality, but rather affirms 'a fundamental identity: the creature of God, and by grace, his child and heir to eternal life'. From this comes 'the realization that a homosexual person, as every human being, deeply needs to be nourished at many different levels simultaneously'.[31]

6. It *acknowledges* that people do not choose their sexual orientation, but that 'everyone, man and woman, should acknowledge and accept his sexual *identity*'.[32] The homosexual inclination of a person 'is not a sin' in itself, although it is classified as 'a more or less strong tendency ordered toward an intrinsic moral evil'.[33] Earlier the distinction was made between that tendency which 'is transitory', and that which is definite, although that distinction was also unfortunately expressed in terms of 'curable' and 'incurable'.[34]
7. It *observes* that homosexuality 'has taken a great variety of forms through the centuries and in different cultures. Its psychological genesis remains largely unexplained'.[35]

THEOLOGIES OF THE TWENTIETH CENTURY

Throughout the history of Christianity a rich range of theologies developed in every age as the church was faced with new situations. In this twentieth century a concern for justice has been taken on passionately as humanity has had to face two world wars, the Jewish Holocaust, overwhelming global poverty, the proliferation of military dictatorships and the abuse of human rights, the rapid destruction of the environment and the massive movement of refugees. Within this framework of justice important and vibrant theologies have emerged in order to help people find new directions for living.

Beginning in South and Central America, and later influencing peoples in Asia and Africa, **liberation theology** has rallied the poor to the extent that they 'have gradually become active agents of their own destiny'. This is 'an expression of the poor to "think their faith"'.[36] This 'quest for freedom and the aspiration to liberation' is recognised by the *Magisterium* as being 'among the principle signs of the time in the modern world'.[37]

A **feminist theology** has emerged from the work of women biblical scholars and from a rejection of the patriarchal structures of the Christian church. In this theology 'women collectively have claimed to be church and have claimed the tradition of the exodus community as a community of liberation from patriarchy'.[38] This theology has sought not only to give women an increased and critical role in the church, but also to address those many issues that deny the dignity and rights of all women. Pope John Paul II calls this 'the great process of women's liberation' which 'has been substantially a positive one', although he admits that more needs to be done. He holds that 'there is an urgent need to achieve *real equality* in every area' since 'this is a matter of justice and also of necessity'.[39]

Creation theology reflects a greater awareness of the finite quality of the created world, and a stronger sense of responsibility for it as each generation must entrust it to future generations. It emerges from the 'intuitive understanding' of ordinary Christians who see 'that love and respect for God involves love and respect for God's creation'. It is supported by an 'understanding of Jesus, and God revealed in Jesus, and of a consequent understanding of humankind and other creatures'.[40] This 'growing attention being paid to the *quality of life* and to *ecology*, especially in more developed societies', is seen as 'another welcome sign' by Pope John Paul II.[41]

For fifty years before the Second Vatican Council, the ecumenical movement was assumed to be theologically Protestant, because Catholics did not see the need to search for Christian unity since they were in union with the chair of Peter in Rome and considered themselves to already possess the fullness of Christian truth. **Ecumenical theology** gained momentum from the Vatican Council that was called by Pope John XXIII specifically to hasten the unity of all Christians. The Council admitted that there were faults on all sides when the unity of the church was severely ruptured by the Great Schism in the East in the thirteenth century, separating Orthodox Christians and the Bishop of Rome from each other. This division was further exacerbated by the Protestant Reformation in the West in the sixteenth century. This ecumenical theology has been one of the most vibrant of all the modern ones because 'ecumenical dialogue is of essential importance'.[42]

What is important to note about these twentieth-century theologies is that while they are part of Catholic theology today, each of them began under a cloud of suspicion or even in the face of great hostility. Slowly as each one was developed, tested by time and research, and refined by dialogue and argument, and not without some considerable pain, the *Magisterium* came to acknowledge their value and place in the life of the community. This is something to be kept in mind as people are beginning to articulate a **gay and lesbian theology**.

A GAY AND LESBIAN THEOLOGY

Like the other theologies of this century, this theology is emerging from the lives of gay and lesbian people themselves and not from the halls of academia. It is faithful to the wish of the Second Vatican Council to develop ministries of 'like to like', among the lay members of the Church acting on their own responsibilities. It is a theology driven by two convictions: an understanding that homosexuality is a gift from God, and that gay and lesbian people 'want to stay within the church'.[43]

Like the liberation, feminist, creation and ecumenical theologies, this one is also firmly rooted in the virtue of justice. It is in partnership with those other movements for justice that have been a mark of our own times: the black civil rights movement in the United States, the anti-apartheid movement in South Africa, the people power of the Philippines, the international green movement and the anti-nuclear movement. This gay and lesbian theology is at a healthy stage, because those who for so long have endured alienation from the Church and society are now taking the initiative to move out of a 'victim' mentality. They have pride in themselves, and they speak of their experience of spirituality and sexuality with growing confidence. The pioneers of this theology will leave for the next generation of gay men and lesbian women an important role model and heritage.

Meanwhile the first and second generations of the Stonewall era gays and lesbians will probably still carry the scars of their rejection of and by the Church for a long time. Many vow that they will never return to the Church, and so the Church must find ways of returning to them. For some their pain is so deep that they are driven by a fury against the Church, even to the point of disrupting church services and desecrating the Sacrament of Communion. The development of a gay and lesbian theology by the whole Church community would be another kind of liberation for the Church itself: a liberation from self-satisfaction and moral complacency.

In the light of all that has gone before, what then could we expect to find in a new gay and lesbian theology?

Homosexuality would be recognised as a God-given gift. Since such orientation helps shape love between people of the same sex it would be honoured because of its divine origin, because 'God is love'.[44] It would be recognised as a further manifestation of God himself in all his wondrous complexity and simplicity, in his tenderness and passion. Understanding that 'God is the ultimate source of genuine love and when people experience love at the human level they are absorbing something of the divine love',[45] homosexuality would be recognised as part of God's creation, and not condemned as a consequence of original sin.

Homosexuality would be recognised as one aspect of human sexuality. While different from, it would be seen as complementary to, heterosexuality. It would not be seen as a threat to heterosexuality, but rather the two would interact and would inform each other of the rich symbolism of human relationships and responsible loving.

Homosexuality would inform a sexual ethic based on friendship. It would highlight the 'wholeness' of the person. The body would be understood as the entry to the spirit of the other, and at the same time as the manifestation of the affection and love of the person. The fundamental role of feelings in human relationships would be acknowledged and respected because 'our feelings are the most important aspects of our life. Feelings are as real as atoms, tables and chairs'.[46]

Gay men and lesbian women would be fully accepted in the Church and welcomed into its ministries. Their creative energies and sensitive perceptions would ennoble worship and sensitise service to others. Rather than having to remain hidden, gay men and lesbian women, as priests and religious, would be able, along with their heterosexual brothers and sisters, to demonstrate an 'affective maturity' which 'presupposes an awareness that love is central to human life'.[47] Those called to a celibate life in priesthood or consecrated life would be able to be a special role model for chastity for other gay men and lesbian women, rescuing sexuality from a sterile 'self-centredness that is content with one's fidelity to purity'.[48] The present-day anxiety about the number of priests and religious who are gay or lesbian would be replaced by appreciation of their person and ministry. Openly gay and lesbian members, including those in relationships, would be able to be received into the employment of the Church, and offer their gifts through many forms of lay ministry.

Gay men and lesbian women would shape a Christian sexual ethic that would base their life-style on justice. Their moral theology would develop responsible relationships and challenge the self-indulgent aspect of gay culture (which is also found among heterosexual persons). They would draw on the rich wisdom of the Church seen in its traditions of worship, teaching and service to others. The sexual ethic they help to shape will be of unique importance to future generations of gay and lesbian Church members. They would move beyond *victim status* in an intolerant Church, to become *active members* participating in its constant and vibrant development and renewal.

Gay men and lesbian women would find support, not condemnation, from the Scriptures. Understanding that all are made in the image and likeness of God, and that everything God made 'indeed was very good (*Genesis* 1:31), they would find in the Scriptures an affirmation of their dignity and worth. The writer of *Wisdom* declared: 'Yes, you love all that exists. You hold nothing of what you have made in abhorrence, for had you hated anything, you would not have formed it' (*Wisdom* 11:24). The Scriptures would offer affirmation of their friendships and relationships in the examples of love and devotion between David and Jonathan (*2 Samuel* 1:17–27); Ruth and Naomi (*Ruth* 1:16–18); Jesus and John (*John* 13:23); Jesus and Lazarus (*John* 11:1–44); Paul and Timothy (*2 Timothy* 1:1–5). The baptism by Philip of the Ethiopian eunuch (*Acts* 8:26–44), the sexual outcast who was the first Gentile to be baptised, is particularly poignant for gay and lesbian Christians.

Gay men and lesbian women would have their relationships honoured and blessed by the Church community. 'The promises that their love generates [*sic*]' would be protected by the Church. Such relationships would be able to demonstrate a spiritual, emotional and societal fruitfulness. Gay and lesbian relationships would offer no threat to marriage and family life, but rather would complement them.

CONSEQUENCES FOR THE CHURCH

Developing such a moral theology for gay and lesbian Christians would have far-reaching consequences for the Catholic Church and beyond.

A gay and lesbian theology would highlight the inclusiveness of the Gospel of Jesus Christ. John Paul II observes that 'our cities risk becoming societies of people who are rejected, marginalized, uprooted and oppressed'.[49] On the other hand the Church is constituted as the people of God through baptism in which there is a genuine equality of dignity. The Church cannot exclude gay men and lesbian women on the grounds of their sexuality, which is not yet fully understood. Nor can they be excluded because of their relationships which they experience as graced by God and live faithfully in good conscience. The Catholic bishops of the United States, England and Wales, and of Australia have all spoken of the needs and rights of gay and lesbian members to have an active role in the Church, to share the Sacraments and to receive respectful acceptance.

A gay and lesbian theology would mark a new phase in the discussion of human sexuality. Rather than focusing on heterosexuality as the ideal to which all must or should aspire, the Church would be open to evaluating the basic goodness of all sexuality, which is manifested in both heterosexuality and homosexuality. The distinction between homosexual orientation and homosexual acts (which acts the *Magisterium* never defines) is suspected by the bishops of The Netherlands to be 'the heart of the matter in evaluating homosexuality', but the bishops do not attempt to elaborate further.[50] As recently as 1990 the American Catholic bishops acknowledged that this distinction is 'not always clear and convincing'. They also point out that single people (and this includes gay and lesbian people) are left 'without a distinctive "theology" of the single state', while theologies have been developed for marriage and for vowed celibacy. For the single person 'chastity . . . is not synonymous with an interior calling to perpetual celibacy'.[51] Yet celibacy is demanded of gay men and lesbians. Psychotherapist Richard Sipe, who has carried out extensive research on celibacy among American Catholic clergy, says that we 'must abandon the simplistic assumption that the distinction between homosexual orientation and behavior is sufficient to define the reality accurately'.[52] The Netherlands bishops reject the sense 'that homosexual people and non-homosexual people in their social relationships are in opposition to each other as if they were two separate worlds'. They conclude: 'They have basic similarities; there is a great variety of mutual points of contact in this one world where people live together'. The Church needs to recognise and understand these 'mutual points of contact'.[53]

A gay and lesbian theology would stimulate further consideration of the purpose of sexuality. Present Catholic teaching holds as one 'the two meanings of the conjugal act: the unitive meaning and the procreative meaning'.[54] They are based on the two accounts of creation: 'God blessed them, saying to them, "be fruitful, multiply, fill the earth and conquer it"' (*Genesis* 1:28), and 'It is not good that man should be alone. I will make him a helpmate' (*Genesis* 2:18). Paul's advice to widows and single people that 'if they cannot control their sexual urges, they should get married, since it is better to be married than to be tortured' (*1 Corinthians* 7:9), once highlighted in Church teaching, is now omitted from the marriage service. The prescription to 'increase and multiply' is given to humanity in general, and not to each person in particular. If it cannot be fulfilled by those for whom there is no attraction towards people of the opposite sex, must they also be denied support of a loving partner, since God himself declared that it was not good 'to be alone'? Infertile heterosexual couples are not denied companionship embracing sexual expression. We hear double talk from Fr Jon Visser, one of the authors of the Vatican's *1975 Declaration* which states homosexual acts are 'intrinsically disordered and can in no case be approved of'. He is quoted as saying that for people who are predominantly homosexual 'one can recommend them to seek a partnership and one accepts this relationship as the best they can do in their present situation'.[55]

A *gay and lesbian theology would promote a richer understanding of the virtue of friendship*. Since 'the virtue of chastity blossoms in *friendship*', it 'represents a great good for all' as it 'develops between persons of the same or opposite sex'.[56] Since all are called to chastity appropriate to their situation in life, friendship is of fundamental importance in human sexuality. It rescues it from selfishness and becomes a foundation for relationships. It helps to rescue marriage and family life from a naturalistic and biological definition. For gay men and lesbian women the question stands: does friendship for them always mean celibate friendship? Feelings of love draw people together to an exclusive and intimate friendship expressed and sealed sexually. Must homosexual people be denied these longings which are common to all humanity, and not only to those of heterosexual orientation? Freedom to enter a committed, faithful relationship of friendship, which may include sexual expression of love, would release gay men and lesbian women from the mistake of entering heterosexual marriage in order to deny their own orientation, or to hide it from the world. Religious and secular writers see in the Church's refusal to acknowledge and support the goodness of such relationships an abandonment of gay and lesbian people to other influences of promiscuity and self-centredness. Writer and AIDS activist Larry Kramer is scathing in his attack on the pronouncements of the Catholic Church, through which 'we have been estranged from our families, and we have been forced to create a ghetto. We have been forced to suffer. We were forced into AIDS'.[57]

A *gay and lesbian theology would empower the Catholic Church to align itself with another group that experiences alienation*. It would take the Church away from the constraints of conventional norms and identify it with those whom many despise. Working for justice has been a special mark of the Catholic Church, and Christianity in general, especially during the twentieth century. Called by the Vatican Council to be a Church *in* the modern world it has sought to alleviate many forms of human suffering through solidarity with those who have become voiceless. This reaffirmation of an inclusive Church would demonstrate that the Church refuses to accept artificial definitions as to who could and would be accepted into mainstream society. It would then enable the Church to begin to address the crucial issue of youth suicide, especially as it relates to adolescents' evolving sexuality.

FACING OUR PREJUDICES

There is much anecdotal evidence that gay men and lesbian women are living in loving, stable, committed relationships for many years. Take the story of two men in Melbourne. They had met in a secret gay bar in Berlin in 1943, and were still together more than fifty years later. When people live out their relationships with fidelity and endurance in the face of civil penalties, church condemnation, society's disapproval, employment discrimination and family rejection, then something of God must be present to sustain such love with rich friendship and confidence. The tragedy is that so many happy and emotionally secure gay and lesbian couples in our societies live hidden to the extent that no one is encouraged, inspired or humbled by their example. True, the public perception and church prejudice is fuelled by flamboyant and hedonistic images of an insatiable sexual appetite, and an abandonment to pleasure and self-indulgence. Those elements are present in the gay community, but they are also present in the heterosexual community where, while not approved of, they are met with much more tolerance. There is something in the gay culture that is 'over the top'. It *celebrates* life, often times quite innocently. But because it is outrageous, it is quickly scorned by a generally more conservative society. The churches fall guilty of judging by appearance, shaping a hardening opposition to homosexuality and homosexual people on that ground. Perhaps here is a 'religious blasphemy' among heterosexuals of the kind spoken of by an English Jewish Rabbi: 'loving one's own more by loving others less'.[58] In order to love marriage and family life, the church, and the Catholic *Magisterium* and fundamentalist communities in particular, feels that it must love its gay and lesbian members less!

Our Western societies are often marked today by a masculineness that entrenches aggression, physical strength, domination, power and roughness. Male homosexuality challenges that image. It refuses to accept such categories. Perhaps the real issue is not so much homosexuality in its various forms, but images and expectations of the male. So many of those who express the greatest contempt for male homosexuality are those who also advocate a return of capital punishment, longer gaol sentences for offenders, and support for the gun lobby. They thrill at the more violent forms of sport, want politicians and business leaders to be tougher on those they consider lazy in the community, and stay largely indifferent towards and silent about war and the abuse of civil rights in the world. They are quite simply afraid of tenderness between men. They cannot even begin to comprehend the strength of character found in the affection, trust, commitment and love that hold two men together in a relationship.

There are those in the churches who believe themselves to be tolerant and understanding when they say 'hate the sin and love the sinner'. They are quite insensitive to the harsh judgemental nature of such a statement. There are those who say that they accept homosexuals as long as they are not 'active'. Yet they never talk about 'active heterosexuals'. They constantly speak a double language. A male–female couple may kiss in the park and go unheeded, but two men or two women holding hands are accused of flaunting their sexuality. Explicit heterosexual love scenes on television raise no comment, but a gay and lesbian mardi gras evokes a storm of protest. Marriage is honoured as noble, but gay and lesbian relationships for all their goodness are scorned as perverted. A young heterosexual man can 'sow his wild oats' but a sexually active young gay man is considered promiscuous.

And what of lesbianism? Society remains substantially silent about lesbian women, as it has about women's sexuality in general throughout history. The limited research into the lives of lesbians highlights the general misogyny that pervades society, found even among women themselves. Church documents carry a definite *masculine* tone to them, and are very rarely nuanced to the special conditions and needs of lesbians. The one significant attempt by the *Magisterium* to respond to lesbian women—in the American bishops' letter pastoral on women's issues—was sabotaged by Vatican officials so that the final draft took on the judgemental and masculine language of the *1986 Letter*. The whole Christian church needs to be sensitised to the aspirations of lesbian women.

If we are going to call for and participate in a more generous dialogue about homosexuality, then we must face our own prejudices and fears. The old wedding ceremony enshrined what all people live in hope for: 'to have and to hold'. This is the 'skin-hunger' that moves human beings out of isolation into relationships. And gay and lesbian people feel it as much as their straight brothers and sisters.

AND SO INTO THE FUTURE

When God's people are in disagreement, we are never abandoned. We live with so much ambiguity and uncertainty. Such situations can overwhelm us, sap energy and stifle creativity. But as history shows us, and this century is no exception, they can give a thirst for knowledge, urge us into action, drive us with hope, and sustain us with an open mind. The churches, and perhaps the Catholic Church in particular, have allowed themselves to be overwhelmed by what they see as the 'problem' of homosexuality. The Gospel however, is an invitation to look on life with love. Love summons us all to see in homosexuality a remarkable gift from the hand of a creating God. In this gift men and women are drawn from their isolation and the bitterness of loneliness to find in the companionship and love of relationship the mysterious presence of the God of love.

Dialogue about homosexuality by the Catholic community with other people of faith and goodwill has the potential to lead us to a *gracious theology* shaped by a new language, celebrating love, recognising this remarkable gift, while building upon the pioneering work of Catholic and Christian gay and lesbian liberationists. God is in the lives of gay and lesbian people, and they have reached a *kairos*, a moment of grace. With the church they stand on the edge of 'a significant boundary', and the dialogue to follow will certainly 'make us wise'. In the search for a fuller truth and a more liberating love, the words of the late Dag Hammarskjöld, former Secretary-General of the United Nations, carry great power:

> For all that has been, thanks!
> For all that shall be, Yes![59]

NOTES

CHAPTER 1 OPENING THE DIALOGUE

1 Brent Hartinger, 'Holy Row: Homosexuality and the Catholic Church', *Torso*, May 1991, p. 19.
2 Congregation for the Doctrine of the Faith, *Letter to the Bishops of the Catholic Church on the Pastoral Care of Homosexual Persons*, Vatican Polyglot Press, Vatican City, 1986, art. 17.
3 B. R. Simon Rosser, 'A Scientific Understanding of Sexual Orientation with Implications for Pastoral Ministry', *Word and World*, 1994, p. 17.
4 From the Congregation for the Doctrine of the Faith: the 1975 *Declaration on Certain Questions Concerning Sexual Ethics*; the 1986 *Letter*; the 1992 *Some Considerations Concerning the Response to Legislative Proposals on the Non-discrimination of Homosexual Persons*; as well as three paragraphs in the *Catechism of the Catholic Church* published in 1994. A reference is found in the encyclical letter *Veritatis Splendor* of Pope John Paul II, in 1993, and hinted at in the 1995 letter *Evangelium Vitae*. He also spoke on the matter in an address to the American bishops in 1987, and in his *Angelus Address* on 20 February 1994 (John Paul II, 1994). The Congregation for Catholic Education in *Educational Guidance In Human Love* of 1984, and the Pontifical Council for the Family in *The Truth and Meaning of Human Sexuality* of 1996, both briefly addressed the issue in the context of teaching young people. The subject of homosexual persons presenting themselves for formation for the priesthood or the religious life is addressed by the Congregation for Institutes of Consecrated Life and Societies of Apostolic Life in the 1990 document *Directives on Formation in*

Religious Institutes, and the Congregation for the Clergy in the 1994 document *Directory on the Ministry and Life of Priests*.

5 Congregation for the Doctrine of the Faith, *Declaration on Certain Questions Concerning Sexual Ethics*, St Paul Publications, Homebush NSW, 1976, art. 8.
6 *1986 Letter*, arts 3, 7, 8.
7 Congregation for the Doctrine of the Faith, 'Some Considerations Concerning the Response to Legislative Proposals on the Non-discrimination of Homosexual Persons', *Catholic International*, vol. 3, no. 18, October 1992, pp. 857–60, art. 14.
8 *1986 Letter*, art. 7.
9 ibid. arts 8, 9.
10 *1992 Considerations*, arts 16, 15.
11 ibid. art. 14.
12 *Catechism of the Catholic Church* (English translation for Australia), St Paul Publications, Homebush NSW, 1994, art. 2359.
13 *1986 Letter*, arts 17, 3.
14 Catholic Bishops Conference of New Zealand, *Dignity, Love, Life: Statement on Homosexuality*, New Zealand Catholic Bishops Conference, Wellington, 1986.
15 Pontifical Biblical Commission, *The Interpretation of the Bible in the Church*, St Paul Books and Media, Boston, 1993, pp. 75 and 113.
16 *1986 Letter*, arts 4, 5.
17 *Catechism*, art. 2357, and footnote 140 naming *Genesis* 19:1–29; *Romans* 1:24–27; *1 Corinthians* 6:10; and *1 Timothy* 1:10.
18 Second Vatican Council, '*Gaudium et spes*', in *Vatican Council II: The Conciliar and Post Conciliar Documents*, ed. Austin Flannery OP, Costello Publishing Company, Northport, 1987, art. 16.
19 *1975 Declaration*, art. 8.
20 *1986 Letter*, art. 11.
21 Gayle Rubin, 'Thinking Sex', in *The Lesbian and Gay Studies Reader*, eds Henry Abelove et al., Routledge, New York, 1993, p. 17.
22 William Doty, *Myths of Masculinity*, Crossroad, New York, 1993, p. 77.
23 Pope John Paul II, *Redemptor Hominis*, Daughters of St Paul, Boston, 1979, art. 19.
24 *Catechism*, art. 2038.
25 *The New Shorter Oxford English Dictionary*, ed. Lesley Brown, Clarendon Press, Oxford, 1993, p. 661.
26 Second Vatican Council, *Dignitatis humanae*, art. 3.
27 John Paul II, *Ut Unum Sint: That They May All Be One*, St Paul Publications, Homebush NSW, 1995, arts 28 (original italics), 36.
28 *Gaudium et spes*, art. 1.
29 *Luke* 10:26.
30 *Gaudium et spes*, art. 27.

31 Second Vatican Council, *Nostra aetate*, art. 5.
32 *Gaudium et spes*, arts 29, 26.
33 *Dignitatis humanae*, art. 3.
34 Second Vatican Council, *Apostolicam actuositatem*, art. 14.
35 *Gaudium et spes*, arts 3, 4, 11.
36 ibid. arts 43, 28.
37 *Dignitatis humanae*, art. 7.
38 *Gaudium et spes*, art. 5.
39 ibid. arts 44, 54, 62.
40 ibid. arts 44, 43, 62.
41 *Apostolicam actuositatem*, arts 7, 24, 13.
42 Second Vatican Council, *Lumen Gentium*, art. 37.
43 *Gaudium et spes*, art. 43.
44 Second Vatican Council, *Unitatis redintegratio*, arts 4, 11.
45 ibid. art. 23.
46 *Ut Unum Sint*, art. 68.
47 *Unitatis redintegratio*, arts 23, 13.
48 Second Anglican–Roman Catholic International Commission, *Life in Christ: Morals, Communion and the Church*, Church House Publishing, London, 1994, p. v, and arts 83, 84.
49 *Ut Unum Sint*, arts 33, 34, 35, 36.
50 Pope Paul VI, *Ecclesiam Suam*, quoted by Bishop Sullivan, 'Introduction', in *A Challenge to Love: Gay and Lesbian Catholics in the Church*, ed. Robert Nugent, Crossroad, New York, 1983, p. xiii.
51 Eric Marcus, *Making History: The Struggle for Gay and Lesbian Equal Rights, 1945–1990*, HarperPerennial, New York, 1992, p. vii.
52 See Richard Plant, *The Pink Triangle*, Henry Holt and Company, New York, 1986; Heinz Heger, *The Men with the Pink Triangle*, Gay Modern Classic Publishers Ltd, London, 1989; Pierre Seel, *I, Pierre Seel, Deported Homosexual: A Memoir of Nazi Terror*, trans. Joachim Neugroschel, Basic Books, New York, 1995.
53 Quoted in John Lauritsen and David Thorstad, *The Early Homosexual Rights Movement*, Times Change Press, New York, 1974, pp. 53–4, 56.
54 Margaret Cruikshank, *The Gay and Lesbian Liberation Movement*, Routledge, New York, 1992, pp. 61, 63–7, 69–72.
55 Ritch Savin-Williams, 'Coming Out', in *Encyclopedia of Homosexuality*, ed. Wayne Dynes, Garland Publishing Inc., New York, 1990, p. 252.
56 Wayne Dynes, 'Inversion', in Dynes (1990), p. 610.
57 Wayne Dynes, 'Homophile', in Dynes (1990), p. 552.
58 Rosser (1994), p. 12.
59 Cruikshank (1992), p. 119.
60 Wayne Dynes, 'Queer', 'Preface', 'Homosexuality' and 'Orientation, Sexual', in Dynes (1990).

61 Robert Nugent, 'Sexual Orientation in Vatican Thinking', in *The Vatican and Homosexuality: Reactions to the Letter to the Bishops of the Catholic Church on the Pastoral Care of Homosexual Persons*, eds Jeannine Gramick and Pat Furey, Crossroad, New York, 1988, p. 55.

CHAPTER 2 A GAY AND CHRISTIAN IDENTITY

1 St Teresa of Avila, quoted in John McNeill, *Freedom, Glorious Freedom: The Spiritual Journey To The Fullness Of Life For Gays, Lesbians And Everybody Else*, Beacon Press, Boston, 1995, p. 101.
2 Marcus, p. 90, citing *Time*.
3 Fenton Johnson, 'God, Gays and the Geography of Desire', in *Wrestling With The Angel: Faith And Religion In The Lives Of Gay Men*, ed. Brian Bouldrey, Riverhead Books, New York, 1995, p. 245.
4 Alfred Corn, 'What is the Sexual Orientation of a Christian?', in Bouldrey (1995), p. 205.
5 Leroy Aarons, *Prayers for Bobby: A Mother's Coming to Terms with the Suicide of Her Gay Son*, HarperSanFrancisco, San Francisco, 1995, pp. 92, 162.
6 John McNeill, (1995), p. 104, and his *Taking a Chance on God: Liberating Theology for Gays, Lesbians, and their Lovers, Families and Friends*, Beacon Press, Boston, 1988, p. 74.
7 Bruce Bawer, *A Place At The Table: The Gay Individual in American Society*, Poseidon Press, New York, 1993, p. 125.
8 Michael Nava, 'Coming Out and Born Again', in Bouldrey (1995), p. 177.
9 Rev. R. Roberts, in *Gay Priests*, ed. James Wolf, Harper & Row, San Francisco, 1989, p. 146.
10 'Sheila's Story' and 'Carla's Story', in *A Book of Revelations: Lesbian and Gay Episcopalians Tell Their Own Stories*, ed. Louie Crew, Integrity Inc, Washington, 1991, pp. 85, 72.
11 Joseph Chetcuti, 'Personally Speaking For Myself', in *Being Different*, ed. Garry Wotherspoon, Hale & Iremonger, Sydney, 1986, p. 127.
12 Brian McNaught, *On Being Gay: Thoughts on Family, Faith, and Love*, St Martin's Press, New York, 1988, p. 145.
13 Andrew Holleran, 'The Sense of Sin', in Bouldrey (1995), p. 83.
14 Tony D'Agio, in *The Homosexuals*, ed. Alan Ebert, Macmillan Publishing Co. Inc, New York, 1976, p. 269.
15 Hilda Hidalgu, 'Curriculum Vitae', p. 166, Mary Hunt, 'Loving Well Means Doing Justice', p. 114, Margaret Cruikshank, 'Less Catholic than the Pope' p. 162, and Julien Murphy, 'Coming Out of Catholicism', p. 82, in *A Faith of One's Own: Explorations by Catholic Lesbians*, ed. Barbara Zanotti, The Crossing Press, Trumansburg NY, 1986.

16 Mary Brady, 'Finding My Way' p. 192, Terry, 'Crozier That Way', p. 164, and Wendy Sequoia, 'Voices From Ghosts, Including The Holy' p. 41, in *Lesbian Nuns: Breaking Silence*, eds Rosemary Curb and Nancy Manahan, The Women's Press Ltd, London, 1993.
17 Sister Jean, in *Profiles in Gay and Lesbian Courage*, eds Troy Perry and Thomas Swicegood, St Martin's Press, New York, 1991, p. 109.
18 Cruikshank (1992), pp. 46, 47, 120.
19 McNeill (1995), p. 68.
20 Bawer (1993), pp. 127, 81, 68.
21 Evelyn Whitehead and James Whitehead, *Seasons of Strength: New Visions of Adult Christian Maturing*, Image Books/Doubleday, Garden City NY, 1986, p. 142.
22 C. Jung, *Collected Works*, Pantheon, New York, 1959, pp. 86–7.
23 John McNeill, 'Homosexuality', in *The New Dictionary of Catholic Spirituality*, ed. Michael Downey, The Liturgical Press, Collegeville, 1993, p. 505.
24 Edward Schillebeeckx, *Ministry: Leadership in the Community of Jesus Christ*, Crossroad, New York, 1981, p. 106.
25 John Struzzo, 'Pastoral Counselling and Homosexuality', in *Homosexuality and Religion*, ed. Richard Hasbany, Harrington Park Press, New York, 1989, p. 199.
26 John Daniel, 'Kindness can kill', the *Tablet*, vol. 249, no. 8100, 4 November 1995, p. 1398.
27 Patrick Arnold, *Wildmen, Warriors and Kings: Masculine Spirituality and the Bible*, Crossroads, New York, 1992, pp. 172–3.
28 McNeill (1995), p. 77.
29 Philip Gambone, 'Searching for Real Words', in Bouldrey (1995), p. 231.
30 Quoted by McNeill (1995), p. 36.
31 Jonathan Emerson, 'The Silent Muse', in *Amazing Grace: Stories of Lesbian and Gay Faith*, eds Malcolm Boyd and Nancy Wilson, The Crossing Press, Freedom CA, 1991, p. 46.
32 Cruikshank (1986), pp. 164, 163.
33 M. R. Ritley, 'Set Apart, Called into the Midst', in Boyd and Wilson (1991), p. 117.
34 Richard Woods, *Another Kind Of Love: Homosexuality And Spirituality*, The Thomas More Press, Chicago, 1977, p. 101.
35 *2 Timothy* 1:7.
36 *Luke* 4:18.
37 Richard Woods, *Another Kind Of Love: Homosexuality And Spirituality*, Knoll Publishing Co Inc, Ft Wayne IN, 1988, p. 39.
38 Lesbian and Gay Christian Movement, *Christianity & Homosexuality: A Short Introduction*, Lesbian and Gay Christian Movement, London, undated, p. 4.

39 McNeill (1988b), p. 181.
40 *1986 Letter*, art. 17.
41 Dignity: House of Delegates, *Letter on Pastoral Care of Gay and Lesbian Persons*, Dignity Inc, Washington, 1987, p. 1.
42 David Donaldson, 'Dignity Inc: An Alternative Experience of church', in *Homosexuality and Religion and Philosophy*, eds Wayne Dynes and Stephen Donaldson, Garland Publishing Inc, New York, 1992, p. 161.
43 Leonard Schmidt, quoted in 'Acceptance? . . . Denial? . . . Rejection?' *Tabletalk*, July/September 1990, p. 12.
44 Mary Hunt, 'Sexual Ethics: A Lesbian Perspective', *Open Hands*, vol. 4, no. 3, Winter 1989, p. 10.
45 Johnson, in Bouldrey (1995), pp. 251–3.
46 *The Code of Canon Law*, Collins, Sydney, 1983, canon 215.
47 *Apostolicam actuositatem*, art. 24.
48 William Coffin, 'The Most Divisive Issue Since Slavery', *Open Hands*, Winter 1993, p. 6.
49 The principal organisations are: Reconciling Congregations (United Methodist Church); Reconciled in Christ Program (Lutheran Church); Open and Affirming Program (United Church of Christ); and More Light Churches Network (Presbyterian Church).
50 Malcolm Boyd, 'Underground Christians', in Boyd and Wilson (1991), p. 7.
51 McNeill (1995), p. 73.
52 McNeill (1995), p. 4.
53 Robert Nugent and Jeannine Gramick, *Building Bridges: Gay and Lesbian Reality and the Catholic Church*, Twenty-Third Publications, Mystic, Connecticut, 1992, pp. 103–4.
54 Ben Fletcher, *Clergy under Stress: A Study of Homosexual and Heterosexual Clergy in the Church of England*, Mowbray, London, 1990, pp. 65, 87.
55 Elizabeth Stuart, *Chosen: Gay Catholic Priests Tell Their Stories*, Geoffrey Chapman, London, 1993, p. 5.
56 Marianne Duddy, Kevin Calegari, Scott Trepania, and Anonymous, 'Gay men and lesbians describe spiritual journeys', *National Catholic Reporter*, 2 September 1994, pp. 8–10.
57 Robert Arpin, *Wonderfully, Fearfully Made: Letters on Living with Hope, Teaching Understanding, and Ministering with Love, from a Gay Catholic Priest with AIDS*, HarperSanFrancisco, San Francisco, 1993, p. 28.
58 Sister Agatha and Sister Marla, in Curb and Manahan (1993), pp. 122, 126.
59 Sister Mary Louise St John OSB, 'Patient Weavers', in Gramick (1989), p. 112.
60 Malcolm Boyd, 'Survival with Grace', in *Gay Soul: Finding the Heart of Gay Spirit and Nature: With Sixteen Writers, Healers, Teachers, and*

Visionaries, Mark Thompson, ed. HarperSan Francisco, New York (1994), p. 236.

61 *Luke* 12:50.

62 Bawer (1993), p. 254.

63 John Boswell, *Same-Sex Unions In Premodern Europe*, Villard Books, New York, 1994, pp. 280–2.

64 Mark Kowalewski, *All Things To All People: The Catholic Church Confronts The AIDS Crisis*, State University of New York Press, Albany NY, 1994, p.20.

65 Howard Carter, *AIDS: The Plague to End all Plagues?* Logos Forum Pty Ltd, Blackheath NSW, 1987, p. 35.

66 Australian Catholic Bishops Conference, *The AIDS Crisis: A message to the Australian people*, St Paul Publications, Homebush NSW, 1988.

67 Gavin Reid, *Beyond AIDS*, Kingsway Publications, Eastbourne, 1987, p. 30, citing Anglican Bishop of Edinburgh, Scotland.

68 John Daniel, 'Kindness can kill', the *Tablet*, 4 November 1995, p. 1398.

69 'Letters: Living with AIDS', the *Tablet*, vol. 249, no. 8, 17 June 1995, p. 775.

70 Bernie, in *Gay Catholics Down Under: The Journeys in Sexuality and Spirituality of Gay Men in Australia and New Zealand*, ed. B. R. Simon Rosser, Praeger, Westport, Con., 1992, p. 171.

71 Peter, in *Wise Before Their Time: People living with AIDS and HIV tell their stories*, eds Ann Richardson and Dietmar Bolle, Collins Dove, North Blackburn Vic., 1992, p. 127.

72 Bernard Lynch, *A Priest on Trial*, Bloomsbury, London, 1992, p. 190 citing Sr Patrice Murphy.

73 Mark King, 'I Don't Get Baptized Anymore', *Open Hands*, vol. 8, no. 1, Summer 1992, p. 6.

74 Cruikshank (1992), p. 184.

75 Keri, in Rosser (1992), p. 74.

76 William Amos, *When AIDS Comes To Church*, The Westminster Press, Philadelphia, 1988, p. 66.

77 Sister Hilda, 'I Don't Want Anyone From The Church', *AIDS: The Church as Enemy and Friend*, ed. Alan Cadwallader, Collins Dove, North Blackburn Vic., 1992, p. 75.

78 Gary Bouma, 'Faith, Scripture and Community in the Development of an AIDS-Relevant Theology', in Cadwallader (1992), pp. 154, 155, 151.

79 Elizabeth Stuart, *Just Good Friends: Towards A Lesbian And Gay Theology Of Relationships*, Mowbray, London, 1995, p. xviii, citing James Nelson.

80 *The Churches Speak On: AIDS: Official Statements from Religious Bodies and Ecumenical Organizations*, Gordon Melton ed., Gale Research Inc, Detroit, 1989, p. xxii.

81 *John* 15: 15.
82 St Aelred of Rievaulx, *Spiritual Friendship*, trans. Mary Eugenia Laker SSND, Cistercian Publications, Kalamazoo Michigan, 1977, p. 74.

CHAPTER 3 A CLASH OF LOYALTIES

1 Peter Coleman, *Gay Christians: A Moral Dilemma*, SCM Press, London, 1989, pp. 1, 188, 161.
2 Coleman (1989), p. 150 (original italics).
3 Marion Soards, *Scripture & Homosexuality: Biblical Authority and the Church Today*, Westminster John Knox Press, Louisville, 1995, pp. 41–2.
4 Marvin Ellison, 'Homosexuality and Protestantism', in *Homosexuality and World Religions*, ed. Arlene Swidler, Trinity Press International, Valley Forge Pennsylvania, 1993, p. 171.
5 Derrick Sherwin Bailey, *Homosexuality and the Western Christian Tradition*, Archon Books, Hamden Conn., p. x (original italics).
6 A Group of Friends, *Towards a Quaker View of Sex*, Friends Home Service Committee, London, 1971, pp. 7, 46, 51.
7 Adrian Thatcher, *Liberating Sex: A Christian Sexual Theology*, SPCK, London, 1993, p. 49.
8 Lance Pierson, *No-Gay Areas: Pastoral Care of Homosexual Christians*, Grove Books Ltd, Bramcotes Notts, 1992, p. 9.
9 Max Stackhouse, 'The Heterosexual Norm', in *Homosexuality and the Christian Community*, ed. Choon-Leong Seow, Westminster John Knox Press, Louisville, 1996, p. 136.
10 Victor Furnish, 'The Bible and Homosexuality: Reading the Text in Context', in *Homosexuality in the Church: Both Sides of the Debate*, ed. Jeffrey Siker, Westminster John Knox Press, Louisville, 1994, pp. 22, 23, 31.
11 Jeffrey Siker, 'Homosexual Christians, the Bible, and Gentile Inclusion: Confessions of a Repenting Heterosexist', in Siker (1994), p. 184.
12 *Genesis*, 18:16–20:29 (NRSV).
13 Victor Furnish, *The Moral Teaching of Paul: Selected Issues*, Abingdon Press, Nashville, 1985, p. 64.
14 Furnish, in Siker (1994), p. 20.
15 L. William Countryman, *Dirt, Greed & Sex: Sexual Ethics in the New Testament and Their Implications for Today*, Fortress Press, Philadelphia, 1990, p. 39.
16 Robin Scroggs, *The New Testament and Homosexuality: Contextual Background for Contemporary Debate*, Fortress Press, Philadelphia, 1983, p. 73.
17 Scroggs (1983), pp. 29–44, 52, 89.

18 *1 Corinthians* 6: 9–11 (NRSV).
19 Furnish (1985), pp. 68–9; and Scroggs (1983), pp. 106, 64.
20 Dale Martin, '*Arsenokoites* and *Malakos*: Meaning and Consequences', in *Biblical Ethics and Homosexuality: Listening to Scripture*, ed. Robert Brawley, Westminster John Knox Press, Louisville, 1996, pp. 124–5.
21 Furnish (1985), p. 69.
22 Scroggs (1983), pp. 107–8.
23 Martin (1996), pp. 118–23.
24 Countryman (1990), p. 119; and John Gaden, *A Vision of Wholeness*, ed. Duncan Reid, E. J. Dwyer, Alexandria NSW, 1994, p. 212.
25 Soards (1995), p. 19.
26 *1 Timothy* 1: 8–11 (NRSV).
27 Scroggs (1983), p. 118.
28 Soards (1995), p. 20.
29 *Romans* 1: 26–27 (NRSV).
30 Furnish (1985), p. 77.
31 Countryman (1990), p. 117.
32 Soards (1995), p. 22.
33 Pierson (1992), p. 13 (original italics).
34 David Field, *The Homosexual Way—A Christian Option?*, Grove Books Limited, Bramcote Nottingham, 1980, p. 16.
35 Gaden (1994), p. 212; Thatcher (1993), p. 20; Soards (1995), p. 22.
36 James Nelson, *Between Two Gardens: Reflections on Sexuality and Religious Experience*, The Pilgrim Press, New York, 1983, p. 93.
37 Scroggs (1983), p. 84.
38 Scroggs (1983), p. 127 (original italics).
39 Ruth Tiffany Barnhouse, *Homosexuality: A Symbolic Confusion*, The Seabury Press, New York, 1979, p. 179; Field (1980), p. 17.
40 Marva Dawn, 'Are Christianity and Homosexuality Incompatible?', in *Caught in the Crossfire: Helping Christians Debate Homosexuality*, eds Sally Geis and Donald Messer, Abingdon Press, Nashville, 1994, pp. 97, 95, 92, 97.
41 Pierson (1992), p. 16.
42 Various church statements in *The Churches Speak On: Homosexuality: Official Statements from Religious Bodies and Ecumenical Organizations*, ed. Gordon Melton, Gale Research Inc, Detroit, 1991.
43 Robert Dawidoff, 'Kill a Queer for Christ', in Thompson (1994b), p. 146.
44 Mel White, *Stranger at the Gate: To be Gay and Christian in America*, Simon & Schuster, New York, 1994, p. 224, quoting Gerry Falwell.
45 Lutheran Church, 'Sex, Marriage and Family' and 'Human Sexuality', in Melton (1991), pp. 113, 139.

46 Evangelical Lutheran Church study, quoted by Ellison in Swindler (1993), pp. 158–9.
47 'Appendix: Selected Denominational Statements on Homosexuality', in Siker (1994), p. 197.
48 Lance Steike, 'Homosexuality and the Church', *The Lutheran*, 23 January 1995, p. 7.
49 Lutheran Church in Australia General Synod, 'Statement on Homosexuality 1975', ed. B. Schwarz, LCA Commission on Social and Bioethical Questions, 1993, p. 2.
50 United Church of Christ, various statements, in Melton (1991), pp. 203, 208–10, 237.
51 The Uniting Church in Australia Assembly Committee on Homosexuality and the Church, *Homosexuality And The Church*, ed. Gordon Dicker, Uniting Church Press, Melbourne, 1985, p. 7.
52 Social Justice Commission of the Uniting Church in Australia, Synod of South Australia, *Homosexuality And The Church: A Response* (mimeo), undated, p. 10.
53 Uniting Church in Australia, 'Decisions of the Assembly Standing Committee', The Joint Board of Christian Education, Melbourne, in *Homosexuality and the Church: Responses*, 1987, p. 43.
54 Uniting Church in Australia Assembly Task Group on Sexuality, *Interim Report on Sexuality*, Uniting Church Press, Melbourne, 1996.
55 Coleman (1989), pp. 127, 160.
56 General Synod Board for Social Responsibility, Church of England, *Homosexual Relationships: A Contribution to Discussion*, CIO Publishing, London, 1979, art. 168.
57 House of Bishops of the General Synod of the Church of England, *Issues in Human Sexuality*, Church House Publishing, London, 1991, arts 3, 8–12, 21–2, 33, 37, 45, 47–8.
58 See Coleman (1989), pp. 178–9.
59 Episcopal Church, 'Statement on Homosexuality' (1979), in Melton (1991), pp. 89–90.
60 Episcopal Church, 'Report of the Task Force on Changing Patterns of Sexuality and Family Life', in Melton (1991), p. 101.
61 Episcopal Church, 'Resolution on Dialogue on Human Sexuality', in Melton (1991), pp. 104–5.
62 Patricia Lefevere, 'Panel accuses Episcopal bishop of heresy', *National Catholic Reporter*, 22 March 1996, p. 3; and 'Episcopal Church Court Rules', *Open Hands*, vol. 12, no. 1, Summer 1996, p. 32.
63 Anglican Diocese of Sydney Ethics and Social Questions Committee, *Report on Homosexuality*, 1973, pp. 14, 16.
64 Archbishop Loane, quoted in *Report on Homosexuality* (1973), p. 19.
65 Anglican Diocese of Melbourne Synod Social Questions Committee, *Report on Homosexuality*, 1971, p. 26.

66 Anglican Diocese of Melbourne Social Questions Committee, 'The Church, Homosexuality and the AIDS Crisis' Appendix A, in *Social Questions Committee Annual Report to Synod 1985: The Church, Homosexuality and the AIDS Crisis*, pp. 1, 7.
67 'Appendix: A Christian discussion on sexuality', in *A Theology of the Human Person*, eds Margaret Rodgers and Maxwell Thomas for The Anglican Church of Australia General Synod Doctrine Commission, Collins Dove, North Blackburn Victoria, 1992, pp. 95–7.
68 Leanne Payne, *The Broken Image: Restoring Sexual Wholeness Through Healing Prayer*, Kingsway Publications, Eastbourne E. Sussex, 1992, p. 13; Briar Whitehead, *Craving for Love: Relationship addiction, homosexuality and the God who heals*, Monarch Publications, Tunbridge Wells Kent, 1993, p. 134; Andrew Comiskey, *Pursuing Sexual Wholeness*, Monarch Publications, Tunbridge Wells Kent, 1990, p. 104.
69 Campion Decent, 'Spirituality + Sexuality: When the spirit is willing but the flesh is honest', in *Sydney Star Observer*, 24 July 1992, p. 18.
70 Martin St. John, 'Rising from the Ashes', in Thompson (1994b), p. 86; Perry and Swicegood (1990), p. 89; and Cruikshank (1992), p. 22.
71 Editor's comment in Melton (1991), p. 254.
72 Nelson (1982), p. 12.
73 Countryman (1988), p. 244.
74 Nelson (1983), p. 117.
75 Pierson (1992), p. 19.
76 *Ut Unum Sint*, arts 47, 31, 68.

CHAPTER 4 DEVELOPING CATHOLIC SEXUAL THEOLOGY

1 *Lumen Gentium*, art. 25.
2 Richard McBrien, *Catholicism*, Collins Dove, North Blackburn Vic., 1994, p. 66.
3 Congregation for the Doctrine of the Faith, *Instruction on the Ecclesial Vocation of the Theologian*, St Paul Books and Media, Boston, 1990, art. 21.
4 Bernard Haring, 'The Role of the Catholic Moral Theologian', in *Moral Theology: Challenges for the Future*, ed. Charles Curran, Paulist Press, New York, 1990, p. 33.
5 *Ecclesial Vocation Theologian*, art. 30.
6 Second Vatican Council, *Dei Verbum*, art. 12.
7 *The Interpretation of the Bible*, p. 114.

8 Daniel Helminiak, *What The Bible Really Says About Homosexuality*, Alamo Square Press, San Francisco, 1994, p. 31.
9 Vincent Genovesi, *In Pursuit of Love: Catholic Morality and Human Sexuality*, Gill and Macmillan, Dublin, 1987, p. 266.
10 Gareth Moore, *The Body in Context: Sex and Catholicism*, SCM Press Ltd, London, 1992, p.187; Gerald Coleman, *Human Sexuality: An All-Embracing Gift*, Alba House, New York, 1992, p. 248.
11 Helminiak (1994), pp. 52–3.
12 Dick Westley, *Morality and Its Beyond*, Twenty-Third Publications, Mystic CT, 1988, p. 224.
13 Genovesi (1987), p. 268.
14 Helminiak (1994), p. 87.
15 Brendan Byrne, 'Paul and the AIDS Crisis', in Cadwallader (1992), p. 170.
16 *Human Sexuality: New Directions in American Catholic Thought*, eds Anthony Kosnik et al., Paulist Press, New York, 1977, p. 195.
17 Helminiak (1994), pp. 69, 71, 75.
18 Genovesi (1987), p. 272.
19 Byrne, in Cadwallader (1992), p. 179.
20 St Augustine quoted in Kosnik (1977), p. 196.
21 St Thomas Aquinas, *Summa Theologica* (question 153, 2, third article), quoted in *Homosexuality and Ethics*, ed. Edward Batchelor, The Pilgrim Press, New York, 1980, p. 43.
22 Bernard Haring, *The Law of Christ: Moral Theology for Priests and Laity*, vol. 3, The Mercier Press, Cork, 1967, pp. 305–6.
23 John Harvey, 'Homosexuality', in *New Catholic Encyclopedia*, vol. vii, ed. William McDonald, The Catholic University of America, Washington, 1967, p. 117.
24 John Harvey, *Pastoral Care of the Homosexual*, Knights of Columbus, New Haven, 1977, p. 17.
25 John Harvey, 'Arguments from Revelation', in *Dialogue About Catholic Sexual Teaching*, eds Charles Curran and Richard McCormick, Paulist Press, New York, 1993, pp. 319, 311, 318, 321.
26 John Harvey, *The Homosexual Person: New Thinking in Pastoral Care*, Ignatius Press, San Francisco, 1987, pp. 100–1.
27 Edward Malloy, *Homosexuality and the Christian Way of Life*, University Press of America Inc, Lanham MD, 1981, pp. 324, 360, 359.
28 Lisa Cahill, 'Moral Methodology: A Case Study', in Nugent (1983), pp. 88–9.
29 Ronald Lawler, *Catholic Sexual Ethics: A Summary, Explanation, and Defence*, Our Sunday Visitor Inc, Huntington Ind., 1985, pp. 199–201.
30 John McNeill, *The Church and the Homosexual*, Beacon Press, Boston, 1988, pp. 217–41, 66.
31 ibid, pp. 85, 87, 103, 108, 130, 131.
32 McNeill (1995), p. xii.

33 Kosnik (1977), pp. xi, 187–8, 210–1, 214–8.
34 Charles Curran, *The Living Tradition of Catholic Moral Theology*, University of Notre Dame Press, Notre Dame Ind., 1992, p. 41.
35 Philip Keane, *Sexual Morality: A Catholic Perspective*, Paulist Press, New York, 1977, pp. 80, 84–9.
36 Charles Curran, *Catholic Moral Theology in Dialogue*, Fides Publishers, Inc, Notre Dame Ind., 1972, pp. 187, 197, 195.
37 Charles Curran, *Transition and Tradition in Moral Theology*, University of Notre Dame Press, Notre Dame Ind., 1979, pp. 69, 67–8.
38 Charles Curran, *Critical Concerns in Moral Theology*, University of Notre Dame Press, Notre Dame Ind., 1984, p. 79.
39 Charles Curran, *Contemporary Problems in Moral Theology*, Fides Publishers Inc, Notre Dame Ind., 1970, pp.176–7.
40 Curran (1972), pp. 204, 217.
41 Curran (1977), pp. 71, 73, 76–7.
42 Curran (1984), pp. 92, 83–4.
43 Curran (1992), p. 41.
44 Andrew Greeley, quoted on back cover, Richard McCormick, *The Critical Calling: Reflections on Moral Dilemmas Since Vatican II*, Georgetown University Press, Washington, 1989.
45 McCormick (1989), pp. 289–90, 307–8 (original italics).
46 Moore (1992), pp. 183, 186, 191, 193–4, 196, 198, 200.
47 Evelyn Whitehead and James Whitehead, *Christian Life Patterns: The Psychological Challenges And Religious Invitations Of Adult Life*, Doubleday and Image, New York, 1982, p. 111.
48 James Whitehead and Evelyn Whitehead, 'The Shape of Compassion: Reflections on Catholics and Homosexuality', *Spirituality Today*, 1987, p. 130, 133, 135.
49 Evelyn Whitehead and James Whitehead, *A Sense of Sexuality: Christian Love and Intimacy*, Doubleday, New York, 1989, pp. 15–16, 37, 266, 240 (original italics).
50 Elizabeth Stuart, *Daring to Speak Love's Name: A Gay and Lesbian Prayer Book*, Hamish Hamilton, London, 1992.
51 Stuart (1995), pp. 233, 109, 48, 234.

CHAPTER 5 UNCERTAIN BISHOPS STRUGGLE AS TEACHERS AND PASTORS

1 *Lumen Gentium*, art. 24.
2 For a full list see *The HarpersCollins Encyclopedia of Catholicism*, ed. Richard McBrien, HarperCollins, New York, 1995, pp. 1126–30.

3 Francis Firth, 'Catholic Sexual Morality in the Patristic and Medieval Periods', in *Human Sexuality and Personhood*, ed. John Leies, Pope John Center, Braintree, Massachusetts, 1990, p. 42.
4 James Hitchcock, 'The Development of Catholic Doctrine Concerning Sexual Morality, 1300–1918', in Leies (1990), p. 61.
5 *1917 Code of Canon Law*, Canon 1013:1, quoted by John Gallagher, 'Magisterial Teaching From 1918 to the Present', in Leies (1990), p. 191.
6 *Gaudium et spes*, art. 48.
7 Pope Paul VI, *Humanae Vitae: Of Human Life*, St Paul Books and Media, Boston, 1968, art. 12.
8 *Catechism*, arts 2333, 2363.
9 *1975 Declaration*, arts 1, 8.
10 Congregation for Catholic Education, *Educational Guidance in Human Love: Outlines for Sex Education*, St Paul Publications, Homebush NSW, 1984, art. 101.
11 *1986 Letter*.
12 Pope John Paul II, 'Los Angeles meeting of the Pope with U.S. Bishops', in *Origins*, vol. 17, no. 16, 1 October 1987, p. 267.
13 Joaquim Navarro-Valls, 'Responding to Legislative Proposals on Discrimination Against Homosexuals', *Origins*, vol. 22, no. 10, 20 August 1992, p. 175.
14 *1992 Considerations*, pp. 857–60.
15 Pope John Paul II, 'Fidei Depositum' (Apostolic Constitution), in *Catechism*, 3.
16 *Catechism*, arts 2357–9, 2347, 2333 (original italics).
17 Pope John Paul II, *Veritatis Splendor: On Certain Fundamental Questions of the Church's Moral Teaching*, St Paul Publications, Homebush, 1993, arts 47, 50 (original italics).
18 Pope John Paul II, 'Legitimizing deviant kinds of behaviour distorts the true meanings of the family and leads to decadence', *L'Osservatore Romano*, no. 8 (1329), 23 February 1994, arts 1, 2, 8 (original italics).
19 Pope John Paul II, *Evangelium Vitae: The Gospel of Life*, St Paul Publications, Homebush, 1995, arts 10, 12, 21.
20 Pontifical Council for the Family, *The Truth and Meaning of Human Sexuality: Guidelines for Education within the Family*, St Paul Publications, Homebush, 1996, arts 104, 125.
21 National Conference of Catholic Bishops, *Principles to Guide Confessors in Questions of Homosexuality*, National Conference of Catholic Bishops, Washington, 1973.
22 National Conference of Catholic Bishops, 'To Live in Christ Jesus', in *Homosexuality and the Magisterium: Documents from the Vatican and the U.S. Bishops 1975–1985*, ed. John Gallagher, New Ways Ministry, Mt Rainier, 1986, p. 9.

23 Various statements, Gallagher (1986).
24 Various statements, Gallagher (1986).
25 Medeiros, pp. 16–17, Hickey, p. 96, in Gallgher (1986).
26 Bishop Untener, quoted in Jim Bowman, 'Lavender & Purple', *Commonweal*, April 1992, p. 6.
27 Archbishop Quinn, in Gallagher (1986), p. 23; Bishop Sullivan, in Nugent (1983), p. xii.
28 National Conference of Catholic Bishops, *Human Sexuality: A Catholic Perspective for Education and Lifelong Learning*, United States Catholic Conference, Washington, 1990, p. 56.
29 Roman Catholic Church in Baltimore, in Gallagher (1986), pp. 38–9.
30 *Human Sexuality*, p. 52.
31 San Francisco Senate of Priests, in Gallagher (1986), pp. 59, 63–4.
32 National Conference of Catholic Bishops, *Called to Compassion and Responsibility: A Response To The HIV/AIDS Crisis*, United States Catholic Conference, Washington, 1989, p. 17.
33 Bishops of California, 'A Pastoral Letter On AIDS', in *Origins*, vol. 16, no. 45, 23 April 1987, p. 788.
34 National Conference of Catholic Bishops Administrative Board, *The Many Faces of AIDS: A Gospel Response*, United States Catholic Conference, Washington, 1987, p. 13.
35 Archibishiop Hickey, in Gallagher (1986), p. 96.
36 Archbishop John Quinn, 'Civil Rights of Gay and Lesbian Persons', *Origins*, vol. 22, no. 11, 20 August 1994, p. 204.
37 Florida State Catholic Conference, 'On Discrimination Against Homosexual Persons', *Origins*, vol. 28, no. 20, 28 October 1993, p. 360; Cardinal Anthony Bevilacqua, 'Domestic Partnership Bills Opposed', *Origins*, vol. 23, no. 3, 3 June 1993, p. 48.
38 Dawn Gibeau, 'Gumbleton hears gay stories, some angry', *National Catholic Reporter*, vol. 31, no. 4, 11 November 1994, p. 3; Tom Roberts, 'He's not disordered, he's my brother', *National Catholic Reporter*, vol. 31, no. 3, 4 November 1994, p. 2; Editorial, 'Bishop Gumbleton opens doors for all to pass through', *National Catholic Reporter*, vol. 31, no. 4, 18 November 1994, p. 20.
39 National Conference of Catholic Bishops *Ad Hoc* Committee, 'Partners in the Mystery of Redemption: A Pastoral Response to Women's Concerns for the Church and Society. First Draft', *Origins*, vol. 17, no. 45, 21 April 1988.
40 McNeill (1995), p. 15.
41 Bishop Francis Murphy, 'Let's Start Over: A Bishop Appraises the Pastoral on Women', *Commonweal*, 25 September 1992, pp. 11–15.
42 National Conference of Catholic Bishops *Ad Hoc* Committee (1988), p. 771.

43 National Conference Catholic Bishops *Ad Hoc* Committee, 'One in Christ Jesus: A Pastoral Response to the Concerns of Women for Church and Society. Second Draft', *Origins*, vol. 19, no. 44, 4 April 1990, p. 727.

44 National Conference of Catholic Bishops *Ad Hoc* Committee, 'Called to be One in Christ Jesus: Pastoral Concerns of Women. Third Draft', *Origins*, vol. 21, no. 46, 23 April 1992, p. 770 (original italics).

45 National Conference of Catholic Bishops *Ad Hoc* Committee, 'Response to Women's Concerns: One in Christ Jesus. Fourth Draft', *Origins*, vol. 22, no. 13, 10 September 1992, p. 231.

46 National Conference of Catholic Bishops, 'Women's Concerns: One in Christ Jesus. Final Document', *Origins*, vol. 22, no. 29, 31 December 1992, p. 499 (author's italics).

47 Archbishop Weakland, 'Who is my Neighbour?', in Gallagher (1986) p. 35.

48 Bishop Sullivan, in Nugent (1983), p. xiv.

49 Baltimore Diocese, in Gallagher (1986), p, 41.

50 Archbishop Godfrey and the bishops of England and Wales, quoted by Australian Catholic Bishops Conference, 'Homosexuality', in *Australian Catholic Bishops' Statements Since Vatican II*, ed. Nicholas Kerr, St Paul Publications, Homebush, 1985, p. 169.

51 Catholic Social Welfare Commission, 'An Introduction to the Pastoral Care of Homosexual People', in *Created Design—Some Pastoral Guidelines for the Care of Lesbian and Gay People*, Pastoral AIDS Series no. 1, Catholic AIDS Link, London, 1994.

52 Cardinal Basil Hume, 'Observations on the Catholic Church's Teaching Concerning Homosexual People', in *Created Design-Some Pastoral Guidelines for the Care of Lesbian and Gay People*, Pastoral AIDS, Series no. 1, Catholic AIDS Link, London, 1994.

53 Cardinal Basil Hume, *A Note on the Teaching of the Catholic Church Concerning Homosexual People*, Archbishop's House, Westminster, London, 1995.

54 Australian Catholic Bishops Conference, 'Homosexuality', in Kerr (1985), pp. 168, 170–1.

55 Australian Catholic Bishops Conference, 'The Australian Broadcasting Corporation and the entitlements of staff in homosexual relationships', in Kerr (1985), p. 172.

56 Archbishop Gleeson, quoted by Tim Reeves, 'The 1972 Debate on Male Homosexuality in South Australia', in *Gay Perspectives II: More Essays in Australian Gay Culture*, ed. Robert Aldrich, University of Sydney, Sydney, 1993, p. 155.

57 Cardinal Freeman, quoted by Miranda Morris, *Pink Triangle: The Gay Law Reform Debate in Tasmania*, University of New South Wales Press, Sydney, 1995, pp. 52–3.

58 Archbishop Foley, 'Homosexuality', *The Record* (Perth), no. 2660, 2 November 1989, p. 1.
59 Bishop Gerry, 'Homosexuality . . . Law, morality and the Church', *The Catholic Leader* (Brisbane), 12 July 1990.
60 Archbishop D'Arcy, 'Archbishop D'Arcy's statement: Don't decriminalise sodomy!', *AD 2000* (Melbourne), September 1991, p. 3.
61 Australian Catholic Bishops Conference, *The AIDS Crisis*, pp. 2, 5.
62 Australian Catholic Bishops Conference, *AIDS: A challenge to love*, St Paul Publications, Homebush, 1989, pp. 2, 1.
63 Australian Catholic Bishops Conference, *Submission: HIV/AIDS National Strategy*, Australian Catholic Bishops Conference, Canberra, 9 September 1994, pp. 1–2.
64 Australian Catholic Bishops' Central Commission, *Letter of Archbishop Little to Attorney General Michael Lavarch*, 27 October 1994.
65 Cardinal Clancy, 'Letters to the Editor', *The Australian*, 3 May 1994, p. 12.
66 Australian Catholic Social Justice Council, *Tolerance: A Christian Perspective on the International Year for Tolerance*, Dove Publications, North Blackburn Vic., 1995, p. 18.
67 *1986 Letter*, arts 4–6.
68 Archbishop Quinn, 'A Pastoral Letter', in Gallagher (1986), pp. 27, 30.
69 Archbishop Weakland, 'Who is my neighbour?', in Gallagher (1986), pp. 34–5.
70 Archbishop Hunthausen, 'Archbishop Addresses Issue of Homosexuality', in Gallagher (1986), p. 84.
71 Catholic Council for Church and Society, *Homosexual People in Society: A contribution to the dialogue within the faith community*, New Ways Ministry, Mt Ranier, 1980, p. 20.

CHAPTER 6 BROADENING THE DIALOGUE: THE CONTRIBUTION TO MODERN SOCIAL THEORY

1 David Greenberg, *The Construction of Homosexuality*, The University of Chicago Press, Chicago, 1988, p. 26.
2 Gilbert Herdt, *Guardians of the Flutes*, Idioms of Masculinity, vol. 1, The University of Chicago Press, Chicago, 1994, pp. xiv, 2, 302.
3 Saikaku Ihara, *Comrade Loves of the Samurai*, trans. E. Powys Mathers, Charles Tuttle Co, Rutland, Vermont, 1972.
4 Greenberg (1988), pp. 42, 44.
5 Tomas Almaguer, 'Chicano Men', in Abelove et al. (1993), pp. 255–60.
6 Greenberg (1988), p. 73.
7 C. Tripp, *The Homosexual Matrix*, Quartet Books, London, 1977, p. 74.

8 George Chauncey et al., 'Introduction', in *Hidden From History: Reclaiming the Gay and Lesbian Past*, ed. Martin Duberman et al., Penguin Books, London, 1989, p. 9.
9 Greenberg (1988), pp. 141, 263.
10 John Boswell, *Christianity, Social Tolerance, and Homosexuality: Gay People in Western Europe from the Beginning of the Christian Era to the Fourteenth Century*, The University of Chicago Press, Chicago, 1980, pp. 5–7, 128, 171, 270.
11 John D'Emilio, 'Capitalism and Gay Identity', in Abelove et al. (1993), pp. 470, 472, 468.
12 Rubin, in Abelove et al. (1993), p. 17.
13 Robert Padgug, 'Sexual Matters', in Duberman et al. (1989), p. 60.
14 R. Connell, *Masculinities*, Allen & Unwin, St Leonards NSW, 1995, p. 143.
15 John De Cecco and David Allen Parker, 'The Biology of Homosexuality: Sexual Orientation or Sexual Preference?', in *Sex, Cells, and Same-Sex Desire: The Biology of Sexual Preference*, eds John De Cecco and David Allen Parker, Harrington Park Press, Binghamton NY, 1995, p. 11.
16 Sigmund Freud, *On Sexuality: Three Essays on the Theory of Sexuality and Other Works*, The Penguin Freud Library, vol. 7, ed. Angela Richards, Penguin Books, London, 1977, p. 56.
17 See Kenneth Lewes, *The Psychoanalytic Theory of Male Homosexuality*, Simon & Schuster, New York, 1988, p. 77; Greenberg (1988), p. 425.
18 Freud, quoted in Lewes (1988), pp. 28–9.
19 Freud (1977), p. 61.
20 Freud, 'Letter', published first in *American Journal of Psychiatry*, 1951, and quoted in Lewes (1988), p. 32.
21 Warren Johansson, 'Psychiatry', in Dynes (1990), p. 1072.
22 All quoted in Lewes (1988).
23 Quoted by Henry Abelove, 'Freud, Male Homosexuality and the Americans', in Abelove et al. (1993), p. 385.
24 Irving Bieber et al., *Homosexuality: A Psychoanalytic Study*, Basic Books, New York, 1962, p. 220.
25 All quoted in Lewes (1988), p. 215.
26 Lewes (1988), p. 222; Robert Hopcke, *Jung, Jungians & Homosexuality*, Shambhala, Boston, 1991, p. 5.
27 Tripp (1977), pp. 83–99.
28 Allan Bell, Martin Weinberg and Sue Hammersmith, *Sexual Preference: Its Development in Men and Women*, Indiana University Press, Bloomington, 1981.
29 Richard Isay, *Being Homosexual: Gay Men and Their Development*, Avon Books, New York, 1989.
30 Richard Friedman, *Male Homosexuality: A Contemporary Psychoanalytic Perspective*, Yale University Press, New Haven, 1988.

31 Isay (1989), p. 12.
32 Wayne Dynes, 'Psychotherapy', in Dynes (1990), p. 1082.
33 Christine Downing, *Myths and Mysteries of Same-Sex Love*, Continuum, New York, 1989, pp. 111–13, 123.
34 C. Jung, (1959), pp. 86–7.
35 All quoted in Hopcke (1991).
36 Alfred Kinsey et al., *The Sexual Behavior in the Human Male*, W. B. Saunders Company Ltd, Philadelphia, 1948, p. 639.
37 Kinsey (1948).
38 Alfred Kinsey et al., *Sexual Behavior in the Human Female*, W. B. Saunders Company Ltd, Philadelphia, 1953.
39 Isay (1989), pp. 12–13.
40 Allan Bell, 'The Homosexual as Patient', in *Sex Research Studies from the Kinsey Institute*, ed. Martin Weinberg, Oxford University Press, New York, 1976, p. 202.
41 Shere Hite, *The Hite Report On The Family: Growing Up Under Patriarchy*, Bloomsbury, London, 1994, pp. 288, 332.
42 John Cornwell, 'Sexual Matters of the Mind', *The Tablet* 21 May 1994, pp. 625–6.
43 Simon LeVay, *The Sexual Brain*, The MIT Press, Cambridge Massachusetts. 1993, 1, 31, 108.
44 Simon LeVay and Dean Hamer, 'Evidence for a Biological Influence in Male Homosexuality', *Scientific American*, vol. 270, no. 5, May 1994, pp. 45–7.
45 William Byne, 'The Biological Evidence Challenged', *Scientific American*, vol. 270, no. 5, May 1994, p. 53.
46 Adam Carr, 'The Gay Gene Myth: Interview by Adam Carr with Professor Steven Rose', *Outrage* (Melbourne), p. 17.
47 See LeVay and Hamer (1994), p. 47; Byne (1994), p. 54; LeVay (1993), p. 112.
48 Byne (1994), p. 54.
49 Dean Hamer and Peter Copeland, *The Science of Desire: The Search for the Gay Gene and the Biology of Behavior*, Simon & Schuster, New York, 1994.
50 Steve Dow, 'Gay "gene" more likely among men: scientists', *The Age* (Melbourne), 19 May 1995, p. 9.
51 Quoted by John Cornwell, 'Ourselves and our genes', *The Tablet*, 27 May 1995, p. 658.
52 Friedman (1988), p. 32.
53 Byne (1994), p. 55.
54 Cornwell (1994), p. 626.
55 Ruth Hubbard, 'False genetic markers', *New York Times*, 2 August 1995, p. 5.

56 Martin Weinberg et al., *Dual Attraction: Understanding Bisexuality*, Oxford University Press, New York, 1994.
57 Michael Ross, *The Married Homosexual Man: A psychological study*, Routledge & Kegan Paul, London, 1983, p. 25.
58 Brenda Maddox, *The Marrying Kind: Homosexuality & Marriage*, Granada, London, 1982, p. 17.
59 Downing (1989), p. 7.
60 Bell et al., 1981, p. 7.
61 Dolores Maggiore, 'Lesbianism', in Dynes (1990), p. 709.
62 Downing (1989), p. 10.
63 Richard Friedman and Jennifer Downing, 'Psychoanalysis, Psychobiology and Homosexuality', *Journal of the American Psychoanalytic Association* (Madison Ct), vol. 41, no. 4, 1993, pp. 1188–90.
64 Downing (1989), pp. 7, 10–11.
65 Friedman and Downing (1993), p. 1190.
66 Andy Metcalf, 'Introduction', in *The Sexuality of Men*, eds Andy Metcalf and Martin Humphries, Pluto Press, London, 1985, p. 2.
67 John Sanford and George Lough, *What Men Are Like: The psychology of men, for men and the women who live with them*, Paulist Press, New York, 1988, p. 7.
68 Cruikshank (1992), pp. 3, 118.
69 George Weinberg, *Society and the Healthy Homosexual*, Anchor Books, Garden City New York, 1973, pp. 70–1.
70 Michel Foucault, *The Use of Pleasure: The History of Sexuality*, vol. 2, trans. Robert Hurley, Penguin Books, London, 1992, pp. 3–4.
71 Michel Foucault, *The History of Sexuality: An Introduction*, vol. 1, trans. Robert Hurley, Penguin Books, London, 1990, p. 43.
72 Zygmunt Bauman, *Intimations of Postmodernity*, Routledge, London, 1992, p. 189.
73 Gertrude Himmelfarb, *On Looking into the Abyss: Untimely Thoughts on Culture and Society*, Alfred A. Knopf, New York, 1994, p. 137.
74 Kwok Wei Leng, 'Theorising Corporeality: Bodies, Sexuality and the Feminist Academy: An Interview with Elizabeth Grosz', in *Melbourne Journal of Politics: Sexuality*, vol. 22, 1994, p. 8.
75 Lauren Berlant and Elizabeth Freeman, 'Queer Nationality', in *Fear of a Queer Planet: Queer politics and social theory*, ed. Michael Warner, University of Minnesota Press, Minneapolis, 1993, p. 198.
76 Bruce Bawer, 'Introduction' and 'Notes on Stonewall', in *Beyond Queer: Challenging Gay Left Orthodoxy*, ed. Bruce Bawer, The Free Press, New York, 1996, pp. ix–xv, 4–15.
77 Paul Gibson, 'Gay Male and Lesbian Youth Suicide', in *Death by Denial: Studies of suicide in gay and lesbian teenagers*, ed. Gary Remafedi, Alyson Publications Inc, Boston, 1994, pp. 16, 45, 57.
78 Tripp (1977), p. 268.

CHAPTER 7 FINDING A NEW DIRECTION THROUGH DIALOGUE

1 *Catechism*, art. 2414.
2 *Nostra aetate*, art. 4.
3 *Catechism*, art. 2432; *Gaudium et spes*, art. 80.
4 *Galatians* 2:11 (Jerusalem Bible).
5 *Dignitatis humanae*, art. 3; *Apostolicam actuositatem*, art. 14; *Ut Unum Sint*, art. 36.
6 *Gaudium et spes*, art. 26.
7 *Gaudium et spes*, art. 62.
8 *Redemptor Hominis*, art. 10.
9 *Catechism*, art. 2357.
10 Charles Birch, *Feelings*, University of New South Wales Press, Sydney, 1995, pp. 108, 110 (original italics).
11 McNeill (1995), p. 187.
12 Boyd (1984), p. 168.
13 Boyd, in *Gay Soul: Finding the Heart of Gay Spirit and Nature*, ed. Mark Thompson, HarperSanFrancisco, New York, 1994, p. 244.
14 Richard Cleaver, *Know My Name: A Gay Liberation Theology*, Westminster John Knox Press, Louisville Kentucky, 1995, p. 142.
15 Paul Monette, 'On Being', in Thompson (1994a), p. 23.
16 Ritley, in Boyd and Wilson (1991), p. 118.
17 Johnson, in Bouldrey (1995), p. 256.
18 White (1994), p. 39.
19 John Fortunato, *Embracing the Exile: Healing Journeys of Gay Christians*, The Seabury Press, New York, 1982, p. 17.
20 Lorna Hochstein, 'Mirroring God', in Zanotti (1986), p. 8.
21 Chris Glaser, *Come Home: Reclaiming Spirituality and Community as Gay Men and Lesbians*, Harper & Row, San Francisco, 1990, pp. 181–2.
22 Andrew Sullivan, *Virtually Normal: An Argument About Homosexuality*, Picador, London, 1995, pp. 202–3.
23 Pope John Paul II, *Familiaris Consortio: The Role of the Christian Family in the Modern World*, St Paul Publications, Homebush, 1982, art 41; also arts 18–27, 42–8, and 49–64.
24 Cindy Wooden, 'Vatican quiet on final document in Beijing', *National Catholic Reporter*, 22 September 1995, p. 13.
25 Australian Catholic Bishops Conference, *Families Our Hidden Treasure: A Statement on Family Life in Australia*, Aurora Books, Melbourne, 1993, p. 5.
26 *1986 Letter*, art. 2.
27 *Catechism*, art. 2358.
28 *1992 Considerations*, arts 11–13, 15.
29 *1986 Letter*, art. 11.

30 *1986 Letter*, art. 12 (original italics).
31 *1986 Letter*, art. 16.
32 *Catechism*, arts 2358, 2333 (original italics).
33 *1986 Letter*, art. 3.
34 *1975 Declaration*, art. 8.
35 *Catechism*, art. 2358.
36 Gustavo Gutierrez, 'Option for the Poor', in *Mysterium Liberationis: Fundamental Concepts in Liberation Theology*, ed. Ignatio Ellacuria SJ and Jon Sobrino SJ, Orbis Books, Maryknoll New York and Collins Dove, Blackburn Victoria, 1993, p. 236.
37 Congregation for the Doctrine of the Faith, *Instruction on Christian Freedom and Liberation*, St Paul Publications, Homebush NSW, 1986, art. 5.
38 Rosemary Radford Ruether, *Women–Church: Theology and Practice of Feminist Liturgical Communities*, Harper & Row, San Francisco, 1985, pp. 22–3.
39 Pope John Paul II, *Letter of Pope John Paul II to Women*, Vatican Polyglot Press, Vatican City, 1995, arts 6, 4.
40 Denis Edwards, *Jesus the Wisdom of God: An Ecological Theology*, St Paul Publications, Homebush NSW, 1995, pp. 2, 13–14.
41 *Evangelium Vitae*, art. 27 (original italics).
42 *Ut Unum Sint*, art. 32.
43 Brian McNaught, *A Disturbed Peace: Selected Writings of an Irish Catholic Homosexual*, Dignity Inc, Washington, 1982, p. 90.
44 *1 John* 4:8.
45 *Pastoral Care*, p. 4.
46 Birch (1995), p. 35.
47 Pope John Paul II, *Pastores Dabo Vobis: I Will Give You Shepherds*, St Paul Books and Media, Boston, 1992, art. 44.
48 Congregation for Institutes of Consecrated Life and Societies of Apostolic Life, *Directives on Formation in Religious Institutes*, St Paul Publications, Homebush NSW, 1990, art. 13.
49 *Evangelium Vitae*, art. 18.
50 *Homosexual People in Society*, p. 17.
51 *Human Sexuality*, pp. 56, 54, 51.
52 A. W. Richard Sipe, *Sex, Priests, and Power: Anatomy of a Crisis*, Cassell, London, 1995, p. 133.
53 *Homosexual People in Society*, p. 20.
54 *Humanae Vitae*, art. 12.
55 A. W. Richard Sipe, *A Secret World: Sexuality and the Search for Celibacy*, Brunner/Mazel Publishers, New York, 1990, p. 106, quoting Fr Jon Visser from the *London Clergy Review* (1976).
56 *Catechism*, art. 2347 (original italics).

57 Larry Kramer, *Report from the Holocaust: the making of an AIDS activist*, St Martin's Press, New York, 1989, p. 180.

58 Lionel Blue, 'Only the best will do', *The Tablet*, vol. 249, no. 8105, 9 December 1995, p. 1576.

59 Dag Hammarskjöld, quoted by Michael Piazza, *Holy Homosexuals: The Truth About Being Gay or Lesbian and Christian*, Sources of Hope Publishing House, Dallas, 1995, p. 112.

BIBLIOGRAPHY

Aarons, Leroy. 1995 *Prayers for Bobby: A Mother's Coming to Terms with the Suicide of Her Gay Son*. HarperSanFrancisco, New York.

Abelove, Henry. 1993 'Freud, Male Homosexuality and the Americans' *The Lesbian and Gay Studies Reader*. eds. Henry Abelove et al., Routledge, New York, pp. 381–93.

Abelove, Henry, et al., eds. 1993 *The Lesbian and Gay Studies Reader*. Routledge, New York.

Aelred of Rievaulx. 1977 *Spiritual Friendship*. Trans. Mary Eugenia Laker SSND. With an Introduction by Douglass Roby. Cistercian Fathers Series no. 5. Cistercian Publications, Kalamazoo, Michigan.

Aldrich, Robert, ed. 1993 *Gay Perspectives II: More Essays in Australian Gay Culture*. Department of Economic History with The Australian Centre for Gay and Lesbian Research, University of Sydney, Sydney.

Aldrich, Robert, and Garry Wotherspoon, eds. 1992 *Gay Perspectives: Essays in Australian Gay Culture*. Department of Economic History, The University of Sydney, Sydney.

Almaguer, Tomas. 1993 'Chicano Men' *The Lesbian and Gay Studies Reader* eds. Henry Abelove et al., Routledge, New York, pp. 255–73.

Altman, Dennis. 1993 (1971) *Homosexual Oppression and Liberation*. With an introduction by Jeffrey Weeks. Serpent's Tail, London.

Amos Jr., William E. 1988 *When AIDS Comes to Church*. The Westminster Press, Philadelphia.

Anglican Church of Australia General Synod Doctrine Commission 1989 'Appendix: A Christian discussion on sexuality' *General Synod Paper no. 3, 1989*. General Synod Office, pp. 83–100.

—— 1992 A *Theology of the Human Person*. Margaret Rodgers and Maxwell Thomas, eds. Collins Dove, North Blackburn Vic.

Anglican Diocese of Melbourne Synod Social Questions Committee 1971 *Report on Homosexuality*. Anglican Diocese of Melbourne.

—— 1985 *Social Questions Committee Annual Report to Synod 1985: The Church, Homosexuality and the AIDS Crisis*. Anglican Diocese of Melbourne.

Anglican Diocese of Sydney Ethics and Social Questions Committee 1973 *Report on Homosexuality*. Anglican Diocese of Sydney.

'*Apostolicam actuositatem: Decree on the Apostolate of Lay People*' 1987 (1965) *Vatican Council II: The Conciliar and Post Conciliar Documents*. A Study Edition. Austin Flannery OP, ed. Costello Publishing Company, Northport.

Archdiocesan Gay/Lesbian Outreach of Baltimore. 1986 *Homosexuality: A Positive Catholic Perspective: Questions and Answers in Lesbian/Gay Ministry*. Archdiocese of Baltimore.

Arnold, Patrick M. 1992 *Wildmen, Warriors And Kings: Masculine Spirituality and the Bible*. With a Foreword by Robert Bly. Crossroad, New York.

Arpin, Robert L. 1993 *Wonderfully, Fearfully Made: Letters on Living with Hope, Teaching Understanding, and Ministering with Love, from a Gay Catholic Priest with AIDS*. HarperSanFrancisco, San Francisco.

Australian Catholic Bishops' Central Commission 1994 *Letter of Archbishop Little to Attorney General Michael Lavarch*. Australian Catholic Bishops' Central Commission, Canberra. 27 October 1994.

Australian Catholic Bishops Conference 1985 (1971) 'Homosexuality' *Australian Catholic Bishops' Statements Since Vatican II*. Nicholas Kerr, ed. St. Paul Publications, Homebush, pp. 168–71.

—— 1985 (1984) 'The Australian Broadcasting Corporation and the entitlements of staff in homosexual relationships' *Australian Catholic Bishops' Statements Since Vatican II*. Nicholas Kerr, ed. St Paul Publications, Homebush, pp. 171–72.

—— 1988 *The AIDS Crisis: A message to the Australian people*. St Paul Publications, Homebush.

—— 1989 *AIDS: a challenge to love*. St Paul Publications, Homebush.

—— 1993 *Families Our Hidden Treasure: A Statement on Family Life in Australia*. Aurora Books, Melbourne.

—— 1994 *Submission: HIV/AIDS National Strategy*. Australian Catholic Bishops Conference, Canberra. 9 September 1994.

Australian Catholic Social Justice Council. 1995 *Tolerance: A Christian Perspective on the International Year for Tolerance*. Dove Publications, North Blackburn Vic.

Back, Gloria Guss. 1985 *Are You Still My Mother? Are You Still My Family?* Warner Books Inc, New York.

Bailey, Derrick Sherwin. 1975 *Homosexuality and the Western Christian Tradition*. Archon Books, Hamden Conn.

Barnhouse, Ruth Tiffany. 1979 *Homosexuality: A Symbolic Confusion*. The Seabury Press, A Crossroad Book, New York.

Batchelor Jr, Edward, ed. 1980 *Homosexuality and Ethics*. The Pilgrim Press, New York.

Bauman, Zygmunt. 1992 *Intimations of Postmodernity*. Routledge, London.

Bawer, Bruce. 1993 *A Place At The Table: The Gay Individual in American Society*. Poseidon Press, New York.

—— 1996 *Beyond Queer: Challenging Gay Left Orthodoxy*. The Free Press, New York.

Bell, Allan. 1976 'The Homosexual as Patient' *Sex Research Studies from the Kinsey Intitute*. Martin Weinberg, ed. Oxford University Press, New York, pp. 202–29.

Bell, Allan P., Martin S. Weinberg, and Sue Kiefer Hammersmith. 1981 *Sexual Preference: Its Development in Men and Women*. Indiana University Press, Bloomington.

Berger, Maurice, et al., eds. 1995 *Constructing Masculinity*. Routledge, New York.

Berlant, Lauren, and Elizabeth Freeman. 1993 'Queer Nationality' *Fear of a Queer Planet: Queer Politics and Social Theory*. Michael Warner, ed. University of Minnesota Press, Minneapolis, pp. 193–229.

Bevilacqua, Cardinal Anthony. 1993 'Domestic Partnership Bills Opposed'. *Origins* vol. 23, no. 3, 3 June 1993, p. 48.

Bible: The Complete Parallel Bible Containing the Old and New Testaments with Apocryphal/Deuterocanonical Books: New Revised Standard Version, Revised. English Bible, New American Bible, New Jerusalem Bible 1993 Oxford University Press, New York.

Bible: The Jerusalem Bible. 1996 Alexander Jones, ed. Darton, Longman & Todd, London.

Bieber, Irving, et al., 1962 *Homosexuality: A Psychoanalytic Study*. Basic Books, New York.

Birch, Charles. 1995 *Feelings*. University of New South Wales Press, Sydney.

Bishops of California. 1987 'A Pastoral Letter On AIDS'. *Origins*. vol. 16, no. 45, 23 April 1987, p. 788.

Blue, Lionel. 1995 'Only the best will do'. *The Tablet*. (London) vol. 249, no. 8105, 9 December 1995, p. 1576.

Borhek, Mary V. 1979 *My Son Eric: A mother struggles to accept her gay son and discovers herself*. The Pilgrim Press, New York.

Boswell, John. 1980 *Christianity, Social Tolerance, and Homosexuality: Gay People in Western Europe from the Beginning of the Christian Era to the Fourteenth Century*. The University of Chicago Press, Chicago.

—— 1988 *The Kindness of Strangers: The Abandonment of Children in Western Europe from Late Antiquity to the Renaissance*. Penguin Books, London.

—— 1989 'Homosexuality and Religious Life: A Historical Approach'. *Homosexuality and the Catholic Church*. Jeannine Gramick, ed. The Thomas More Press, Chicago, pp. 3–20.

—— 1994 *Same-Sex Unions In Premodern Europe*. Villard Books, New York.

Bouldrey, Brian, ed. 1995 *Wrestling With The Angel: Faith and Religion in the Lives of Gay Men*. Riverhead Books, New York.

Bouma, Gary. 1992 'Faith, Scripture and Community in the Development of an AIDS-Relevant Theology' *AIDS: The Church as Enemy and Friend: Ambiguities in the Church's Response to AIDS*. Allan Cadwallader, ed. With a Foreword by Fr Bill Kirkpatrick. Collins Dove, North Blackburn Vic, pp. 147–61.

Bowman, Jim. 1992 'Lavender and Purple'. *Commonweal*. April 1992, pp. 5–6.

Bowman, Mark, et al., 1993 'Birth of a Movement'. *Open Hands*. Winter, 1993, pp. 8–9.

Boyd, Malcolm. 1984 *Take off the Masks*. With a Foreword by Harry Britt. New Society Publishers, Philadelphia.

—— 1991 'Underground Christians' *Amazing Grace: Stories of Lesbian and Gay Faith*. Malcolm Boyd and Nancy Wilson, eds. The Crossing Press, Freedom CA, pp. 1–16.

—— 1994 'Survival with Grace' *Gay Soul: Finding the Heart of Gay Spirit and Nature: With Sixteen Writers, Healers, Teachers, and Visionaries*. Mark Thompson, ed. HarperSanFrancisco, New York, pp. 228–45.

Boyd, Malcolm, and Nancy L. Wilson, eds. 1991 *Amazing Grace: Stories of Lesbian and Gay Faith*. The Crossing Press, Freedom CA.

Brawley, Robert L. 1996 *Biblical Ethics and Homosexuality: Listening to Scripture*. Westminster John Knox Press, Louisville.

Bromell, David, et al., eds. 1991 *Love Unbounded: On being Gay or Lesbian and Christian*. Colcom Press, Hibiscus Coast New Zealand.

Brown, Lesley, ed. 1993 *The New Shorter Oxford English Dictionary*. Clarendon Press, Oxford.

Byne, William. 1994 'The Biological Evidence Challenged'. *Scientific American* (New York) vol. 270, no. 5, May 1994, pp. 50–5.

Byrne SJ, Brendan. 1992 'Paul and the AIDS Crisis' *AIDS: The Church as Enemy and Friend: Ambiguities in the Church's Response to AIDS*. Allan Cadwallader, ed. With a Foreword by Fr Bill Kirkpatrick. Collins Dove, North Blackburn Vic, pp. 163–81.

Cadwallader, Allan H., ed. 1992 *AIDS: The Church as Enemy and Friend: Ambiguities in the Church's Response to AIDS*. With a Foreword by Fr Bill Kirkpatrick. Collins Dove, North Blackburn Vic.

Cahill, Lisa Sowle. 1983 'Moral Methodology: A Case Study' *A Challenge to Love: Gay and Lesbian Catholics in the Church*. Robert Nugent, ed. Crossroad, New York, pp. 78–92.

Carr, Adam. 1994 'The Gay Gene Myth: Interview by Adam Carr with Professor Steven Rose'. *Outrage*. (Melbourne).

Carter, Howard. 1987 *AIDS: The Plague to End all Plagues?*. Logos Forum Pty Ltd, Blackheath NSW.

Catechism of the Catholic Church. 1994 English translation for Australia. St Paul Publications, Homebush NSW.

Catholic Bishops Conference of New Zealand. 1986 *Dignity, Love, Life: Statement on Homosexuality*. New Zealand Catholic Bishops Conference, Wellington.

Catholic Council For Church And Society (The Netherlands). 1980 (1979) *Homosexual People in Society: A Contribution to the Dialogue Within the Faith Community*. Second printing. New Ways Ministry, Mt Rainier.

Catholic Social Welfare Commission: Catholic Bishops of England and Wales. 1994 (1979) 'An Introduction to the Pastoral Care of Homosexual People' *Created Design—Some Pastoral Guidelines for the Care of Lesbian and Gay People*. Pastoral AIDS Series no. 1. Catholic AIDS Link, London.

Chauncey Jnr., George, et al. 1989 'Introduction' *Hidden From History: Reclaiming the Gay and Lesbian Past*. Martin Duberman et al., eds. Penguin Books, London, pp. 1–13.

Chetcuti, Joseph. 1986 'Personally Speaking For Myself' *Being Different*. Garry Wotherspoon, ed. Hale & Iremonger, Sydney, pp. 125–44.

Church-Acceptance Dialogue Group. 1996 *We are the Church, Too? Towards an Understanding of Being Catholic and Gay*. Archdiocese of Brisbane, Brisbane.

Clancy, Cardinal Edward. 1994 'Homosexuals: where to attach culpability' in 'Letters to the Editor'. The *Australian* 3 May 1994, p. 12.

Clark, J. Michael, 1993 *Beyond Our Ghettos: Gay Theology in Ecological Perspective*. The Pilgrim Press, Cleveland.

Clarke, Don. 1977 *Loving Someone Gay*. A Signet Book, New American Library, New York.

Cleaver, Richard. 1995 *Know My Name: A Gay Liberation Theology*. Westminster John Knox Press, Louisville.

The CMI Journal. 1988 *Nurturing The Gift: Gay and Lesbian Persons in Seminary & Religious Formation*. Communication Ministry Inc., New York.

The Code of Canon Law 1983 Collins Liturgical Publications, Sydney.

Coffin, William Sloane. 1993 'The Most Divisive Issue Since Slavery'. *Open Hands* Winter, p. 6.

Coleman, Peter. 1989 *Gay Christians: A Moral Dilemma*. SCM Press, London.

Coleman SS, Gerald D. 1992 *Human Sexuality: An All-Embracing Gift*. Alba House, New York.

—— 1995 *Homosexuality: Catholic Teaching and Pastoral Practice*. Paulist Press, New York.

Comiskey, Andrew. 1990 *Pursuing Sexual Wholeness*. With a Foreword by Leanne Payne. First British edition. Monarch Publications, Tunbridge Wells Kent.

Comstock, Gary David. 1993 *Gay Theology Without Apology*. The Pilgrim Press, Cleveland.

Congregation for Catholic Education. 1984 *Educational Guidance In Human Love: Outlines for Sex Education*. Australian edition. St Paul Publications, Homebush NSW.

Congregation for Institutes of Consecrated Life and Societies of Apostolic Life. 1990 *Directives on Formation in Religious Institutes*. St Paul Publications, Homebush NSW.

Congregation for the Clergy. 1994 *Directory on the Ministry and Life of Priests*. St Paul Publications, Homebush NSW.

Congregation for the Doctrine of the Faith. 1975 *Declaration on Certain Questions Concerning Sexual Ethics*. St Paul Publications, Homebush NSW.

—— 1986 *Letter to the Bishops of the Catholic Church on the Pastoral Care of Homosexual Persons*. Vatican Polyglot Press, Vatican City.

—— 1986 *Instruction on Christian Freedom and Liberation*. St Paul Publications, Homebush NSW.

—— 1990 *Instruction on the Ecclesial Vocation of the Theologian*. St Paul Books and Media, Boston.

—— 1992 'Some Considerations Concerning the Response to Legislative Proposals on the Non-discrimination of Homosexual Persons' *Catholic International*. vol. 3, no. 18, October 1992, pp. 857–60.

Conigrave, Timothy. 1995 *Holding the Man*. McPhee Gribble Publishers, Ringwood Victoria.

Connell, R. W. 1995 *Masculinities*. Allen & Unwin, St Leonards NSW.

Corn, Alfred. 1995 'What is the Sexual Orientation of a Christian?' *Wrestling With The Angel: Faith and Religion in the Lives of Gay Men*. Brian Bouldrey, ed. Riverhead Books, New York, pp. 203–20.

Cornwell, John. 1994 'Sexual Matters of the Mind'. The *Tablet* (London) 21 May 1994, pp. 625–26.

—— 1995 'Ourselves and Our Genes'. The *Tablet* (London) 27 May 1995, pp. 656–8.

Cotter, Jim. 1993 *Pleasure, Pain & Passion: Some Perspectives on Sexuality and Spirituality*. Cairns Publications, Sheffield.

Countryman, L. William. 1990 (1988) *Dirt, Greed & Sex: Sexual Ethics in the New Testament and Their Implications for Today*. Paperback edition. Fortress Press, Philadelphia.

Crew, Louie, ed. 1991 *A Book of Revelations: Lesbian and Gay Episcopalians Tell Their Own Stories*. With a Foreword by Bishop George N. Hunt. Integrity Inc, Washington.

Cruikshank, Margaret. 1986 'Less Catholic than the Pope' *A Faith of One's Own: Explorations by Catholic Lesbians*. Barbara Zanotti, ed. The Crossing Press Feminist Series. The Crossing Press, Trumansburg New York, pp. 161–5.

—— 1992 *The Gay and Lesbian Liberation Movement*. Revolutionary thought/Radical movements, series ed. Roger S. Gottlieb, Routledge, New York.

Curb, Rosemary, and Nancy Manahan, eds. 1993 (1985) *Lesbian Nuns: Breaking Silence*. Great Britain edition. The Women's Press Ltd, London.

Curran, Charles E. 1970 *Contemporary Problems in Moral Theology*. Fides Publishers, Inc., Notre Dame Ind.

—— 1972 *Catholic Moral Theology in Dialogue*. Fides Publishers, Inc., Notre Dame Ind.

—— 1977 *Transition and Tradition in Moral Theology*. University of Notre Dame Press, Notre Dame Ind.

—— 1984 *Critical Concerns in Moral Theology*. University of Notre Dame Press, Notre Dame Ind.

—— 1992 *The Living Tradition of Catholic Moral Theology*. University of Notre Dame Press, Notre Dame Ind.

—— ed. 1990 *Moral Theology: Challenges for the Future*. Paulist Press, New York.

Curran, Charles E., and Richard McCormick SJ. 1993 *Dialogue About Catholic Sexual Teaching*. Readings in Moral Theology no. 8. Paulist Press, New York.

Daniel, John. 1995 'Kindness can kill'. The *Tablet* (London) 4 November 1995, p. 1398.

D'Arcy, Archbishop Eric. 1991 'Archbishop D'Arcy's statement: Don't decriminalise sodomy!'. *AD 2000* (Melbourne) September 1991, pp. 3–4.

Dawidoff, Robert. 1994 'Kill a Queer for Christ' *Long Road to Freedom: The Advocate History of The Gay and Lesbian Movement*. Mark Thompson, ed. St Martin's Press, New York, pp. 145–6.

Dawn, Marva. 1994 'Are Christianity and Homosexuality Incompatible?' *Caught in the Crossfire: Helping Christians Debate Homosexuality*. Sally Geis and Donald E. Messer, eds. Abingdon Press, Nashville, pp. 89–98.

DeCecco, John P., and John P. Elia. 1993 *If You Seduce A Straight Person, Can You Make Them Gay? Issues in Biological Essentialism versus Social Constructionism in Gay and Lesbian Identities*. Harrington Park Press, Binghamton New York.

De Cecco, John P., and David Allen Parker, 1995 'The Biology of Homosexuality: Sexual Orientation or Sexual Preference?' *Sex, Cells and Same-Sex Desire: The Biology of Sexual Preference*. John De Cecco and David Parker, eds. Harrington Park Press, Binghamton New York, pp. 1–27.

—— eds. 1995 *Sex, Cells and Same-Sex Desire: The Biology of Sexual Preference*. Harrington Park Press, Binghamton, New York.

Decent, Campion. 1992 'Spirituality + Sexuality: When the spirit is willing but the flesh is honest'. *Sydney Star Observer* 24 July 1992, pp. 18–19.

'*Dei verbum:* Dogmatic Constitution on Divine Revelation' 1987 (1965) *Vatican Council II: The Conciliar and Post Conciliar Documents*. A Study Edition. Austin Flannery OP, ed. Costello Publishing Company, Northport.

D'Emilio, John. 1993 'Capitalism and Gay Identity' *The Lesbian and Gay Studies Reader* Henry Abelove et al., eds. Routledge, New York, pp. 467–78.

Dessaix, Robert. 1994 *A Mother's Disgrace*. Angus & Robertson, Pymble NSW.

—— 1996 *Night Letters: A Journey through Switzerland and Italy*, Igor Miaznow, ed. Macmillan, Sydney.

'*Dignitatis humanae:* Declaration on religious Liberty' 1987 (1965) *Vatican Council II: The Conciliar and Post Conciliar Documents*. A Study Edition. Austin Flannery OP, ed. Costello Publishing Company, Northport.

Dignity: House of Delegates. 1987 *Letter on Pastoral Care of Gay and Lesbian Persons*. Dignity Inc, Washington. 23 July 1987.

—— 1993 *Statement of Position and Purpose*. Dignity Inc, Washington.

Donaldson, David. 1992 'Dignity Inc: An Alternative Experience of Church' *Homosexuality and Religion and Philosophy*. Studies in Homosexuality, A Garland Series, vol. xii. Wayne Dynes and Stephen Donaldson, eds. Garland Publishing, Inc, New York, pp. 161ff.

Doty, William G. 1993 *Myths of Masculinity*. Crossroad, New York.

Dow, Steve. 1995 'Gay "gene" more likely among men: scientists'. *The Age* (Melbourne). 19 May 1995, p. 9.

Downey, Michael, ed. 1993 *The New Dictionary of Catholic Spirituality*. A Michael Glazier Book, The Liturgical Press, Collegeville, Minnesota.

Downing, Christine. 1989 *Myths and Mysteries of Same-Sex Love*. Continuum, New York.

Duberman, Martin Bauml, Martha Vicinus, and George Chauncey Jr., eds. 1989 *Hidden From History: Reclaiming the Gay and Lesbian Past*. Penguin Books, London.

Duddy, Marianne T., Kevin Calegari, Scott Trepania, and Anonymous. 1994 'Gay men and lesbians describe spiritual journeys'. *National Catholic Reporter* 2 September 1994, pp. 7—10.

Dynes, Wayne, ed. 1990 *Encyclopedia of Homosexuality* vol. 1 and 2. Garland Publishing Inc, New York.

Dynes, Wayne R., and Stephen Donaldson, eds. 1992 *Homosexuality and Religion and Philosophy*. Studies in Homosexuality, A Garland Series, vol. xii. Garland Publishing Inc, New York.

Ebert, Alan. 1976 *The Homosexuals*. Macmillan Publishing Co Inc, New York.

Edwards, Denis. 1995 *Jesus the Wisdom of God: An Ecological Theology*. St Paul Publications, Homebush NSW.

Edwards, George R. 1984 *Gay/Lesbian Liberation: A Biblical Perspective*. With a Foreword by Norman K. Gottwald. The Pilgrim Press, New York.

Ellacuria SJ, Ignacio, and John Sobrino SJ, eds. 1993 *Mysterium Liberationis: Fundamental Concepts of Liberation Theology*. Orbis Books, Maryknoll NY.

Ellison, Marvin. 1993 'Homosexuality and Protestantism' *Homosexuality and World Religions*. Arlene Swidler, ed. Trinity Press International, Valley Forge, Pennsylvania, pp. 149–79.

Emerson, Jonathan. 1991 'The Silent Muse' *Amazing Grace: Stories of Lesbian and Gay Faith*. Malcolm Boyd and Nancy Wilson, eds. The Crossing Press, Freedom CA, pp. 39–56.

Ferry, James. 1994 *In The Courts Of The Lord: A Gay Priest's Story*. With a Foreword by Bishop John S. Spong. Crossroad, New York.

Field, David. 1980 *The Homosexual Way—A Christian Option?* New edition. In Grove Booklets on Ethics. Grove Books Limited, Bramcote Nottingham.

Fletcher, Ben (C.). 1990 *Clergy under Stress: A Study of Homosexual and Heterosexual Clergy in the Church of England*. With a Foreword by Dr Jack Dominian. Mowbray, London.

Florida State Catholic Conference. 1993 'On Discrimination Against Homosexual Persons'. *Origins*. vol. 23, no. 20, 28 October 1993, pp. 359–60.

Foley, Archbishop William J. 1989 *Homosexuality and the Acceptance of Homosexuals*. Catholic Archdiocesan Chancery Office, Perth Western Australia. 1 November 1989.

—— 1989 'Homosexuality'. *The Record*. (Perth Western Australia) no. 2660, 2 November 1989, p. 1.

Fortunato, John E. 1982 *Embracing the Exile: Healing Journeys of Gay Christians*. The Seabury Press, New York.

Foster, John. 1993 *Take Me To Paris, Johnny: A Life Accomplished in the Era of AIDS*. Minerva Australia, Port Melbourne.

Foucault, Michel. 1990 (1976) *The History of Sexuality: An Introduction* vol. 1. Trans. Robert Hurley. Reprinted English edition. Penguin Books, London.

—— 1992 (1984) *The Use of Pleasure: The History of Sexuality* vol. 2. Trans. Robert Hurley. Reprinted English edition. Penguin Books, London.

Freud, Sigmund, 1991 (1977) *On Sexuality: Three Essays on the Theory of Sexuality and Other Works*. The Penguin Freud Library, vol. 7. Angela Richards, ed. James Strachey, transl. ed., Penguin Books, London.

Fricke, Aaron, and Walter Fricke. 1991 *Sudden Strangers: The Story of a Gay Son and His Father*. St Martin's Press, New York.

Friedman, Richard C. 1988 *Male Homosexuality: A Contemporary Psychoanalytic Perspective*. Yale University Press, New Haven.

Friedman, Richard, and Jennifer Downing. 1993 'Psychoanalysis, Psychobiology and Homosexuality'. *Journal of the American Psychoanalytic Association* (Madison, Ct.), vol. 41, no. 4, 1993, pp. 1159–98.

Furnish, Victor Paul. 1985 *The Moral Teaching of Paul: Selected Issues*. Second edition, revised. Abingdon Press, Nashville.

—— 1993 'What Does Scripture Say? How Shall We Listen? The Bible and Homosexuality'. *Open Hands*. vol. 9, no. 1, Summer 1993.

—— 1994 'The Bible and Homosexuality: Reading the Text in Context' *Homosexuality in the Church: Both Sides of the Debate*. Jeffrey Siker, ed. Westminster John Knox Press, Louisville, pp. 18–35.

Gaden, John. 1994 *A Vision of Wholeness*. Duncan Reid, ed. E. J. Dwyer, Alexandria NSW.

Gallagher, John, ed. 1986 *Homosexuality and the Magisterium: Documents from the Vatican and the U.S. Bishops 1975–1985*. New Ways Ministry, Mt Rainier.

Gambone, Philip. 1995 'Searching for Real Words' *Wrestling With The Angel: Faith and Religion in the Lives of Gay Men*. Brian Bouldrey, ed. Riverhead Books, New York, pp. 221–42.

'*Gaudium et spes*: Pastoral Constitution on the Church in the Modern World' 1987 (1965) *Vatican Council II: The Conciliar and Post Conciliar Documents*. A Study Edition. Austin Flannery OP, ed. Costello Publishing Company, Northport.

Geis, Sally B., and Donald E. Messer. 1994 *Caught in the Crossfire: Helping Christians Debate Homosexuality*. Abingdon Press, Nashville.

General Synod Board for Social Responsibility, Church of England. 1979 *Homosexual Relationships: A Contribution to Discussion*. CIO Publishing, London.

Genovesi SJ, Vincent J. 1987 *In Pursuit of Love: Catholic Morality and Human Sexuality*. Gill and Macmillan, Dublin.

Gerry, Bishop John. 1990 'Homosexuality . . . Law, morality and the Church' *The Catholic Leader* (Brisbane, Queensland). 12 July 1990, p. 1.

Gibeau, Dawn. 1994 'Gumbleton hears gay stories, some angry'. *National Catholic Reporter*. vol. 31, no. 4, 11 November 1994, pp. 3–4.

Gibson, Paul. 1994 'Gay Male and Lesbian Youth Suicide' *Death by Denial: Studies of Suicide in Gay and Lesbian Teenagers*. Gary Remafedi, ed. Alyson Publications Inc, Boston, pp. 15–68.

Glaser, Chris. 1988 *Uncommon Calling: A Gay Man's Struggle to Serve the Church*. With a Foreword by Virginia Ramey Mollenkott, and an Introduction by John Boswell. HarperSanFrancisco, New York.

—— 1990 *Come Home: Reclaiming Spirituality and Community as Gay Men and Lesbians*. Harper & Row, San Francisco.

—— 1994 *The Word is Out: The Bible Reclaimed for Lesbians and Gay Men: 365 Daily Meditations*. HarperSanFrancisco, San Francisco.

Goss, Robert. 1993 *Jesus Acted Up: A Gay And Lesbian Manifesto* HarperSanFrancisco, New York.

Gould, Allan. 1995 *What Did They Say About Gays?* ECW Press, Toronto.

Gramick, Jeannine, ed. 1983 *Homosexuality and the Catholic Church*. The Thomas More Press, Chicago.

—— 1989 *Homosexuality in the Priesthood and the Religious Life*. Crossroad, New York.

Gramick, Jeannine, and Pat Furey, eds. 1988 *The Vatican and Homosexuality: Reactions to the 'Letter to the Bishops of the Catholic Church on the Pastoral Care of Homosexual Persons'*. Crossroad, New York.

Grau, Gunter, ed. 1995 *Hidden Holocaust: Gay and Lesbian Persecution in Germany 1933–45*. Trans. Patrick Camiller. With a Contribution by Claudia Schoppmann. Cassell, London.

Greenberg, David F. 1988 *The Construction of Homosexuality*. The University of Chicago Press, Chicago.

Group of Friends, A. 1971 *Towards A Quaker View Of Sex*. Revised edition, second reprint. Friends Home Service Committee, London.

Gutierrez, Gustavo. 1993 'Option for the Poor' *Mysterium Liberationis: Fundamental Concepts of Liberation Theology*. Ignacio Ellacuria SJ and John Sobrino SJ, eds. Orbis Books, Maryknoll NY, pp. 235–50.

Hamer, Dean, and Peter Copeland. 1994 *The Science of Desire: The Search for the Gay Gene and the Biology of Behavior*. Simon & Schuster, New York.

Hanigan, James P. 1988 *Homosexuality: The Test Case For Christian Sexual Ethics*. Theological Inquiries Series. Lawrence Boadt CSP, general ed. Paulist Press, Mahwah NJ.

Hannon, Howard. 1996 *Agony in the Garden: The Story of a Gay Minister*. With a Foreword by Herman Waetjen. OutWrite Publishing, Portland, Oregon.

Haring CSSR, Bernard. 1967 *The Law of Christ: Moral Theology for Priests and Laity*. Three volumes. The Mercier Press, Cork.

—— 1990 'The Role of the Catholic Moral Theologian' *Moral Theology: Challenges for the Future*. Charles Curran, ed. Paulist Press, New York, pp. 32–47.

Hartinger, Brent. 1991 'Holy Row: Homosexuality and the Catholic Church'. *Torso* (New York) May 1991, pp. 19–22.

—— 1991 'A Case For Gay Marriage: In Support of Loving & Monogamous Relationships' *Commonweal*. vol. cxviii, no. 20, 22 November 1991.

Harvey OSFS, John F. 1967 'Homosexuality' *New Catholic Encyclopedia*. William J. McDonald, ed. The Catholic University of America, Washington. vol. vii, p. 117.

—— 1977 *Pastoral Care of the Homosexual*. Knights of Columbus, New Haven.

—— 1979 *A Spiritual Plan to Redirect One's Life: For Today's Homosexual*. DSP Pamphlets, Boston.

—— 1987 *The Homosexual Person: New Thinking in Pastoral Care*. Ignatius Press, San Francisco.

—— 1993 'Arguments from Revelation' *Dialogue About Catholic Sexual Teaching*. Charles Curran and Richard McCormick, eds. Readings in Moral Theology no. 8. Paulist Press, New York, pp. 309–25.

Hasbany, Richard, ed. 1989 *Homosexuality and Religion*. Harrington Park Press, New York.

Heger, Heinz. 1989 (1972) *The Men with the Pink Triangle*. Trans. David Fernbach. Fourth impression. Gay Modern Classic Publishers Ltd, London.

Helminiak, Daniel. 1994 *What the Bible Really Says About Homosexuality*. With a Foreword by Bishop John S. Spong. Alamo Square Press, San Francisco.

Herdt, Gilbert. 1994 (1981) *Guardians of the Flutes*. Idioms of Masculinity, vol. 1. With a Foreword by Robert A. LeVine. The University of Chicago Press, Chicago.

Hidalgu, Hilda. 1986 'Curriculum Vitae' *A Faith of One's Own: Explorations by Catholic Lesbians*. Barbara Zanotti, ed. The Crossing Press Feminist Series. The Crossing Press, Trumansburg NY, pp. 166–8.

Higgins, Patrick, ed. 1993 *A Queer Reader*. Fourth Estate, London.

Hilda, Sister. 1992 'I Don't Want Anyone From The Church' *AIDS: The Church as Enemy and Friend: Ambiguities in the Church's Response to AIDS*. Allan Cadwallader, ed. With a Foreword by Fr Bill Kirkpatrick. Collins Dove, North Blackburn Vic, pp. 73–9.

Hill, James and Rand Cheadle. 1996 *The Bible Tells Me So: Uses and Abuses of Holy Scripture*, Anchor Books/Doubleday, New York.

Hilton, Bruce. 1993 *Can Homophobia Be Cured? Wrestling With Questions That Challenge The Church*. Abingdon Press, Nashville.

Himmelfarb, Gertrude. 1994 *On Looking into the Abyss: Untimely Thoughts on Culture and Society*. Alfred A. Knopf, New York.

Hite, Shere. 1994 *The Hite Report On The Family: Growing Up Under Patriarchy*. Bloomsbury, London.

Hochstein, Lorna. 1986 'Mirroring God' *A Faith of One's Own: Explorations by Catholic Lesbians*. Barbara Zanotti, ed. The Crossing Press Feminist Series. The Crossing Press, Trumansburg NY, pp. 8–13.

Hodge, Dino. 1996 *The Fall Upwood: Spirituality in the Lives of Lesbian Women and Gay Men*. Little Gem Publications, Casuarina Northern Territory.

Holleran, Andrew. 1995 'The Sense of Sin' *Wrestling With The Angel: Faith and Religion in the Lives of Gay Men*. Brian Bouldrey, ed. Riverhead Books, New York, pp. 83–96.

Hopcke, Robert H. 1991 (1989) *Jung, Jungians & Homosexuality*. First paperback edition, Shambhala Boston.
House of Bishops of the General Synod of the Church of England. 1991 *Issues in Human Sexuality*, Church House Publishing, London.
Hubbard, Ruth. 1995 'False genetic markers'. *New York Times* 2 August 1995.
Hume, Cardinal Basil. 1994 'Observations on the Catholic Church's Teaching Concerning Homosexual People' *Created Design—Some Pastoral Guidelines for the Care of Lesbian and Gay People*. Pastoral AIDS Series no. 1. Catholic AIDS Link, London, pp. 20–4.
—— 1995 *A Note on the Teaching of the Catholic Church Concerning Homosexual People*. Archbishop's House, Westminster London.
Hunt, Mary. 1986 'Loving Well Means Doing Justice' *A Faith of One's Own: Explorations by Catholic Lesbians*. Barbara Zanotti, ed. The Crossing Press Feminist Series. The Crossing Press, Trumansburg NY, pp. 114–24.
—— 1989 'Sexual Ethics: A Lesbian Perspective'. *Open Hands* vol. 4, no. 3, Winter 1989, p. 10.
Ihara, Saikaku. 1972 *Comrade Loves of the Samurai*. Trans. E. Powys Mathers. Charles Tuttle Co, Rutland Vermont.
Isay, Richard A. 1989 *Being Homosexual: Gay Men and Their Development*. Avon Books, New York.
James, David C. 1996 *What are they saying about Masculine Spirituality?* With an Introduction by Richard Rohr. Paulist Press, Mahwah NJ.
Johansson, Warren. 1990 'Psychiatry' *Encyclopedia of Homosexuality*. Wayne Dynes, ed. Garland Publishing Inc, New York, pp. 1072–5.
John Paul II, Pope. 1979 *Redemptor Hominis: The Redeemer of Man*. Daughters of St Paul, Boston.
—— 1982 *Familiaris Consortio: The Role of the Christian Family in the Modern World*. St Paul Publications, Homebush.
—— 1987 'Los Angeles Meeting of the Pope with U.S. Bishops: The Pope's Address: Part IV'. *Origins* 1 October 1987, vol. 17, no. 16, pp. 258–67.
—— 1992 *Pastores Dabo Vobis: I Will Give You Shepherds: Post-Synodal Apostolic Exhortation*. St Paul Books and Media, Boston.
—— 1993 *Veritatis Splendor: On Certain Fundamental Questions of the Church's Moral Teaching*. St Paul Publications, Homebush.
—— 1994 'Apostolic Constitution: *Fidei Depositum*', *Catechism of the Catholic Church*. St Paul Publications, Homebush.
—— 1994 'Legitimizing deviant kinds of behaviour distorts the true meaning of the family and leads to decadence'. *L'Osservatore Romano* no. 8 (1329), 23 February 1994, pp. 1 and 8.
—— 1995 *Evangelium Vitae: The Gospel of Life*. St Paul Publications, Homebush.
—— 1995 *Ut Unum Sint: That They May All Be One*. St Paul Publications, Homebush.

—— 1995 *Letter of Pope John Paul II to Women*. Vatican Polyglot Press, Vatican City.

Johnson, Fenton. 1995 'God, Gays and the Geography of Desire' *Wrestling With The Angel: Faith and Religion in the Lives of Gay Men*. Brian Bouldrey, ed. Riverhead Books, New York, pp. 243–58.

Jung, C. G. 1959 *Collected Works*. Pantheon, New York.

Keane SS, Philip S. 1977 *Sexual Morality: A Catholic Perspective*. Paulist Press, New York.

Kerr, Nicholas, ed. 1985 *Australian Catholic Bishops' Statements Since Vatican II*. St Paul Publications, Homebush.

King, Mark. 1992 'I Don't Get Baptized Anymore'. *Open Hands* vol. 8, no. 1, Summer 1992, p. 6.

Kinsey, Alfred, et al., 1948 *The Sexual Behavior in the Human Male*. W. B. Saunders Company Ltd, Philadelphia.

Kinsey, Alfred, et al., 1953 *Sexual Behavior in the Human Female*. W. B. Saunders Company Ltd, Philadelphia.

Kosnik, Anthony, et al., eds. 1977 *Human Sexuality: New Directions in American Catholic Thought: A Study Commissioned by The Catholic Theological Society of America*. Paulist Press, New York.

Kowalewski, Mark R. 1994 *All Things to All People: The Catholic Church Confronts the AIDS Crisis*. State University of New York Press, Albany NY.

Kramer, Larry. 1989 *Report from the Holocaust: The Making of an AIDS Activist*. St Martin's Press, New York.

Lauritsen, John, and David Thorstad. 1974 *The Early Homosexual Rights Movement (1864–1935)*. Times Change Press, New York.

Lawler OFM, Ronald, et al., 1985 *Catholic Sexual Ethics: A Summary, Explanation, & Defense*. Our Sunday Visitor Inc, Huntington Ind.

Lefevere, Patricia. 1996 'Panel accuses Episcopal bishop of heresy'. *National Catholic Reporter*. 22 March 1996.

Leies SM, John A, ed. 1990 (1981) *Human Sexuality and Personhood: Proceedings of the Workshop for the Hierarchies of the United States and Canada Sponsored by the Pope John Center*. With a Preface by Archbishop Bernard Law. Revised edition. Pope John Center, Braintree, Massachusetts.

Leng, Kwok Wei. 1994 'Theorising Corporeality: Bodies, Sexuality and the Feminist Academy: An Interview with Elizabeth Grosz'. *Melbourne Journal of Politics: Sexuality*. vol. 22, 1994, pp. 29–33.

Lesbian and Gay Christian Movement. *Christianity & Homosexuality: A Short Introduction*. Lesbian and Gay Christian Movement, London (undated).

—— *Catholic Caucus: An Introduction*. Lesbian and Gay Christian Movement, London (undated).

—— *The Evangelical Fellowship within the Lesbian and Gay Christian Movement*. Lesbian and Gay Christian Movement, London (undated).

LeVay, Simon. 1993 *The Sexual Brain*. A Bradford Book, The MIT Press, Cambridge Massachusetts.

LeVay, Simon, and Dean H. Hamer. 1994 'Evidence for a Biological Influence in Male Homosexuality'. *Scientific American* vol. 270, no. 5, May 1994, pp. 40–9.

Lewes, Kenneth. 1988 *The Psychoanalytic Theory of Male Homosexuality*. Simon & Schuster, New York.

Little, Archbishop T. F. 1986 'The Pastoral Care of Homosexual Persons'. *The Advocate* (Melbourne Victoria) 13 November 1986, p. 7.

'*Lumen Gentium*: Dogmatic Constitution on the Church' 1987 (1964) *Vatican Council II: The Conciliar and Post Conciliar Documents*. A Study Edition. Austin Flannery OP, ed. Costello Publishing Company, Northport.

Lutheran Church in Australia General Synod. 1993 'Statement on Homosexuality 1975' *Bible Study Resource Paper Series no. 17 Homosexuality*. B. Schwarz, ed. LCA Commission on Social and Bioethical Questions. No page numbers.

Lynch, Bernard. 1992 *A Priest on Trial*. Bloomsbury, London.

McBrien, Richard. 1994 (1980) *Catholicism*. Revised and updated edition. Collins Dove, North Blackburn Victoria.

—— ed. 1995 *The HarperCollins Encyclopedia of Catholicism*. HarperCollins Publishers, New York.

McCormick SJ, Richard A. 1989 *The Critical Calling: Reflections on Moral Dilemmas Since Vatican II*. Georgetown University Press, Washington.

McDonald, Helen B., and Audrey I. Steinhorn. 1993 *Understanding Homosexuality: A Guide for Those Who Know, Love, or Counsel Gay and Lesbian Individuals*. With a Foreword by William Van Ornum. The Crossroad Publishing Company, New York.

McDonald William J., ed. 1967 *New Catholic Encyclopedia*. vol. vii. The Catholic University of America, Washington.

McNaught, Brian. 1982 (1981) *A Disturbed Peace: Selected Writings of an Irish Catholic Homosexual*. Dignity Inc, Washington.

—— 1988 *On Being Gay: Thoughts on Family, Faith, and Love*. St Martin's Press, New York.

McNeill, John J. 1988a (1976) *The Church and the Homosexual*. Third updated and expanded edition. Beacon Press, Boston.

—— 1988b *Taking a Chance on God: Liberating Theology for Gays, Lesbians, and their Lovers, Families and Friends*. Beacon Press, Boston.

—— 1993 'Homosexuality' *The New Dictionary of Catholic Spirituality*. Michael Downey, ed. A Michael Glazier Book, The Liturgical Press, Collegeville Minnesota, p. 505.

—— 1995 *Freedom, Glorious Freedom: The Spiritual Journey to the Fullness of Life for Gays, Lesbians, and Everybody Else*. Beacon Press, Boston.

Maddern, Rev. John. 1990 *Homosexuality and Leadership in the Church: Statement by Rev. John Maddern, Moderator, Uniting Church in SA*. The Uniting Church of Australia Synod of South Australia, Adelaide. 9 July 1990.

Maddox, Brenda. 1982 *The Marrying Kind: Homosexuality & Marriage*. Granada, London.

Maggiore, Dolores. 1990 'Lesbianism' *Encyclopedia of Homosexuality* Wayne Dynes, ed. Garland Publishing Inc, New York, pp. 708–21.

Malloy, Edward A. 1981 *Homosexuality and the Christian Way of Life*. University Press of America Inc, Lanham MD.

Marcus, Eric. 1992 *Making History: The Struggle for Gay and Lesbian Equal Rights 1945–1990: An Oral History*. HarperPerennial, New York.

—— 1993 *Is It A Choice? Answers to 300 of the Most Frequently Asked Questions about Gays and Lesbians*. HarperSanFrancisco, New York.

Martin, Dale B. 1996 '*Arsenokoites* and *Malakos*: Meaning and Consequences' *Biblical Ethics and Homosexuality: Listening to Scripture*. Robert L. Brawley, ed. Westminster John Knox Press, Louisville.

Melton, Gordon, 1991 'The Churches' Ethical Dilemma with Homosexuality' *The Churches Speak On: Homosexuality: Official Statements from Religious Bodies and Ecumenical Organizations*. Gordon Melton, ed. Gale Research Inc, Detroit, pp. xv–xxxi.

—— ed. 1989 *The Churches Speak On: AIDS: Official Statements from Religious Bodies and Ecumenical Organizations*. Gale Research Inc, Detroit.

—— 1991 *The Churches Speak On: Homosexuality: Official Statements from Religious Bodies and Ecumenical Organizations*. Gale Research Inc, Detroit.

Metcalf, Andy. 1985 'Introduction' *The Sexuality of Men*. Andy Metcalf and Martin Humphries, eds. Pluto Press, London, pp. 1–14.

Metcalf, Andy, and Martin Humphries, eds. 1985 *The Sexuality of Men*. Pluto Press, London.

Mohr, Richard D. 1992 *Gay Ideas: Outing and Other Controversies*. Beacon Press, Boston.

Mondimore, Francis Mark. 1996 *A Natural History of Homosexuality*. The John Hopkins University Press, Baltimore.

Monette, Paul. 1994 'On Being' *Gay Soul: Finding the Heart of Gay Spirit and Nature: with Sixteen Writers, Healers, Teachers, and Visionaries*. Mark Thompson, ed. HarperSanFrancisco, New York, pp. 18–31.

Moore OP, Gareth. 1992 *The Body In Context: Sex and Catholicism*. SCM Press Ltd, London.

Morris, Miranda. 1995 *Pink Triangle: The Gay Law Reform Debate in Tasmania*. University of New South Wales Press, Sydney.

Murphy, Bishop Francis. 1992 'Let's Start Over: A Bishop Appraises the Pastoral on Women'. *Commonweal*. 25 September 1992, pp. 11–15.

Murphy, Julien. 1986 'Coming Out of Catholicism' *A Faith of One's Own: Explorations by Catholic Lesbians*. Barbara Zanotti, ed. The Crossing Press Feminist Series. The Crossing Press, Trumansburg NY, pp. 81–92.

National Catholic Reporter 1994 'Editorial: Bishop Gumbleton opens door for all to pass through'. vol. 31, no. 5, 18 November 1994, p. 20.

National Conference of Catholic Bishops. 1973 *Principles to Guide Confessors in Questions of Homosexuality*. National Conference of Catholic Bishops, Washington.

—— 1989 *Called to Compassion and Responsibility: A Response To The HIV/AIDS Crisis*. National Conference of Catholic Bishops, Washington.

—— 1990 *Human Sexuality: A Catholic Perspective For Education And Lifelong Learning*. United States Catholic Conference, Washington.

National Conference of Catholic Bishops *Ad Hoc* Committee. 1988 'Partners in the Mystery of Redemption: A Pastoral Response to Women's Concerns for the Church and Society. First Draft'. *Origins* vol. 17, no. 45, 21 April 1988, pp. 766–71.

—— 1990 'One in Christ Jesus: A Pastoral Response to the Concerns of Women for Church and Society. Second Draft' *Origins* vol. 19, no. 44, 4 April 1990, p. 727.

—— 1992 'Called to be One in Christ Jesus: Pastoral Concerns of Women. Third Draft'. *Origins* vol. 21, no. 46, 23 April 1992, pp. 770–1.

—— 1992 'Response to Women's Concerns: One in Christ Jesus. Fourth Draft'. *Origins* vol. 22, no. 13, 10 September 1992, p. 231.

—— 1992 'Women's Concerns: One in Christ Jesus. Final Document'. *Origins* vol. 22, no. 29, 31 December 1992, pp. 497–9.

National Conference of Catholic Bishops Administrative Board. 1987 *The Many Faces of AIDS: A Gospel Response*. United States Catholic Conference, Washington.

Nava, Michael. 1995 'Coming Out and Born Again' *Wrestling With The Angel: Faith and Religion in the Lives of Gay Men*, Brian Bouldrey, ed. Riverhead Books, New York, pp. 175–82.

Navarro-Valls, Joaquim. 1992 'Responding to Legislative Proposals on Discrimination Against Homosexuals'. *Origins* vol. 22, no. 10, 20 August 1992. pp. 173, 175–7.

Nelson, James B. 1979 *Embodiment: An Approach to Sexuality and Christian Theology*. SPCK, London.

—— 1983 *Between Two Gardens: Reflections on Sexuality and Religious Experience*. The Pilgrim Press, New York.

—— 1988 *The Intimate Connection: Male Sexuality, Masculine Spirituality*. Westminster Press, Philadelphia.

Nelson, James B., and Sandra P. Longfellow. 1994 *Sexuality and the Sacred: Sources For Theological Reflection*. Mowbray, London.

'*Nostra aetate*: Declaration on the Relationship of the Church to Non-Christian Religions' 1987 (1965) *Vatican Council II: The Conciliar and*

Post Conciliar Documents. A Study Edition. Austin Flannery OP, ed. Costello Publishing Company, Northport.

Not A Day Goes By: Report on the GLAD Survey into Discrimination and Violence Against Lesbians and Gay Men in Victoria 1994. Gay Men and Lesbians Against Discrimination, Melbourne.

Nugent, Robert, ed. 1983 *A Challenge to Love: Gay and Lesbian Catholics in the Church*. With an Introduction by Bishop Walter F. Sullivan. Crossroad, New York.

—— 1988 'Sexual Orientation in Vatican Thinking' *The Vatican and Homosexuality: Reactions to the 'Letter to the Bishops of the Catholic Church on the Pastoral Care of Homosexual Persons'*. Jeannine Gramick and Pat Furey, eds. Crossroad, New York, pp. 48–58.

Nugent SDS, Robert C., Jeannine Gramick SSND, and Thomas Oddo CSC. 1982 *Homosexual Catholics: A New Primer For Discussion*. Dignity Inc, Washington.

Nugent SDS, Robert C., and Jeannine Gramick SSND, eds. 1987 *A Time To Speak: A Collection of Contemporary Statements from the U.S. Catholic Sources on Homosexuality, Gay Ministry and Social Justice*. New Ways Ministry, Mt Rainier MD.

—— 1992 *Building Bridges: Gay and Lesbian Reality and the Catholic Church*. With a Foreword by Charles Curran. Twenty-Third Publications, Mystic Connecticut.

O'Neill, Craig, and Kathleen Ritter. 1992 *Coming Out Within: Stages of Spiritual Awakening for Lesbians and Gay Men: The Journey from Loss to Transformation*. HarperSanFrancisco, New York.

Padgug, Robert. 1989 'Sexual Matters' *Hidden From History: Reclaiming the Gay and Lesbian Past*. Martin Duberman et al., eds. Penguin Books, London, pp. 54–64.

Paul VI, Pope. 1968 *Humanae Vitae: Of Human Life*. St Paul Books and Media, Boston.

Payne, Leanne. 1992 *The Broken Image: Restoring Sexual Wholeness Through Healing Prayer*. Kingsway Publications Ltd, Eastbourne E. Sussex.

Perry, Troy D., with Thomas I, P. Swicegood. 1990 *Don't Be Afraid Anymore: The story of Reverend Troy Perry and the Metropolitan Community Churches*. St Martin's Press, New York.

—— 1991 *Profiles in Gay and Lesbian Courage*. St Martin's Press, New York.

Piazza, Michael S. 1995 (1994) *Holy Homosexuals: The Truth About Being Gay or Lesbian and Christian*. Sources of Hope Publishing House, Dallas.

Pierson, Lance. 1992 *No-Gay Areas: Pastoral Care of Homosexual Christians*. Grove Books Ltd, Bramcote Notts.

Plant, Richard. 1986 *The Pink Triangle: The Nazi War Against Homosexuals*. Henry Holt and Company, New York.

The Pontifical Biblical Commission. 1993 *The Interpretation of the Bible in the Church*. St Paul Books and Media, Boston.

Pontifical Council for the Family. 1996 *The Truth and Meaning of Human Sexuality: Guidelines for Education within the Family*. St Paul Publications, Homebush.

Positively Called—HIV, Priesthood and Religious Life 1995. Pastoral AIDS Series no. 2. Catholic AIDS Link, London.

Quinn, Archbishop John. 1989 'Homily on Violence Against Gays. *Origins* vol. 19, no. 16, 21 September 1989, pp. 260–2.

—— 1994 'Civil Rights of Gay and Lesbian Persons' *Origins* vol. 22, no. 11, 20 August 1994, p. 204.

Reeves, Tim. 1993 'The 1972 Debate on Male Homosexuality in South Australia' *Gay Perspectives II: More Essays in Australian Gay Culture*. Robert Aldrich, ed. Department of Economic History with The Australia Centre for Gay and Lesbian Research, University of Sydney, Sydney, pp. 149–92.

Reid, Gavin. 1987 *Beyond AIDS*. Kingsway Publications, Eastbourne.

Remafedi, Gary, ed. 1994 *Death by Denial: Studies of Suicide in Gay and Lesbian Teenagers*. Alyson Publications Inc, Boston.

Richardson, Ann, and Dietmar Bolle, eds. 1992 *Wise Before Their Time: People living with AIDS and HIV Tell their Stories*. Forewords by Dr Julian Gold and Sir Ian McKellan. Australian edition, Collins Dove, North Blackburn, Victoria.

Ringer, R. Jeffrey, ed. 1994 *Queer Words, Queer Images: Communication and the Construction of Homosexuality*. New York University Press, New York.

Ritley, M. R. 1991 'Set Apart, Called into the Midst' *Amazing Grace: Stories of Lesbian and Gay Faith*. Malcolm Boyd and Nancy Wilson, eds. The Crossing Press, Freedom CA, pp. 116–30.

Ritter, Kathleen and Craig O'Neill. 1996 *Righteous Religion: Unmasking the Illusions of Fundamentalism and Authoritarian Catholicism*. The Haworth Pastoral Press, New York.

Roberts, Tom. 1994 'He's not disordered, he's my brother'. *National Catholic Reporter*. vol. 31, no. 3, 4 November 1994, pp. 1 and 6.

Ross, Michael W. 1983 *The Married Homosexual Man: A Psychological Study*. Routledge & Kegan Paul, London.

Rosser, B. R. Simon, ed. 1992 *Gay Catholics Down Under: The Journeys in Sexuality and Spirituality of Gay Men in Australia and New Zealand*. With a Foreword by Rev. Dr Felix Donnelly. Praeger, Westport Connecticut.

—— 'A Scientific Understanding of Sexual Orientation with Implications for Pastoral Ministry'. *Word and World* 1994.

Rubin, Gayle. 1993 'Thinking Sex' *The Lesbian and Gay Studies Reader*. Henry Abelove et al., eds. Routledge, New York, pp. 3–44.

Ruether, Rosemary Radford. 1985 *Women-Church: Theology and Practice of Feminist Liturgical Communities*. Harper & Row, San Francisco.

Sanford, John A., and George Lough. 1988 *What Men Are Like: The Psychology of Men, for Men and the Women who Live with Them*. Paulist Press, New York.

Savin-Williams, Ritch. 1990 'Coming Out' *Encyclopedia of Homosexuality*. Wayne Dynes, ed. Garland Publishing Inc, New York.

Scanzoni, Dawson, and Virginia Ramey Mollenkott. 1994 (1978) *Is the Homosexual my Neighbour? A Positive Christian Response*. Revised and updated edition. HarperSanFrancisco, New York.

Schillebeeckx, Edward. 1981 *Ministry: Leadership in the Community of Jesus Christ*. Crossroad, New York.

Scroggs, Robin. 1983 *The New Testament and Homosexuality: Contextual Background For Contemporary Debate*. Fortress Press, Philadelphia.

The Second Anglican-Roman Catholic International Commission 1994 *Life in Christ: Morals, Communion and the Church*. Church Publishing House and Catholic Truth Society, London.

Second Vatican Council. 1987 *Vatican Council II: The Conciliar and Post Conciliar Documents*. A Study Edition. Austin Flannery OP, ed. Costello Publishing Company, Northport.

Seel, Pierre. 1995 *I, Pierre Seel, Deported Homosexual: A Memoir of Nazi Terror*. Trans. Joachim Neugroschel. Basic Books, New York.

Seow, Choon-Leong, ed. 1996 *Homosexuality and the Christian Community*. Westminster John Knox Press, Louisville.

Shilts, Randy. 1988 *And The Band Played On: Politics, People and the AIDS Epidemic*. Penguin Books, London.

Siegel, Stanley, and Ed Lowe Jr. 1995 *Uncharted Lives: Understanding the Life Passages of Gay Men*. A Plume Book, New York.

Siker, Jeffrey S., 1994 'Homosexual Christians, the Bible, and Gentile Inclusion: Confessions of a Repenting Heterosexist' *Homosexuality in the Church: Both Sides of the Debate*. Jeffrey S. Siker, ed. Westminster John Knox Press, Louisville, pp. 178–94.

—— ed. 1994 *Homosexuality in the Church: Both Sides of the Debate*. Westminster John Knox Press, Louisville.

Singer, Bennett L., and David Deschamps, eds. 1994 *Gay & Lesbian Stats*. With an Introduction by Congressman Gerry E. Studds. The New Press, New York.

Sipe, A. W. Richard. 1990 *A Secret World: Sexuality and the Search for Celibacy*. With a Foreword by Robert Coles. Brunner/Mazel New York.

—— 1995 *Sex, Priests, And Power: Anatomy of a Crisis*. With a Foreword by Margaret R. Miles. Cassell, London.

Smith, Richard L. 1994 *AIDS, Gays, and the American Catholic Church*. With a Foreword by Robert N. Bellah. The Pilgrim Press, Cleveland.

Soards, Marion L. 1995 *Scripture & Homosexuality: Biblical Authority and the Church Today*. Westminster John Knox Press, Louisville.

Spencer, Colin. 1995 *Homosexuality: A History*. Fourth Estate, London.

Spong, John Shelby. 1988 *Living in Sin? A Bishop Rethinks Human Sexuality*. With a Foreword by Robert G. Lahita. Harper & Row, San Francisco.

Steicke, Lance G. 1995 'Homosexuality and the Church'. *The Lutheran* 23 January 1995, p. 7.

St John, Martin. 1994 'Rising from the Ashes' *Long Road to Freedom: The Advocate History of The Gay and Lesbian Movement*. Mark Thompson, ed. St Martin's Press, New York, p. 86.

St John, Sr Mary Louise. 1989 'Patient Weavers' *Homosexuality in the Priesthood and the Religious Life*. Jeannine Gramick, ed. Crossroad, New York, pp. 109–17.

Struzzo, John. 1989 'Pastoral Counselling and Homosexuality' *Homosexuality and Religion*. Richard Hasbany, ed. Harrington Park Press, New York, pp. 109–17.

Stuart, Elizabeth. 1992 *Daring to Speak Love's Name: A Gay and Lesbian Prayer Book*. With a Foreword by Rt Revd Dr David Jenkins. Hamish Hamilton, London.

—— 1993 *Chosen: Gay Catholic Priests Tell Their Stories*. Geoffrey Chapman, London.

—— 1995 *Just Good Friends: Towards A Lesbian And Gay Theology Of Relationships*. Mowbray, London.

Sullivan, Andrew. 1995 *Virtually Normal: An Argument About Homosexuality*. Picador, London.

Sullivan, Bishop Walter. 1983 'Introduction' *A Challenge to Love: Gay and Lesbian Catholics in the Church*. Robert Nugent, ed. Crossroad, New York, pp. xi–xiv.

Swindler, Arlene, ed. 1993 *Homosexuality and World Religions*. Trinity Press International, Valley Forge Pennsylvania.

Tablet, The 1995 'Letters: Living with AIDS' (name supplied). vol. 249, no. 8080, 17 June 1995, p. 775

Tabletalk 1990 'Acceptance? . . . Denial? . . . Rejection?' July/September 1990, pp. 10–14.

Thatcher, Adrian. 1993 *Liberating Sex: A Christian Sexual Theology*. SPCK, London.

Thompson, Mark ed. 1994a *Gay Soul: Finding the Heart of Gay Spirit and Nature: with Sixteen Writers, Healers, Teachers, and Visionaries*. HarperSanFrancisco, New York.

—— 1994b *Long Road to Freedom: The Advocate History of The Gay and Lesbian Movement*. With a Foreword by Randy Shilts. St Martin's Press, New York.

Tigert, Leanne McCall. 1996 *Coming Out While Staying In: Struggles and Celebrations of Lesbians, Gays, and Bisexuals in the Church*. United Church Press, Cleveland.

Tripp, C. A. 1977 (1975) *The Homosexual Matrix*. First Great Britain edition. Quartet Books, London.

Uhrig, Larry J. 1986 *Sex Positive: A Gay Contribution To Sexual And Spiritual Union.* Alyson Publications, Boston.

'*Unitatis redintegratio*: Decree on Ecumenism' 1987 (1964) *Vatican Council II: The Conciliar and Post Conciliar Documents.* A Study Edition. Austin Flannery OP, ed. Costello Publishing Company, Northport.

Uniting Church in Australia. 1987 *Homosexuality and the Church: Responses: Responses from the Uniting Church in Australia to a Report of the Assembly Committee on Homosexuality and the Church.* The Joint Board of Christian Education, Melbourne.

Uniting Church in Australia, Assembly Committee on Homosexuality and the Church. 1985 *Homosexuality And The Church: A Report of the Assembly Committee on Homosexuality and the Church*, Gordon S. Dicker, ed. Uniting Church Press, Melbourne.

Uniting Church in Australia Assembly Task Force on Sexuality. 1996 *Interim Report on Sexuality* Uniting Church Press, Melbourne.

Uniting Church in Australia, Social Justice Commission, Synod of South Australia, *Homosexuality And The Church: A Response.* (Mimeo), undated.

Unks, Gerald, ed. 1995 *The Gay Teen: Educational Practice and Theory for Lesbian, Gay, and Bisexual Adolescents.* Routledge, New York.

Vaid, Urvashi. 1995 *Virtual Equality: The Mainstreaming of Gay and Lesbian Liberation.* Anchor Books Doubleday, New York.

Vasey, Michael. 1995 *Strangers and Friends: A New Exploration of Homosexuality and the Bible.* Hodder & Stoughton, London.

Warner, Michael, ed. 1993 *Fear of a Queer Planet: Queer Politics and Social Theory.* University of Minnesota Press, Minneapolis.

Weinberg, George. 1973 *Society and the Healthy Homosexual*, Garden City, Anchor Books, New York.

Weinberg, Martin S., and Colin J. Williams. 1974 *Male Homosexuals: The Problems and Adaptations.* Oxford University Press, New York.

Weinberg, Martin S., et al. 1994 *Dual Attraction: Understanding Bisexuality.* Oxford University Press, New York.

Weinberg, Martin S., ed. 1976 *Sex Research Studies from the Kinsey Institute.* Oxford University Press, New York.

Westley, Dick. 1988 *Morality and Its Beyond.* Third printing. Twenty-Third Publications, Mystic CT.

White, Mel. 1994 *Stranger at the Gate: To be Gay and Christian in America.* With a Foreword by Lyla White. Simon & Schuster, New York.

Whitehead, Briar. 1993 *Craving For Love: Relationship Addiction, Homosexuality and the God who Heals.* With a Foreword by Jeanette Howard. Monarch Publications, Tunbridge Wells Kent.

Whitehead, Evelyn Eaton, and James D. Whitehead. 1982 *Christian Life Patterns: The Psychological Challenges And Religious Invitations Of Adult Life.* Doubleday and Image, New York.

—— 1986 *Seasons of Strength: New Visions of Adult Christian Maturing*. Image Books/Doubleday, Garden City NY.
—— 1987 'The Shape of Compassion: Reflections on Catholics and Homosexuality'. *Spirituality Today* 1987, pp. 126–36.
—— 1989 *A Sense of Sexuality: Christian Love and Intimacy*. Doubleday, New York.
Williams, Robert. 1992 *Just As I Am: A Practical Guide to Being Out, Proud and Christian*. HarperPerennial, New York.
Wilson, Nancy. 1995 *Our Tribe: Queer Folks, God, Jesus, and the Bible*. HarperSanFrancisco, New York.
Wolf, James G., ed. 1989 *Gay Priests*. With a Foreword by Jay R. Feierman. Harper & Row, San Francisco.
Wooden, Cindy. 1995 'Vatican quiet on final document in Beijing'. *National Catholic Reporter* 22 September 1995, p. 13.
Woods OP, Richard. 1977 *Another Kind of Love: Homosexuality and Spirituality*. The Thomas More Press, Chicago.
—— 1988 *Another Kind of Love: Homosexuality and Spirituality*. Third edition. Knoll Publishing Co Inc, Fort Wayne IN.
Wotherspoon, Garry, ed. 1986 *Being Different*. Hale & Iremonger, Sydney.
—— 1996 *Gay and Lesbian Perspectives III: Essays in Australian Culture*. Department of Economic History with The Australian Centre for Lesbian and Gay Research, University of Sydney, Sydney.
Zanotti, Barbara, ed. 1986 *A Faith of One's Own: Explorations by Catholic Lesbians*. The Crossing Press Feminist Series. The Crossing Press, Trumansburg NY.

INDEX